June 12, 2022

McKer

MW01001700

Congratulations on your nursing degree! Always follow God's plan and you will experience life's best!

Your Bethel Holiness Church family

Mountain Trailways

for Youth

Compiled by

Mrs. Chas. E. Cowman

"But you will not mind the roughness nor the steepness of the way,
Nor the chill, unrested morning, nor the searness of the day;
And you will not take a turning to the left or to the right,
But go straight ahead, nor tremble at the coming of the night,
For the trail leads Home."

Published by

THE ORIENTAL MISSIONARY SOCIETY
900 North Hobart Blvd., Los Angeles 27, Calif. U. S. A.

Nineteen Hundred and Forty-seven

Lovingly
Dedicated

to

The Youth of the World

Foreword

On a morning some months ago a leader of youth called at the office of The Oriental Missionary Society, 900 North Hobart Blvd., Los Angeles, California. On what quest had he come?

"Will you give to us a book of daily devotional readings—a book exclusively for youth? We are readers of *Streams in the Desert* and *Springs in the Valley*, and through *Charles Cowman, Missionary Warrior*, many of our youth have caught the vision of missionary service and have responded to the call to the nations. But, we need a book! One with a challenge to youth—for sacrificial living and a complete abandonment to God—a book of our very own!"

What a challenge his request presented! One which seemed to be impossible of fulfillment, as my youthful days had long since flown. But prayer was made, God's will earnestly sought; and now Mountain Trailways for Youth is on its mission to the youth of our generation.

Those who bear the Master's name—whether youthful or aged—must all travel the same highway. Those who have journeyed the longest and farthest are better acquainted with the road, its dangerous windings and its detours, and thus the younger pilgrims on the trail value the words of counsel and the experience of their elders. A poet has beautifully expressed this in the following lines:

THE BRIDGE BUILDER

"An old man, going a lone highway,
Came at the evening, cold and gray,
To a chasm vast and deep and wide,
Through which was flowing a raging tide.
The old man crossed in the twilight dim;
The sullen stream had no fears for him;
But he turned when safe on the other side,
And built a bridge to span the tide.
'Old man,' said a fellow-pilgrim near,
'You are wasting your strength with building here;
Your journey will end with the closing day;
You never again will pass this way.
You've crossed the chasm deep and wide.
Why build you this bridge at eventide?'
The builder lifted his old gray head.
'Good friend, in the path I have come,' he said,
'There followeth after me today
A youth whose feet must pass this way.
This chasm which has been as naught to me,
To that fair-haired youth may a pitfall be;
He, too, must cross in the twilight dim;
Good friend, I am building this bridge for him.'"

It has been a precious privilege—a delightsome task—to compile Mountain Trailways for Youth exclusively for you, my beloved youthful friends. May you find within its pages the spiritual tonic needed to strengthen you for the climb to the heights and courage to keep on climbing until you reach the summit—not somehow, but triumphantly!

Yours in Calvary bonds,

L. B. Cowman.
(Mrs. Chas. E. Cowman)

*Something hidden. Go and find it. Go
and look behind the Ranges—
Something lost behind the Ranges.
Lost and waiting for you. Go!*
                                    —Kipling.

Mountain Trailways

for Youth

January 1

"Now therefore give me this mountain." (Joshua 14: 12.)

YOUTH of the world, fellow mountaineers, roadmates, in the name of our loving Master we greet you on this glorious New Year's morning! Together we stand at the foot of a great mountain range to salute the breaking of the dawn, to renew our covenant with Him, to place anew our hands in His as we begin our journey through the untrodden months ahead. Before us are twelve towering peaks rearing their heads above the snow line. The tang of their icy winds sweeps down upon us. We are awed by their desolate grandeur. Harken! Bugles are sounding. Those who have left the murky mists of the low valleys and have made their way to the peace-crowned summits are beckoning us! The topmost crag challenges us, stirs our blood, and kindles our courage. Our Great Leader cries, "Out! Out! Take the trail!" Multiplied thousands of Christian youth are responding to His call to scale the heights, win the prize, "the high calling of God in Christ Jesus"—triumphant mountaineers who will participate in the conquest of the ages. To them "the mountain shall be thine" (Joshua 17: 18)—His gracious Word of assurance!

There are three things you can do with mountains. You can *climb* them. Mountains look sinister at a distance, but they lose much of their terror when you boldly approach them. Then, you can *take* a mountain. History has been made by men and women who have *taken* mountains that have seemed formidable to others. After you take a mountain you can *use* it. Caleb did that, and *you and I* can become Calebs. (Read the book of Joshua.) The hard climb strengthens the muscles; the problem solved trains the mind; the difficulties conquered build character. There is joy unspeakable in conquering mountains, triumphing in His victory!

Our Lord does not ask us to climb in our human strength. "I will gird thee!" He has not bidden us journey alone. "Lo, I am with you!" One climbs beside you.

Makē you away this very hour to the glory-crowned heights with
God! Who knows what awaits you! *Climb and listen!*

Make me Thy mountaineer; I would not linger
    On the lower slope.
Fill me afresh with hope, O God of hope,
    That undefeated
I may climb the hill
As seeing Him who is invisible.

Make me to be Thy happy mountaineer,
    O God most high;
My climbing soul would welcome the austere;
    Lord, crucify
On rock or scree, ice-cliff or field of snow,
The softness that would sink to things below.

Thou art my Guide; where Thy sure feet have trod
    Shall mine be set;
Thy lightest word my law of life, O God;
    Lest I forget,
And slip and fall, teach me to do Thy will,
Thy mountaineer upon Thy holy hill.
                                    —*Amy Wilson Carmichael.*

January 2

"*. . . Jesus himself drew near, and went with them.*"
                                        (Luke 24:15.)

AT THE gateway of the year now let us kneel to pray—asking God to bless us ere we go upon our way. . . . We dare
not take one step along the road that lies ahead—without a
prayer for guidance on the path that we must tread.
    Let us pray for strength, endurance, courage, fortitude—
so that we may venture out with hope and faith renewed . . . mighty
weapons, final victory.   —*Patience Strong.*

"*Shepherd of tender youth,*
Guiding in love and truth
Through devious ways;

Ever be Thou our Guide,
Our Shepherd and our Pride,
Our Staff and Song;
Jesus, Thou Christ of God,
By Thy perennial Word,
Lead us where Thou hast trod,
Make our faith strong."   —*Hymnal.*

Dr. S. D. Gordon once wrote: "Our Lord has been everywhere that we are called to go. His feet have trodden down smooth a path through every experience that comes to us. He knows each road, and knows it well—the steep path of temptation down through the rocky ravines and slippery gullies, the dizzy road along the heights of victory, the old beaten road of commonplace daily routine."

> *I said to the man who stood*
> *at the gate of the year,*
> *"Give me a light that I may*
> *tread safely into the unknown."*
>
> *And he replied,*
> *"Go out into the darkness and put*
> *your hand*
> *Into the hand of God;*
> *That shall be to you better than light*
> *and safer than a known way."*
> —*M. Louise Haskins.*

(Quoted by His Majesty the King in an Empire broadcast.)

Take the road, the lonely road; be courageous, unafraid; and He will walk with you, as long ago He walked the Emmaus Road.

January 3

". . . Forgetting those things which are behind, and reaching forth unto those things which are before." (Phil 3: 13.)

THE New Year is not present with us. Only a new day! So it will be continually. We shall see but one day at a time. . . . If each day is lived right, the whole year will be right; if each day is wrong, the year will be all wrong. Each day is a white page to be written. Write it beautifully, and the year will be beautiful."

NEW YEAR PRAYER

Lord, Thou hast given me a clean, new year.
Help me to keep its pages pure, unspoiled;
To write upon its scroll but kindly thoughts,
With no unsightly blots to have it soiled.

Let me not mar, in thought or word or deed,
This page, so white, so pure, unsullied, fair.
Help me to know that when I stand in need
Of help from Thee, Thou'rt always standing there.

When duty calls me, Lord, let pleasure wait.
Let me fulfill my calling. Let Thy will,
Not mine, be done. Oh, let me ever hear
Thy calm, approving voice, Thy guidance still.

Lead me, dear Lord, in paths of peacefulness.
But if, perchance, Thy paths should ever lie
O'er mountain trails, though they be rough and bleak,
Then may I answer, "Master, here am I."
—I. S. Ellis.

An artist who was asked, "What is your best picture?" answered, "My next." Make tomorrow your best day!

"Yesterday ended last night."

January 4

"I beseech you therefore, brethren, by the mercies of God, that ye present your bodies a living sacrifice, holy, acceptable unto God, which is your reasonable service." (Rom. 12:1.)

MY NEW YEAR'S GIFT
Laid on Thine altar, O my Lord divine,
Accept my gift this day, for Jesus' sake,
I have no jewels to adorn Thy shrine,
Nor any world-famed sacrifice to make;
But here I bring within my trembling hands,
This will of mine, a thing that seemeth small,
Yet Thou alone, O Lord, canst understand
How when I yield Thee this, I yield my all.

Hidden therein Thy searching gaze can see
Struggles of passion, visions of delight,
All that I have, or am, or fain would be,
Deep loves, fond hopes, and longings infinite;
It hath been wet with tears, and dimmed with sighs,
Clenched in my grasp, till beauty hath it none;
Now from Thy footstool, where it vanquished lies,
The prayer ascendeth, "May Thy will be done."

Take it, O Father, ere my courage fail,
And merge it so into Thine own will, that e'en
If in some desperate hour my cries prevail,
And Thou give back my gift, it may have been
So changed, so purified, so fair have grown,
So one with Thee, so filled with love divine,
I may not know or feel it as my own,
But gaining back my will, may find it Thine.
—Selected.

Not the sundown hours of my life, but all the hours of my life—God's!

January 5

"Hear thou, my son, and be wise, and guide thine heart in the way." (Prov. 23: 19.)

TO a young man who had just graduated from college and had expressed uncertainty as to what course he should follow in the future, Calvin Coolidge made this remark: "You are starting out in life. When you begin any journey you chart your course, you plan which direction and which road will lead to your desired destination. Have a predetermined chart, and then follow it."

General Foch made this statement as he stood before the allied commanders of the World War: "Battles are won the day before." It is the planning that goes into a life that determines how well it will succeed. We must chart the course we expect to take.

"Sailors may make their own journeyings, but not their own map; they may not paint their own horizons on the cabin ceiling; they must obey the stars and a magnetism-out-of-sight, or the ocean lanes become shambles."

A college professor said to a lad on graduation day, "Now, my boy, understand that you are going to launch your craft on a dangerous ocean." "Yes, I know it," said the boy, and taking a Bible out of his pocket and holding it up he added, "but you see, I have a safe compass to steer by."

The starting point of this journey is with God in the consciousness of sins forgiven and the peace that comes to a life fully surrendered.

> Just one thing, O Master, I ask today,
> Now that the old year has passed away,
> And a promising new year, through grace
>   of Thine,
> With all the dreams of youth is mine—
> Just one thing I ask as I onward go,
> That I'll walk with Thee—not too fast,
>   nor slow;
> Just one thing I ask, and nothing more,
> Not to linger behind, nor run before,
> O Master! This is my only plea—
> Take hold of my life and pilot me.

—Selected.

January 6

*"Wilt thou not from this time cry unto me, My father, thou
art the guide of my youth?"* (Jer. 3: 4.)

HAT course pursued will make certain a successful voyage for the sea of life?" was the question put to a professor by a young woman who had entered her freshman
year at a noted university. To her inquiry the professor
replied:
"O choose, young life, the course which you can still be following
a million years from now, and be following it joyfully and in highest profit. 'Tis the set of the sail that sends the ship safe to harbor.
'Tis the set of the soul that sends the youth triumphantly onward
and upward. It is direction that determines destiny."

What course pursued will make certain a successful voyage for
the sea of life?

(1) A definite acceptance of the Creator's plan for a whole lifetime; an utter abandonment to do His will, at any cost, by any
road. (2) A regular, systematic, never-failing prayer-life, *every*
day. (3) A daily feeding of the inner life from the inspired Word.
(4) Fellowship with others of like purpose who are climbing the
heights. (5) Alertness in testimony and loving service. The great
Pilot of the sea of life will take the command of your ship, voyage
with you and bring you safely into port.

OUTWARD BOUND

"The tugging ship is unmoored; her sails are filling with the
breeze; she sniffs the spray in her nostrils; her rigging grows taut
like giant muscles; the course is set; the pilot is at the helm—the
New Year is outward bound!"

As we stand amid the sunrise glories of this new dawn let us be
like Wilfred Campbell's pioneers:

> *"They feared no unknown; saw no horizon dark;*
> *Counted no danger; dreamed all seas their road*
> *To possible futures; struck no craven sail*
> *For sloth or indolent cowardice; steered their keels*
> *O'er wastes of heaving oceans, leagues of brine;*
> *While Hope firm kept the tiller, Faith, in dreams,*
> *Saw coasts of gleaming continent looming large*
> *Beyond the ultimate of the sea's far rim."*

Sail out, O soul of mine!

January 7

". . . That in all things he might have the pre-eminence."
(Col. 1:18.)

WOULD it not be a wise thing, here at the threshold of the New Year to walk through the rooms of your home, to search the chambers of your soul, and find if there are not things which should be submitted to the flames? God's power, in limitless abundance, is waiting to come into the souls that are willing to accept the fire test by surrendering all to Him.

A man in India, as he was searching for a book, felt a pain in his finger like the prick of a pin. He took little notice of it; but soon his arm began to swell, and in a short time he was dead. A small but deadly serpent was found among the books. There are many who receive in a book a bad wound that may seem slight but proves fatal to the soul. Be careful what you read!

Somewhere a story is recorded that the walls of a certain student's room were covered with pictures of a low order. The student's mother visited him. Not a word did she say, but placed on the wall Hofmann's "Christ in the Temple." On another visit she found the objectionable pictures were all gone! The student explained to his mother, "When He went up, *other* things had to come down."

> Dear Master, as the old year dieth soon,
>   Take Thou my harp,
> And prove if anything be out of tune,
>   Or flat, or sharp!
>
> Correct Thou, Lord, for me
>   What ringeth harsh to Thee,
> That heart and life may sing, the New Year long,
>   Thy perfect song!   —Selected.

Keep in tune with the Infinite One!

January 8

". . . And comfort of the scriptures . . ." (Rom. 15: 4.)

YOUTH will be glad to recall Stanley's rededication of himself to his Lord and Master as a result of his reading of the Bible, alone, in the heart of Africa. His own testimony in his autobiography includes the following remarkable paragraphs:

"My sicknesses were frequent, and during my first attack of African fever I took up the Bible to while away the tedious, feverish hours in bed. Though incapacitated from the march, my temperature being constantly at 105 degrees, it did not prevent me from reading, when not light-headed. I read Job and then the Psalms.

"The Bible, with its noble and simple language, I continued to read with a higher and truer understanding than I had ever before conceived. Its powerful verses had a different meaning, a more penetrative influence, in the silence of the wilds. I came to feel a strange glow while absorbed in its pages, and a charm peculiarly appropriate to the deep melancholy of African scenery.

"When I laid down the Book, my mind commenced to feed upon what memory suggested. Then rose the ghosts of bygone yearnings, haunting every cranny of the brain with numbers of baffled hopes and unfulfilled aspirations. Here was I, only a poor journalist, with no friends, and yet possessed by a feeling of power to achieve! How could it ever be! Then verses of Scripture rang iteratively through my mind as applicable to my own being, sometimes full of glowing promise, often of solemn warning.

"Alone in my tent, unseen of men, my mind labored and worked upon itself, and nothing was so soothing and sustaining as when I remembered the long-neglected comfort and support of lonely childhood and boyhood. I flung myself on my knees and utterly poured out my soul in secret prayer to Him from whom I had been so long estranged; to Him who had mysteriously led me here into Africa, there to reveal Himself, and His will. I then became inspired with a fresh desire to serve Him to the utmost, that same desire which, in early days in New Orleans, filled me each morning and sent me joyfully skipping to my work.

"As seen in my loneliness, there was this difference between the Bible and the newspapers. The one reminded me that, apart from God, my life was but a bubble of air, and it bade me remember my Creator; the other fostered arrogance and worldliness. When that vast unheaved sky and mighty circumference of tree-clad earth, or sere downland, marked so emphatically my personal littleness, I felt often so subdued, that my black followers might have discerned, had they been capable of reflection, that Africa was changing me."

"I rejoice at thy word as one that findeth great spoil." exclaimed the Psalmist. Do you know the joy that lies hidden in these neglected pages, the honey that you might eat from this garden of the Lord, these blossoms of truth and promise? Oh, take your Bibles as the living love letters of His heart to you, and ask Him to speak it to you in joy and faith and spiritual illumination, as the sweet manna of your spirit's life and the honey out of the Rock of Ages!

January 9

"Verily, verily I say unto you, . . . the works that I do shall
he do also; and greater works than these shall he do; because
I go unto my Father." (John 14: 12.)
"But ye shall receive power, after that the Holy Ghost is
come upon you: . . ." (Acts 1: 8.)

OD does not ask for personalities; persons will do. That is,
God does not ask for exceptional people. But He needs
them, and can do no great things without them. Then why
does He ask for persons when He wants personalities?
Because the power of Pentecost turns persons into personalities. By the Holy Spirit's indwelling the most ordinary can become extraordinary. All God asks for is *you;* He will see to the
rest."

Two famous men have recently spoken to youth. The Honorable
Winston Churchill says: *"This is a time when the voice of Youth*
will be welcomed in the world." In what accents will that voice
speak?   Will it take the counsel of Field Marshal Montgomery,
who says: *"Learn to build the framework of your life on a Chris-*
tian foundation"?

Do we need to be reminded of what happens when the religious
foundations—the *CHRISTIAN* foundations—are destroyed?

> *"Mourn not for the vanquished ages*
> *With their great historic men,*
> *Who dealt in history's pages*
> *And live in the poet's pen,*
> *For the grandest days are before us,*
> *And the world is yet to see*
> *The noblest work of this whole earth*
> *Is the men and women that are to be."*

"The tools to him that can use them!"

You are God's opportunity in your day. He has waited for ages
for a person just like you. If you refuse Him, then God loses His
opportunity which He sought through you, and He will never have
another, for there will never be another person on the earth just
like you.

> *Bring to God your gift, my brother,*
> *He'll not need to call another,*
> *You will do;*
> *He will add His blessing to it,*
> *And the two of you will do it,*
> *God and you.*
>   —R. E. Neighbour.

January 10

"But when it is sown, it groweth up, and becometh greater than all herbs, and shooteth out great branches; so that the fowls of the air may lodge under the shadow of it." (Mark 4:32.)

WHAT IS THE MOST STIMULATING WORD IN HUMAN SPEECH?

ET the answer to the question be given in two pictures. Here is a boy fourteen years old. He comes down the stairs of his boyhood home with his suitcase in his hand. He sets it down by the door of his mother's room and goes in to bid her good-bye. As long as he can remember, his ambition has been to go to sea, and now the hour has come, and he is bidding his mother farewell. He realizes that it is against her judgment that he go, and as he looks into her face, always sad because she is gradually growing blind, he sees the grief which the thought of his departure is causing her. So instead of bidding her farewell, he goes out, picks up his bag, mounts the stairs and stays at home. The picture that goes with that is of a man astride a horse beneath an elm tree on the edge of a college campus. He is assuming command of the armies of his people whom he is to lead to victory in their fight for independence, a service he is to fulfill as their first President—"first in war, first in peace, and first in the hearts of his countrymen." *The boy became that man.*

Another picture is that of a boy twelve years old on the campus of Phillips-Exeter Academy in New Hampshire; he is crying, partly because he is homesick and partly because his clothes are outlandish, having been made by his mother and dyed with butternut stain. They are different from those of the other fellows who laugh at him; but he wants to go home principally because he is afraid to speak before the school the next Friday afternoon. He does not see how he can speak. He realizes that his father has mortgaged the farm to send him to school, and he dimly realizes that the success of his life in any large sense will depend upon his education, but he is crying with homesickness and with fear of having to speak. The picture that goes with that is of a man on the floor of the Senate of the United States. He is a man of strange and distinctive impressiveness. An English wit said of him that he was the greatest living lie, for nobody could possibly be as great as he looked. Another said that when he walked on Beacon Street in Boston the houses looked smaller, and now as he stands on the floor of the Senate, it has fallen to his lot that he shall define the nationalism of his country in phrases that constitute one of the greatest speeches in American history. *That boy became that man.*

So here we have our word—the great, living, throbbing word—"to become." The greatness of a youth is not in what he does but

in what *he may do*. Before youth is the future in the dawn-mist of
hovering glory and surprise.

—Chapel Talks.

January 11

*". . . See, saith he, that thou make all things according to the
pattern shewed to thee in the mount."* (Heb. 8: 5.)

SONG OF A DREAMER

*I want to see other things than dreams, God—
And yet these, my dreams, must live,
Untouched by the frost of realness—
Shining like hope in my heart.*

*Dream of heroic things,
Courage—and the silver cry of bugles . . .
But let me see the small, unnoticed pain
In the eyes of some war-lonely child.
Help me to find a comfort for him . . .
Some simple thing
To make his unshed tears fall softly
And a smile come back again.*

*Tall, beautiful dreams for Someday,
Covered with the mist of things unformed . . .
God, help me not to be so blind
To all the little ugly things
That I could take so easily inside my heart
For even just an hour or two,
And make them lovely.
Things like unmittened hands,
Hunger and weeping,
The ugliness of want and need.*

*Dream of music, deeper and more sweet
Than any ever made . . .
But I want my listening ears to hear
The sound of a stifled sob,
Tears in a voice that tries to sing,
The desolate echo of a voiceless cry . . .
Help me to give my hand to someone,
Lend my song-dreams to an empty heart,
Weave sweeter music
From the loom of real things—
Harsh, unlovely, small—
But real.*

Dreams, silver–misted, in my heart are dear . . .
Strange that these simple little things of Now
Should somehow make them brighter . . .
Make them suddenly come true.
            —*Marian Vincent Hoffman.*

"Dreams may be spun upon the looms of God, but remember that dreams may be our traitors. Build great castles in the air and then go out to work and put solid foundations beneath them."

Sign your name to your dreams.

January 12

". . . *Hold that fast which thou hast, that no man take thy crown.*" (Rev. 3: 11.)

N a day in the autumn I saw a prairie eagle mortally wounded by a rifle shot. His eye still gleamed like a circle of light. Then he slowly turned his head and gave one more searching and longing look at the sky. He had often swept those starry spaces with his wonderful wings. The beautiful sky was the home of his heart. It was the eagle's domain. A thousand times he had exploited there his splendid strength. In those far away heights he had played with the lightnings, and raced with the winds, and now, so far away from home, the eagle lay dying, done to the death, because for once he forgot and flew too low.
Read the story of Samson (Judges, chapters 13-16).

          "*One deed may mar a life,*
           And one may make it."

January 13

"*But the mountain shall be thine. . . .*" (Joshua 17: 18.)

HE story is told of a great Carthaginian general who summoned his troops to meet in the foothills of the towering Alps. Pointing to the majestic mountains, he said, "*Over the Alps lies Italy!*" Beautiful, sunny Italy—the land of their dreams! The challenge was theirs! A challenge that meant heroism, bravery, determination! Those mountains held a lure for the brave soldiers. But—were they now ready to accept the challenge, to face the difficulties, and to hazard their lives in the undertaking to make their dreams come true?
Their general did not hide from them the perils they must encounter if they were to reach the top. But he told them of the wide horizons that would be theirs at the trail's end—the honors await-

ing them as a reward for their valiant act. A few retreated, preferring to live in the valley and the lowland rather than face the struggle, deadly insensitive to their glorious privilege of winning the prize! But the majority girded themselves for the feat to be accomplished. They had caught the vision and were content to leave the valley roads for high climbing. Day by day, over sharp rocks and crags they went, through toil and pain, fainting oft from hunger and fatigue. Blood drops on the pure white snow marked their tracks. At last—cold, ragged, and hungry—they reached the top and planted their standard on the highest peak of the Alps. The almost insurmountable mountains below them were wreathed in the mystery of the clouds! The peaks around were touched with the glory of the sunrise! Before their vision, of unsurpassing loveliness, were fields of waving grain in the green valley below! Beautiful orchards, sparkling fountains! Italy! They had arrived in the land of their dreams! It lay *"across the Alps."*

"Youth without faith is a day without sun."

January 14

"Search me, O God, and know my heart: try me, and know my thoughts: . . . and lead me in the way everlasting."
(Psalm 139:23, 24.)

TAKING SPIRITUAL INVENTORY

THERE is a proverb in the business world that the man who takes no inventories finally becomes bankrupt.

Bishop Foster said, "If you have no sense of need, you will assuredly make no progress. If, with them of Laodicea, you say, 'I am rich, and increased with goods, and have need of nothing'—I have religion enough, I see no special reason for making so much ado about the matter—if such, or anything resembling this, is your feeling, you will not soon occupy advanced ground. Seek to realize your needs. But how shall you do this? There is but one way. Oh, that we could prevail upon you to be faithful here! Taking the twin lamps of truth, the Bible and conscience, with sincere prayers for the guidance of the Holy Ghost, make that diligent search which the importance of the case requires. Be candid with yourself. Make no extenuations, no apology; use no tenderness. Ferret every recess thoroughly; probe to the bottom; pass through every chamber of your soul; search it through and through with a determination to know your case, to look at yourself stripped of every disguise. What do you find? Are there no idols in the sacred temple, no 'images of gold,' no 'Babylonish garments' no concealed 'spies,' no pride, no envy, no jealousy, no anger, no malice, no undue love of the world, no undue desire for the praise of men, no improper ambition? Does God possess your heart without a rival? Are you wholly the Lord's? Oh, for faithfulness! Have no mercy on yourself; be resolved to know the worst! You may make such discoveries as will astonish and distress you; still, make diligent search. What is your example? Is it all that a Christian's should be? Do you daily exhibit in the family, in the social circle, in your business—everywhere—those tempers which should adorn the Christian character? What is your influence? Is it, so far as it is under your control, always decidedly and undividedly for Christ?"

But no matter how discouraging the results of this inventory may be, let no one give over to everlasting bankruptcy. Confess the need to Christ without any shaming. Press your claim, through the merits of His blood, for immediate help. Believe His promise. Receive His Spirit. Obtain the riches of full salvation today.—*Selected.*

The old German artist Hofmann is said to have visited at intervals the Royal Gallery in Dresden to touch up his paintings there.

January 15

"... Those that seek me early in the morning [Hebrew] shall find me." (Prov. 8: 17.)

PREBENDARY WEBB-PEPLOE once said: *"All great saints have been early risers."* Some of the holiest and busiest of God's children have made the Morning Watch the settled habit of their lives. Sir Henry Havelock, even if he had to march at four in the morning, would rise so as to have two hours of fellowship with the King. The late Lord Cairns made it a rule to have an hour and a half for prayer before meeting the family, and never deviated from this, even if his late duties in Parliament left him no more than two hours' sleep. Wesley and Whitefield were early risers. Frances Ridley Havergal could not have filled earth with so much of the music of heaven, had she not enjoyed what she calls "the one hour at dawn with Jesus."

Can any of us dispense with this Morning Watch? What time is there to gather manna for the soul unless we do it before the sun rises? (Exod. 16:19-21). What time to steal a march upon the enemy, unless like Joshua, we awake right early? (Joshua 6:12).

"Thankfully do I here testify to the value of the Morning Watch and vow to keep the holy tryst" are the words of a noted missionary.

> Some minutes in the morning,
> Ere the cares of life begin,
> Ere the heart's wide door is open
> For the world to enter in.

Oh, then alone with Jesus,
In the silence of the morn,
In heavenly, sweet communion
Let your every day be born,
In the quietude that blesses,
With a prelude of repose,
Let your soul be soothed and softened
As the dew revives the rose.

Some minutes in the morning
Take your Bible in your hand,
And catch a glimpse of glory
From the peaceful promised land.
It will linger still before you
When you seek the busy mart,
And like flowers of hope will blossom
Into beauty in your heart.
The precious words like jewels
Will glisten all the day
With a rare refulgent glory
That will brighten all the way!

—*Selected.*

The morning hour has gold in its hand.

January 16

"Sing unto the Lord, bless his name; show forth his salvation from day to day." (Psalm 96: 2.)

THIS is the day the Lord hath made.' It is the Lord's gift. But for His goodness and mercy I should not have seen Today. His goodness is new upon me each morning.

But why should God give me Today? He has given me so many; rarely have I given one back to Him. He gave me Today that I might honor and serve Him better than on any day I hitherto accepted from His hand.

How strangely wonderful would it be if but a single day could be fully given back to God by me; if on arising in the morning I would call upon Him: 'Cause me to hear Thy lovingkindness in the morning,' and then through Today in all things be guided by His voice, trust Him, love Him, obey Him.

If from youth a man accepts Today as God's gift and lives it by His grace, he exalts the name of God and brings strength to his nation."

TO YOUTH

Here is your armor: the shield of glorious youth,
The keen spurs of the mind, the sword of vision.

Go forth and find the Holy Grail of Truth,
Unmindful of the multitude's derision.

Today is yours, and yours the confidence
Of garnered knowledge and our past mistakes:
Subdue the hosts of ignorance and pretense:
Bring back the only cup our thirsting slakes.

You shall erase the scars of this dark hour,
The lines of hunger and the wounds of pain;
Yours the great spirit that must rise to power
And give a lost world peace and faith again.
—Selected.

When God says "now" let no man say "tomorrow."

Today is better than tomorrow.

January 17

". . . Get thee out of thy country, and from thy kindred, . . .
unto a land that I will shew thee." (Gen. 12: 1.)

NO test is harder to a conscientious Christian than the necessity of separation in matters of conscience and principle from those most dearly loved. They plead so plausibly for our concessions and surrenders that it seems almost harsh to ride rough shod over all their sweet affection and gentle pleading. One of the finest of modern paintings represents a beautiful French girl, on the night preceding the awful massacre of St. Bartholomew, trying to pin a little badge on the breast of her Protestant lover; with tearful eyes and strained entreaty she is pleading with him to wear it as his only defense against the murderous swords of his assassins. With tender love but heavenly courage he is represented as gently holding back her hand and detaching the rosette from his bosom, knowing all the while that it is probably the last time they would ever meet on earth. It is just such little things as this which constitute the difference beween loyalty and treason, between the hero-martyr and the easy time-server of every age."

—Dr. A. B. Simpson.

Beware lest the sympathy of others compete with God for the throne of your life!

In spite of the stares of the wise and the world's derision,
Dare follow the star-blazed road, dare follow the vision.
—Edwin Markham.

January 18

". . . Arise, let us go hence." (John 14:31.)

WHEN nature plants an oak in the forest, she does not say, "Be a lichen, a small ground-creeping thing!" She says, "Grow! Become a tall, strong, mountain tree!" When we hold our baby in our arms we do not say, "My child, be good for nothing." Neither does God say, "Be nothing; do nothing! Just exist as humbly and meekly as you can!" He says, "Quit you like men!"

Each of us is born for a sceptre and a crown. It gives a strange new thrill to life to realize we may long earnestly for high things, and work for them, if our inmost desire is not for self, but for God.
—*The Warrior.*

"We need not live on the marsh and in the mists. The slopes and ridges invite us!"

Teach me the faith of the mountains, serene and sublime,
The deep-rooted joy of just living one day at a time;
Leaving the petty possessions the valley-folk buy
For the glory of glad wind-swept spaces where earth meets the sky.

Teach me the faith of the mountains, their strength to endure,
The breadth and the depth of their vision, unswerving and sure,
Counting the dawn and the starlight as parts of one whole
Wrought by the Spirit Eternal, within His control.
—*Author Unknown.*

Help us to live a mountain-top life!

January 19

". . . I seek not mine own will, but the will of the Father, which hath sent me." (John 5: 30.) *". . . Nevertheless not my will, but thine, be done."* (Luke 22: 42.)

AN ambitious young student heard God's call. This student had plans of his own. He had his own program mapped out, but Christ crossed His path. He must do something with Christ. Christ crossed his path, the inescapable Christ, and the young man yielded. Yielded his life, yielded will, yielded all, and then in a quiet place he wrote:

WHEN I MET THE MASTER

I had walked life's way with an easy tread,
  Had followed where comforts and pleasure led,
Until one day, in a quiet place,
  I met the Master, face to face.

With station and rank and wealth for my goal,
  Much thought for my body, but none for my soul,
I had entered to win in life's big race,
  When I met the Master, face to face.

I had built my castles and reared them high,
  With their towers had pierced the blue of the sky,
I had sworn to rule with an iron mace,
  When I met the Master, face to face.

I met Him and knew Him, and blushed to see
  That His eyes full of sorrow were fixed on me,
And I faltered and fell at His feet that day,
  While my castles melted and vanished away.

Melted and vanished, and in their place
  Naught else did I see but the Master's face,
And I cried aloud, "Oh, make me meet
  To follow the steps of Thy wounded feet!"

My thought is now for the souls of men,
  I have lost my life to find it again,
E'er since that day in a quiet place,
  When I met the Master, face to face.

—Selected.

The greatest hour in any person's life is when he comes face to face with Jesus Christ and hears the Master's call to the fellowship and service of His Kingdom.

January 20

"Therefore if any man be in Christ, he is a new creature: old things are passed away; behold, all things are become new."
(2 Cor. 5:17.)

"The Spirit itself beareth witness . . . , that we are the children of God." (Rom. 8:16.)

 NEW creature! The *new* birth! 'Except a man be born again'—what does it mean? I cannot explain the mystery of birth, but what does it matter? Here is *the child.* I cannot explain the truth that something darting like a flash of lightning into the soul of that Oxford student transformed his whole life, but, explained or unexplained, here is *George Whitefield!"—Boreham.*

"In the evening I went very unwillingly to a society in Aldersgate Street, where one was reading Luther's preface to the Epistle to the Romans. About a quarter before nine, while he was describing the change which God works in the heart through faith in Christ, I felt my heart strangely warmed. I felt I did trust in Christ, Christ alone, for salvation; and an assurance was given me, that He had taken away *my* sins, even *mine*, and saved *me* from the law of sin and death."—*John Wesley's Journal*, May 24, 1738.

I HAVE BEEN CHANGED

And can it be that I should gain an interest in the Saviour's blood?
Died He for me, who caused His pain? For me, who Him to death
pursued?
Amazing love! how can it be that Thou, my Lord, shoulds't die for
me?

Long my imprisoned spirit lay, fast bound in sin and nature's night;
Thine eye diffused a quickening ray; I woke; the dungeon flamed
with light:
My chains fell off, my heart was free, I rose, went forth, and fol-
lowed Thee.

No condemnation now I dread, Jesus, with all in Him, is mine;
Alive in Him, my living Head, and clothed in righteousness divine.
Behold I approach the eternal throne, and claim the crown, through
Christ, my own.
                                    —*Charles Wesley* (1707–1788).

January 21

"As the hart panteth after the water brooks, so panteth my
soul after thee, O God. My soul thirsteth for God . . ."
                                    (Psalm 42:1, 2.)

IF there is in your heart this deep spiritual thirst, thank God! It is the very beginning of the blessing you seek, and already the Holy Spirit is at work preparing you for the answer to your cry.

Dr. A. B. Simpson relates the following story:

"An eastern caravan was once overtaken in the desert with the failure of the supply of water. The accustomed fountains were all dried, the oasis was a desert, and they halted an hour before sunset after a day of scorching heat, to find that they were perishing for want of water. Vainly they explored the usual wells, for they were all dry. Dismay was upon all faces and despair in all hearts, when one of the ancient men approached the sheik and counselled him to unloose two beautiful harts that he was conveying home as a present to his bride, and let them scour the desert in search of water. Their tongues were protruding with thirst, and their bosoms heaving with distress. But as they were led out to the borders of the camp and set free on the boundless plain, they lifted up their heads on high, and sniffed the air with distended nostrils, and then, with unerring instinct, with a course as straight as an arrow and with speed as swift as the wind, they darted off across the desert. Swift horsemen followed close behind; an hour or two later they hastened back with the glad tidings that water had been found, and the camp moved with shouts of rejoicing to the happily discovered fountains."

No instinct can be put in you by the Holy Spirit but one He purposes to fulfill. He who breathes into our hearts the heavenly hope will not deceive nor fail us when we press forward to its realization.

Are you panting for a draught from some cool spring? Follow the "scent of water"! It will lead you to the heavenly springs.

"All that I need is in Jesus!
He satisfies! He satisfies!"

January 22

"Now the Lord had said unto Abram, Get thee out of thy country, . . . unto a land that I will shew thee." (Gen. 12: 1.)

"God has guided the heroes and saints of all ages to do things which were ordinarily regarded by the community as ridiculous and mad. Have you ever taken any risks for Christ?"
—*Chas. E. Cowman*

"There's no sense in going further—it's the edge of cultivation."
So they said, and I believed it—broke my land and sowed my
*   crop—*
Built my barns and strung my fences in the little border station—
Tucked away below the foothills where the trails run out and stop.

Till a voice, as bad as conscience, rang interminable changes
On one everlasting whisper, day and night repeated so:
"Something hidden. Go and find it. Go and look behind the
*   Ranges,*
Something lost behind the Ranges, lost and waiting for you. Go!"
Anybody might have found it, but—His whisper came to me!
*   —Kipling.*

"It is impossible to be a hero in anything unless one is first a hero in faith."

"By faith they...." (Today read the book of Hebrews, chapter eleven.)

Only those who see the invisible shall do exploits!

January 23

". . . and he went forth conquering, and to conquer."
(Rev. 6:2.)

IN the soul of youth there is this mysterious something, this inner and inescapable urge that makes them go forth on quests, and all youth are conscious of it; so they set the inner urge to tingling with their own purposes. Youth's hour, youth's chance has come. Let us venture forth, willing to take up the costly journey to the mountain top, above timberline, of a new vision where we can see the sun rise upon a new world and catch a new vision of the glory that is to be in this, our Father's world!

What does this quest mean in the life of youth? Garibaldi knew what it was in the soul of his young red-shirted warriors when he said: "Follow me. I offer you hardship, suffering, wounds, and death." Our Lord knew when He said: "Seek ye first the kingdom of God, and his righteousness." (Matt. 6: 33.)

". . . Go ye into all the world, and preach the Gospel to every creature." (Mark 16: 15.)

The time has come to make it a reality. The opportunity for the adult generation is rapidly passing away with every clock-tick of Father Time. Youth's opportunity has come! Let us share together the happy and adventurous path!

YOUTH AND HIS DREAM

Youth with his dream went forth,
"I must conquer the world," he said;
Held in his hand a sword,
Soon youth and his dream lay dead.

Youth with his dream went forth,
"Christ must rule o'er the world," he said;
Held in his hand a Cross,
And followed where'er the dream led.
—*Author Unknown.*

"By this sign we'll conquer." (Crusaders' Watchword.)

" 'So few men venture out beyond the blazed trail,'
'Tis he who has the courage to go past this sign
That cannot in his mission fail.
He will have left at least some mark behind
To guide some other brave exploring mind."

January 24

*"And one cried unto another and said, Holy, holy, holy, is the
Lord of hosts: the whole earth is full of his glory." (Isa. 6:3.)*

A BOY went with his father to the zoo. He became so interested in the monkeys that he refused to look at the beautiful birds, the graceful deer, or the powerful buffalo. When
he returned home, he could talk only of the monkeys. Is
it possible that we can go through life looking at so many
trinkets and toys that we never notice God or His many blessings?

> *"Two men were looking at the sea—*
> *But one saw only quantity.*
> *The other soul was filled with awe,*
> *The handiwork of God is what he saw.*
>
> *"And then the singing of a bird—*
> *A noise is all the first one heard.*
> *The other felt uplifted all day long,*
> *And loved the Lord more dearly for the song.*
> *Eyes see when opened by His touch,*
> *And ears unstopped can hear so much."*

The poet Blake stood on the shore watching the sun rise out of
the ocean. Sky and sea were brilliant with a million refracted rays.
The sun's bright disk was just visible above the water when he
noticed a man standing beside him. Blake turned in an ecstasy,
and pointing to the rising sun, he cried,
"Look! Look! What do you see?"
"Oh," returned the other, "I see something that looks like money
—gold money. What do you see?"
"I see the glory of God," replied Blake, "and I hear a multitude
of the heavenly host saying, 'Holy, holy, holy, is the Lord God
Almighty.'"   —*Rev. A. W. Tozer.*

Joses, the brother of Jesus, plodded from day to day
With never a vision within him to glorify his clay;
Joses, the brother of Jesus, was one with the heavy clod,
But Christ was the soul of rapture, and soared, like a lark, with
*   God;*
Joses, the brother of Jesus, was only a worker in wood,
And he never could see the glory that Jesus his brother could.
"Why stays he not in the workshop," he often used to complain,
"Sawing the Lebanon cedar, imparting to woods their stain?
Why must he go thus roaming, forsaking my father's trade,
While hammers are busily sounding, and there is gain to be made?"
Thus ran the mind of Joses, apt with plummet and rule,
And deeming whoever surpassed him either a knave or a fool—

For he never walked with the prophets in God's great garden of
    bliss;
And of all the mistakes of the ages the saddest, methinks, was this:
To have such a brother as Jesus, to speak with him day by day,
Yet never to catch the vision which glorified his clay.
                              —*Harry Kemp.*

January 25

"*Let him know, that he which converteth the sinner from the error of his way, shall save a soul from death, and shall hide a multitude of sins.*" (James 5:20.)

 MISSIONARY once wrote, "Out in India, in the mountains, I have heard in the twilight hour a call from the ridge below. Away through the stillness comes the call, and from the ridge above me comes a response. And then I hear, in a moment more, a faint call from a far ridge, away up and beyond, sounding almost like a distant echo. What did it mean? It meant that the man close above me was passing the word from the man below to the man beyond. The man below could never have reached the other man except for the man who stood on the middle ridge and passed the message on."

Christian youth! you stand on the middle ridge. To you has been committed the tremendous responsibility of reaching the youth on the ridge below. Thousands of them are within your reach every day, in the schoolroom, the office and factory. They must be won for Christ. There is a youth down there who will never hear "the Man" up there, unless you become the youth on the middle ridge.

Resolve this day to become a soul-winner!

"Lord, lay some soul upon my heart,
   And love that soul through me;
And may I humbly do my part
   To win that soul for Thee."

"And they that be wise shall shine as the brightness of the firmament; and they that turn many to righteousness as the stars for ever and ever. (Daniel 12:3.)

"I will make you fishers of men,
   If you follow me."

January 26

"Thine eyes did see my substance, yet being unperfect; and in thy book all my members were written, which in continuance were fashioned, when as yet there was none of them."

(Psalm 139:16.)

IS not my life planned out for me by God? Are not my times in *His* hand? Till the appointed hour strikes on the clocks of heaven, ten thousand may fall at my right hand, but it shall not come nigh me. Man in the center of God's will is immortal till his work is done! God is concerned about my life.

> *Thou art more than a clod;*
> *More than a rough-spun dress;*
> *More than a sheltering pod*
> *For a soul's homelessness;*
>
> *More than a fettered slave*
> *Bound to a master;*
> *Destined to fill a grave;*
> *Born to disaster.*
>
> *Thou art a thought of God;*
> *A long-planned implement,*
> *Designed to fill His hand*
> *And made for His content.*
>
> *Angels with watchful eyes*
> *Have charge of thee,*
> *Lest uncouth hand should chip*
> *Thy frail mortality.*
>
> *Lest uncouth hand should chip*
> *The vase of clay;*
> *Or underling let slip*
> *The pitcher by the way.*
>
> *When thou art broken—when*
> *Thy lamp is lifted high,*
> *Will He who made thee, leave thee then,*
> *Or, heedless, put thee by?*

—Fay Inchfawn.

". . . Ye shall be a peculiar treasure unto me . . ." (Exod. 19: 5.)

". . . Children of God: And if children, then heirs; heirs of God, and joint-heirs with Christ, . . ." (Rom. 8: 16, 17.)

January 27

"Let us go on unto perfection. . . ." (Heb. 6:1.)

THE youth who resolves to concentrate on one important objective and puts forth his best efforts day after day is destined for real achievement.

Ability to do one thing supremely well is better than to possess a score of varied but half-used talents.

You enhance your chances of successfully attaining your objective when you take time to think out the best available means of pursuing it.

Here are some suggestions that will help you to formulate a set of holy New Year's resolutions for yourself:

I resolve by the grace of God:
1. Never to judge others. 1 Cor. 4: 3-5.
2. Never to discuss the faults and failures of absent ones. Prov. 16:28.
3. Never to divulge secrets. Prov. 11: 13.
4. Never to repeat a matter. Prov. 17: 9.
5. Rather to remain silent when there is nothing that I can say to another's advantage. Titus 3:2.
6. To set a watch upon my lips. Psalm 39: 1.
7. Always to attribute the best motives. 1 Cor. 13: 7.
8. To talk less and listen more.
9. To take time to be friendly.
10. To be uniformly courteous.
11. To shun debt.
12. To do an hour's solid reading.
13. To cultivate patience.
14. That should I fail in any one of the above resolutions, to repent and confess it immediately, and if necessary, to ask an injured brother's forgiveness.   —*Anon.*

"Choices are the hinges of destiny."—*Edwin Markham.*

January 28

". . . The people had a mind to work." (Neh. 4:6.)

THERE were no shirkers or lazy workmen in Nehemiah's group. Every man could be depended upon to do his work well and with all his heart. Laziness paralyzes the soul and the body and is a type of slow suicide.

"I refuse to be lazy" wrote a noted university professor. "I refuse to be the slave of ease. I will so command my body that I shall, even at a great sacrifice, complete my plans. I cannot afford an hour of lassitude. I will study most carefully how to rest and refresh myself, but I arise to declare that I am not a slave. 'Father, teach me the power of self-mastery. Help me to train my body to serve perfectly Thy high purpose!'"

God never called a lazy man
To do a task for Him—
He's looking for the men who work
With energy and vim.
For men like that are sure to win
A cause they undertake.
He doesn't want the lazy kind,
He wants men wide awake.
So if you're called to do a task,
To help Him right some wrong,
You just be glad that you are called
To help His cause along.　　—Edward H. Kessler.

"In the morning when thou findest thyself unwilling to rise, consider thyself presently, if it is to go about a man's work, that I am stirred up; or was I made for this, to lay me down and make much of myself in a warm bed."—Marcus Aurelius.

Sunshine and sleep have no inter-fitness. Moonlight and ploughing are badly matched.

The youth of the world who have reached the mountain summit were not pushed into their place of triumph; they *worked* their way there!

January 29

"Thou shalt guide me with thy counsel..." (Psalm 73: 24.)

THERE are test hours which lead on to triumph or failure. *Columbus* had his supreme moment. What a calamity if he had wasted it! *Washington* had his hour which was freighted with tremendous import. *Lincoln* held his watch when destiny itself was in the tick. *Luther* with the Pope's bull above the flames, and *Knox* before Queen Mary, were at moments with an eternity in them.

The battles of men and nations have often hung in the balance on a fraction of time.

"I will instruct thee and teach thee in the way which thou shalt go: I will guide thee with mine eye." (Psalm 32: 8.)

Abraham Lincoln, during the Civil War, said: "I have been driven many times to my knees by the overwhelming conviction that I had nowhere else to go. My own wisdom and that of all about me seemed insufficient for the day."

"When I was hemmed in, thou hast freed me often." (Psalm 4: 1 —Trans.)

January 30

"Whom having not seen, ye love: in whom, though now ye see him not, yet believing, ye rejoice with joy unspeakable and full of glory." (1 Peter 1:8.)

ROFESSOR DRUMMOND in his essay on "The Changed Life" tells of a young girl who practiced living in the presence of Christ. Her perfect grace of character was the wonder of all who knew her. She wore on her neck a golden locket which no one was ever allowed to open. One day, in a moment of unusual confidence, one of her companions was allowed to touch the spring and learn its secret. She saw written these words: *"Whom not having seen, I love."*

The One altogther lovely, the mightiest of magnets!

I have seen Jesus, and my heart is dead to all beside;
I have seen Jesus, and my wants are all supplied;
I have seen Jesus, and my heart is satisfied,
    Satisfied with Jesus.
               —A. B. Simpson.

Young hearts can offer love, pure as a limpid spring. Their sympathy is as responsive as the most sensitive harp and yields to the touch of the tenderest joy and grief. Their smiles in gladness are sweet as sunshine; their tears in sadness are gentle as the dew. All their nature is fresh and unabused; it is like the fresh green of the springtime before the dust or the city grime has fallen upon it. Youth to the Master are as gracious streams and flowers of the field.
               —Selected.

"Show me Thy face—one transient gleam
    Of loveliness Divine,
And I shall never think or dream
    Of other love save Thine:
All lesser light will darken quite,
    All lower glories wane,
The beauty of earth will scarce
    Seem beautiful again.

"Show me Thy face—my faith and love
    Shall henceforth fixed be,
And nothing here have power to move
    My soul's serenity.
My life shall seem a trance, a dream,
    And all I feel and see
Illusive, visionary—Thou
    The one reality!"

(May be sung to the tune of "Drink to Me Only with Thine Eyes.")

January 31

*". . . No man, having put his hand to the plough, and looking
back, is fit for the kingdom of God."* (Luke 9:62.)

THE disciples, asking themselves, "Is not sainthood for rare
and elect souls and beyond the compass of our common
clay?" were tempted to go back from Christ. So, some of
us are tempted to take the lower road, thinking it more
level to our powers, and we settle down into the *second
best!* This is the tragedy of many youth. They have caught gleams
of the summit of Mount Everest; now they are content to live below. The real victory of this life of ours is to keep on climbing to
the end. God's best is not for elect souls but for those who trust
Him wholly.

"A voice said 'CLIMB.' And he said, 'How shall I climb? The
mountains are so steep that I cannot climb.'
"The voice said, 'CLIMB or DIE.'
"He said, 'But how? I see no way up those steep ascents. This
that is asked of me is too hard for me.'

"The voice said, 'CLIMB or PERISH, soul and body of thee, mind
and spirit of thee. There is no second choice for any son of man.
CLIMB or DIE.'

"Then he remembered that he had read in the books of the
bravest climbers on the hills of earth, that sometimes they were
aware of the presence of a Companion who was not one of the
earthly party of climbers on the mountains. How much more certain was the presence of his Guide as he climbed the high places
of the Spirit!

"And he remembered a word in the Book of Mountaineers that
heartened him. 'My soul is continually in my hand.' It heartened
him, for it told him that he was created to walk in precarious places,
not on the easy levels of life."
                —*Amy Wilson Carmichael, in Figures of the True.*

*"I'm going by the upper road, for that still holds the sun,
I'm climbing through night's pastures where the starry rivers run:
If you should think to find me in my old dark abode,
You'll find this writing on the door, 'He's on the Upper Road.' "*

In "Roadmates," by John Oxenham, are these lines:
      *"So make we—all one company,
      Love's golden chord our tether,
      And, come what may, we'll climb the way
      Together—aye, together!"*

February 1

". . . And ye shall know that I am the Lord your God."
(Exod. 16:12.)
". . . And hereby we know that he abideth in us by the Spirit which he hath given us." (1 John 3:24.)

"YOU really don't know *what* you believe," said a captious voice, summing up theological difficulties in a way which the hyper-critic considered unanswerable.

"But I know *WHOM* I have believed," replied the young Christian quietly, to the utter confusion of the skeptic. We can be sure of God!

What clean work the Lord makes of philosophy and "modern thought" when He puts His hand to it! He brings the fine appearance down to nothing; He utterly destroys the wood, hay, and stubble. "For it is written, I will destroy the wisdom of the wise, and will bring to nothing the understanding of the prudent." (1 Cor. 1:19.)

The humblest believer who has found Christ as his Saviour and Lord has an experience which neither men nor devils can overthrow.

Someone asked a young convert how he could believe the Bible was inspired. He said, "It inspires me!" That is a shortcut to inspiration. I would doubt my existence as quickly as I would doubt the truth of that Book.   —*D. L. Moody.*

A foolish child can pull a flower to pieces, but it takes a God to form and paint a flower! Until a man can construct a book that equals the Bible, he would better let the Bible stand in its solitary grandeur and power.—*David Gregg.*

February 2

"Thou therefore endure hardness, as a good soldier of Jesus Christ." (2 Tim. 2:3.)

"THERE are just two types of men in the world," says Robert Louis Stevenson. "The one type is represented by the Alpine cragsman who makes a trail to the heights, and as he makes his trail he plants his feet where it is safe for those who follow him to plant their feet also. So he mounts to the summit where the sky is clear, the horizons are far and spacious, and the air is vigorous and tonic. His blood runs red to the tips of his body, his lungs are full; he is Man at his best, both in his own achievement and as a guide. That is one type.

"The other type is represented by a chemist I knew who dreaded catching cold. Therefore, he stayed in the house and wore a shawl and tin shoes and dieted upon tepid milk. Round and round his little shop he thought only of himself—coddled himself. There were no horizons for him, no heights, no trail upward, no footsteps for others to use in their climbing toward the summits."

> *From prayer that asks that I may be*
> *Sheltered from winds that beat on me,*
> *From fearing when I should aspire,*
> *From faltering when I should climb higher,*
> *From silken self, O Captain, free*
> *Thy soldier who would follow Thee.*
>
> *From subtle love of softening things,*
> *From easy choices, weakenings.*
> *(Not thus are spirits fortified,*
> *Not this way went the Crucified.)*
> *From all that dims Thy Calvary,*
> *O Lamb of God, deliver me.*
>
> *Give me the love that leads the way,*
> *The faith that nothing can dismay,*
> *The hope no disappointments tire,*
> *The passion that will burn like fire.*
> *Let me not sink to be a clod:*
> *Make me Thy fuel, Flame of God.*   —*Gold Cord.*

February 3

"Meditate upon these things; give thyself wholly to them; that thy profiting may appear to all." (1 Tim. 4:15.)

IF YOU have but ten or fifteen minutes night and morning, read *God's Word*—and read it consecutively! In this way you get a grasp of the "whole counsel of God." But this is not *Bible study*! For this, fifteen minutes will not suffice. Try to get two or three hours as often as possible, and then sit down with your Bible, with your concordance, your textbook, a pen, ink, and a ruler. Determine that you will not be diverted from your purpose—and you may expect a feast of rich things! Don't be impatient. Wait, and ponder, and pray. Compare Scripture with Scripture—and as you thus dig, God will unfold to you "precious things."—*S. M.*

"What a Book! Vast and wide as the world, rooted in the abysses of creation, and towering up behind the blue secrets of Heaven. Sunrise and sunset, promise and fulfillment, birth and death, the whole drama of humanity all in this Book!"—*Heinrich Heine.*

Most men have forgotten the importance of Divine Revelation and have gone after fantastic fads for the satisfaction of their souls and the enlightenment of their minds. But we cling to the Bible—the road-lamp of the pilgrim and the guiding chart of the Christian mariner.

THE BOOK, THE PLACE

I entered the world's great library doors,
I crossed their acres of polished floors;
I searched and searched their stacks and nooks,
But I settled at last on the Book of books.

I journeyed north, south, east, and west,
An endless trail, a hopeless quest;
At last, at last, I came to where
Was a little, walled-in place of prayer.   —W. A. C.

February 4

". . . Eye hath not seen, nor ear heard, neither have entered into the heart of man, the things which God hath prepared for them that love him." (1 Cor. 2:9.)

YOUTH has great possibilities. You remember the story of the German teacher who always reverently removed his hat before a company of young people, "not knowing," he said, "what future great man might be among them." Possibilities! Makers of future history!

Do you, young people, ever sit down in the quiet and think, deeply and seriously, about your life—what it is, what wondrous powers are sleeping in your brain, in your heart, in your hands—think what you may become, what you may do in this world?

If you have never sat down before to look at your life, to think of its almost endless possibilities, you have not begun to live. Yes, youth is glorious!

But *Christian* young life, given to Christ and touched by His hand and set apart in holy consecration to be His alone for time and eternity—who can paint its glory, its possibilities, its destiny!

> *Be strong!*
> *We are not here to play, to dream, to drift;*
> *We have hard work to do, and loads to lift.*
> *Shun not the struggle; face it.*
> *'Tis God's gift.*

> *Be strong!*
> *Say not the days are evil—who's to blame?*
> *And fold the hands and acquiesce—O shame!*
> *Stand up, speak out, and bravely,*
> *In God's name.*

Be strong!
It matters not how deep entrenched the wrong,
How hard the battle goes, the day how long,
Faint not, fight on!
    Tomorrow comes the song.
             —*Maltbie D. Babcock.*

February 5

"Put on the whole armour of God, that ye may be able to stand against the wiles of the devil." (Eph. 6:11.)
"Lest Satan should get an advantage of us: for we are not ignorant of his devices." (2 Cor. 2:11.)

AN Indian fable relates that Brahma inquired of the Spirit of Power, "What is stronger than thou?" and he replied, "Cunning." In wickedness, however, we have strength and cleverness, passion and policy, the wrath of the lion and the subtlety of the serpent.

The kingdom of evil reveals genius as well as energy. The Chinese proverb asks, "What would not the lion do if he were the monkey also?" But in evil the lion is the monkey also, the force of the one being combined with the craft of the other.

Marianne North, writing about the forests of Brazil, speaks of the trees as being decorated with "spider-webs, green, gold, or silver, glittering in the morning sun, often spangled with diamond dew." The worst spider (Satan) knows how to weave seductive webs for youth! See those palaces of passion at the street corner—mirrors, music, maidens!

When the mad Queen of Mexico escaped from her prison, her anxious attendants, remembering her passion for roses, strewed roses along roads, and soon the poor Queen was lured back. The pleasures of sin have lured many to an evil destination. (Heb. 11: 25.)

"Yield not to temptation,
    For yielding is sin;
Each victory will help you
    Some other to win;
Fight manfully onward,
    Dark passions subdue;
Look ever to Jesus,
    He will carry you through.

"Ask the Saviour to help you,
    Comfort, strengthen, and keep you;
He is willing to aid you,
    He will carry you through."

February 6

"I am the vine, ye are the branches: He that abideth in me, and I in him, the same bringeth forth much fruit: for without me ye can do nothing." (John 15:5.)

OUR influence with our fellow men in public will always be in exact proportion to the depth of our hidden life with God in secret. It is not what we say, not what we do; it is what we *are* that tells, or rather what Christ is in us. Make room for Christ in your heart, and you need not advertise it. It will be noised that He is in the house.

We cannot say to ourselves too often that Christianity is a personal experience. One evening in a West Point delegation at the Northfield Student Conference, conversation fell on serious lines, and one of the men threw this question into the circle: "What is Christianity, anyway?" After a long pause one of the cadets gave this answer: "Oscar Westover." Exactly! I do not know who he was, only that he was one of the cadets living a kind of life so that when the boys thought of Christianity they defined it in terms of him. That is the only way you ever can define it. It is "Oscar Westover." It is not a creed, nor an organization, nor a ritual. These are important, but they are secondary. They are the leaves; they are not the roots. They are the wires; they are not the message. The *thing itself is life;* it is "Oscar Westover."

> *This I learned from the shadow of a tree,*
> *Which to and fro did sway against a wall.*
> *Our shadow selves, our influence may fall*
> *Where we can never be.*   —*Selected.*

One such example is worth more to earth than the stained triumphs of ten thousand Caesars.

February 7

". . . I will not give to the Lord that which costs me nothing. . . ." (2 Samuel 24:24, Trans.)

WHEN Mary was selecting a gift for her Lord, she did not decide upon the *cheapest* box of perfume which would answer. We can imagine her inquiring as the different qualities were brought out if they had anything better, until the merchant finally showed her the alabaster box, explaining: 'This is the *finest* thing in the market—but it is very expensive! The price is three hundred pence.'

" 'Never mind,' said Mary, 'it is none too good for Jesus!' And she took it home and broke it at the Master's feet, and the perfume of it is spreading still, though losing none of its sweetness."

Christ wants the best. He in the far-off ages
  Once claimed the firstling of the flock, the finest of the wheat,
And still He asks His own with gentlest pleading
  To lay their highest hopes and brightest talents at His feet.
He'll not forget the feeblest service, humblest love;
  He only asks that of our store we give to Him
               The best we have.

Christ gives the best. He takes the hearts we offer,
  And fills them with His glorious beauty, joy and peace;
And in His service as we're growing stronger,
  The calls to great achievements still increase.
The richest gifts for us on earth, or in the heavens above,
  Are hid in Christ. In Jesus we receive
               The best we have.

And is our best too much? O friends, let us remember
  How once our Lord poured out His soul for us,
And in the prime of His mysterious manhood
  Gave up His precious life upon the cross,
The Lord of lords, by whom the worlds were made,
  Through bitter grief and tears gave us
             The best He had.   —*Selected.*

February 8

"But without faith it is impossible to please him: . . . he is a rewarder of them that diligently seek him." (Heb. 11:6.)

IF YOU want your faith to grow, there are four rules that you must adopt. First, be willing to have a great faith. When men say they cannot believe, ask, "Are you willing to believe?" because if the will is toward faith, the Holy Ghost will produce a great faith. Second, use the faith you have; the child with its slender arm muscles, will not be able to wield the sledgehammer unless he begins step by step to use them. Do not, therefore, stand on the boat's edge and wait to be able to swim a mile, but throw yourself out from its side into the water and swim a yard or two; for it is in these smaller efforts that you are to be prepared for the greater and mightier exploits. Third, be sure to put God between yourself and circumstances. Everything depends on where you put God. Fourth, live a life of daily obedience to God's will. Observe these rules and your faith will grow.
                                     —*F. B. Meyer.*

Faith cannot grow in the atmosphere of doubt.

BY FAITH

Ye children of promise, who are awaiting your call to glory, take possession of the inheritance that now is yours. *By faith take the promises.* Live upon them, not upon emotions. Remember feeling is not faith. Faith grasps and clings to the promises. Faith says, "I am certain, not because feeling testifies to it, but because God says it."   —*Mandeville.*

"Our unbelief ties the hands of His omnipotence."

All the scholastic scaffolding falls, as a ruined edifice, before one single word—faith!—*Napoleon I.*

February 9

"Wherefore he is able also to save them to the uttermost that come unto God by him, seeing he ever liveth to make intercession for them." (Heb. 7:25.)

WENDELL PHILLIPS was asked: "Did you ever make a consecration of yourself to God?"

"Yes," he replied, "when I was a boy fourteen years of age I heard a sermon on the theme, 'You Belong to God,' and I went home after the sermon and locking the door, threw myself on the floor in my room, and said: 'God, I belong to you! Take what is Thine own. I ask but this, that whenever a thing is right, it take no courage to do it; that whenever a thing be wrong, it may have no power of temptation over me.' So," said Mr. Phillips, "has it ever been with me since that night."

Are we not ready now to look up into Christ's face and from the heart say to Him, "Christ, I belong to Thee altogether, for time, for eternity. I ask that whatever it may be my duty to do I may do without question, without hesitation; and that whatsoever I may see wrong I may not even be tempted to do."

"The great consecrations of life are apt to come suddenly without warning; while we are patiently and faithfully keeping sheep in the wilderness, the messenger is hurrying toward us with the vial of sacred oil to make us kings."

> Now I belong to Jesus,
> And Jesus belongs to me;
> Not for the years of time alone,
> But for eternity.   —*Youth Chorus.*

"In whom ye also trusted, after that ye heard the word of truth, the gospel of your salvation: in whom also after that ye believed, ye were sealed with that holy Spirit of promise, Which is the earnest of our inheritance until the redemption of the purchased possession, unto the praise of his glory." (Eph. 1: 13, 14.)

February 10

"Remember now thy Creator in the days of thy youth, while the evil days come not, nor the years draw nigh, when thou shalt say, I have no pleasure in them." (Eccl. 12:1.)

YOUTH is a time of accomplishment. Much has been achieved in our world by young men and young women, and many of the great deeds of our time will be done by the youth of today.

Most of you who read these lines at the beginning of this new year are in the morning of life, which is much like the dawn of day—"full of purity and imagery and harmony." You are well and strong and have no aches and pains. You are full of courage and hope and are surrounded with more opportunities than ever offered themselves to any other generation which has ever lived. The pages of history are filled with the records of the accomplishments of the great and good and wise and mighty, and these are largely the doings of *youth.*

Benjamin Franklin was writing for publication at sixteen.

At twenty-two George Whitefield was one of the world's greatest preachers.

Dwight L. Moody was preaching at eighteen, and Charles Spurgeon at sixteen.

William Cullen Bryant wrote "Thanatopsis" at eighteen. Robert Southey was famous at the same age. John Milton wrote one of his best poems at the age of twenty-two.

Henry Wadsworth Longfellow was professor of modern languages at nineteen, a much-loved poet at twenty-six.

Robert Burns was a gifted writer at sixteen.

William Gladstone belonged to the House of Lords at twenty-three.

Demosthenes was the greatest orator of old Greece at twenty-five.

Solomon at eighteen began a reign which was marked by wealth and wisdom.

There is no time like the present. Begin now!

Said Sir Walter Scott, "The three greatest letters in the English alphabet are—N-O-W."

"Behold, now is the accepted time."

February 11

*". . . A wise man . . . built his house upon a rock: And the
rain descended, and the floods came, and the winds blew, and
beat upon that house; and it fell not: for it was founded upon
a rock."* (Matt. 7:24, 25.)

Be true to yourself at the start, young man,
  Be true to yourself and God;
Ere you build your house, mark well the spot,
Test all the ground, and build you not
  On the sand or the shaking sod.

Dig, dig the foundation deep, young man,
  Plant firmly the outer wall;
Let the props be strong and the roof be high,
Like an open turret toward the sky,
  Through which heaven's dews may fall.

Let this be the room of the soul, young man—
  When shadows shall herald care,
A chamber with never a roof or thatch
To hinder the light—or door or latch
  To shut in the spirit's prayer!

Build slow and sure; 'tis for life, young man,
  A life that outlives the breath;
For who shall gainsay the Holy Word?
"Their works do follow them," said the Lord,
  Therein there is no death.

Build deep, and high, and broad, young man,
  As the needful case demands;
Let your title-deeds be clear and bright,
Till you enter your claim to the Lord of Light,
  For the "house not made with hands."
                    —*Moody Monthly* (used by permission).

February 12

"Be strong in the Lord, and in the power of his might."
                              (Eph. 6:10.)

DARE to be different! Dare to stand alone.—Dare to stand
up for your convictions even though the crowd may move
as one body the other way.

The deciding factor for the Christian is not what does a
certain hero think or do, or even what do all the others
say and do, but rather what would Jesus Christ, my Saviour, have
me do? Every decision for our Christian youth today should be

faced in the light of these two questions: (1) Will this bring me closer to Christ? (If not, it should be out of my life.) (2) Will it help me to win others for Christ? (Every possibility of being an offense or a stumbling-block to someone else must be out.)

A cross-bearing Christianity is necessary for our comfortable hero-worshipping age. Today Jesus Christ says to high school Christian young people: "If any man will come after me, let him deny himself, and *take up his cross daily*, and follow me."

Do not misunderstand this cross carrying. To carry the cross is *not* to create suffering for ourselves by our own stubborn self-will. It is *not* to make ourselves obnoxious merely for the sake of becoming objects of persecution. *But the cross is the price we often must pay that the will of God can be done in our lives.* Sometimes high school young people in this day must pay such a price if they dare to be different and follow in the footsteps of Jesus Christ.

Jesus Christ, our Saviour and Lord, is the great Hero that our young people need to worship and adore today. He died on the cross for youth that their hearts might be made clean in His blood. He came to give purpose to their living. In Christ alone our youth can reach their destiny of eternal glory.

Young people, dare to be seeming fools for the sake of Christ! Dare to stand up for your convictions. With the weapon of God's living Word, the Sword of the Spirit, dare to be a crusader for Christ. Dare to carry your cross. Be a Christian with real vertebrae. Only in the power that God gives you through Christ, your Saviour, can you dare to be different. The world desperately needs such youth of faith today.—*Oscar C. Hansen.*

"Must Jesus bear the Cross alone?"

February 13

"Also I heard the voice of the Lord, saying, Whom shall I send, and who will go for us? Then said I, Here am I, send me." (Isa. 6:8.) *"I will go!"* (Fenton's trans.)

THERE was once a day of crisis in Jerusalem, for Uzziah, the father of his people, the great statesman on whose wisdom they had leaned, was dead. It was

*"As when a kingly cedar green with boughs
Goes down with great shout upon the hills,
And leaves a lonesome place against the sky,"*

and everyone felt lost! That day a young man (Isaiah), bewildered like the rest, went to the Temple to beseech God to raise up someone on whom they could lean. He heard the Voice of God saying, "Whom shall I send and who will go for us?" It was as though God was saying to *him*, "And why not *you?*" This came as a sudden and unexpected question!—and the man gazed astounded, hardly crediting his own heart; yet finding it was said in earnest, he rose to his feet, dazed but obedient, saying: "Here am I; send me!"

And today God may be saying to you, why not *you?* And *you?* And *you?* Christ needs *you;* Christ appeals to *you;* Christ follows *you,* entreating for *your* help! God made you for the work of your own generation. Don't throw away your chance!

Your choice is brief and yet endless.—*Carlyle.*

> *The Summons*
> *Set my heart aflame—*
> *I heard God calling*
> *And I came!*
> —*Edwin Osgood Grover.*

February 14

"The Lord is thy keeper: the Lord is thy shade upon thy right hand." (Psalm 121:5.)

THE OIL UNDER THE DOVE'S WING

 YOUNG Christian girl obtained employment in a shop where she had to make a tremendously brave stand, for her colleagues were not Christians. In *this* environment of worldliness and bad language, she was compelled ever to be on her guard.

At one time she was a little fearful that she would fall into their habits or unconsciously let an unchristianlike word escape her lips. But as the days went by she found there was no desire whatever in her heart to enter into their ways. It puzzled her greatly that she could live under such conditions and not be contaminated. One day to an older Christian she expressed her pleasure in being kept pure under such circumstances. This was the explanation given her.

"However much a dove may grovel in the filth and mire of earth it is never contaminated. It always retains its purity and whiteness. The reason is that there is a continual flow of oil through the dove's wings, which acts as a perpetual cleanser."

As the dove is kept pure in that manner so are we kept pure from the vileness of sin by the continual cleansing of the oil of the Holy Spirit. So many young Christians just starting out on the journey of life fear they will be led away from the Christian's pathway. Banish that fear, in your perfect love for Christ. Remember—God is not only a God that can save, but a God that can keep! What a comforting thought!

Pray the prayer of David: "Lord, keep me as the apple of Thine eye," guided and protected from all evil. Whatever your circumstances, have courage, for we are kept by the power of God, through faith. —*Gertrude Hale.*

Kept, as chaste as unsunn'd snow."—*Shakespeare.*

February 15

". . . And they blew the trumpets, and brake the pitchers. . . ."
(Judges 7:19.)

IN England in early times lighted lanterns were hung in some of the church steeples at night, and others in front of dwelling houses. The watchman going his rounds called out, "Hang out your light!" And this is the call of Christ! "Let your light shine! Let the world know by your actions and words that you are My follower!" An unlighted lantern hung out in those days of old was as effective in guiding a traveler along the road as is many a one in these days who has taken the name of *Christian* and yet is unlighted. A follower of Christ who is not making his presence felt for good is a failure.

The cry of the Church today, "Pitchers for the Lamps of God!"

> *A lamp once hung in an ancient town*
>   *At the corner of a street,*
> *There the wind was keen, and the way was dark,*
>   *And the rain would often beat.*
> *And all night long its light would shine*
>   *To guide the travelers' feet.*
>
> *The lamp was rough and plain and old,*
>   *And the storm had beaten it sore;*
> *'Twas not a thing one would care to show,*
>   *Whate'er it had been before,*
> *But no one thought what the lantern was,*
>   *'Twas the light that within it bore.*
>
> *The lamp is a text for young and old,*
>   *Who seek, in a world of pride,*
> *To shine for their Lord and to show Him forth*
>   *And never their light to hide.*
> *You are the lantern, a thing of naught,*
>   *But Christ is the Light inside.*

—G. G.

Where are the youth whose hearts are not captivated, entranced, thrilled when listening to the story of Gideon and his three hundred! (Judges, 7th chapter). What strange weapons were employed! Ordinary earthenware lamps, which, when shattered, revealed a glowing light within! What does the story reveal to the youth of today? Your calling from God and your mission upon earth—to reflect the light! "I am the true light," said Jesus. May you ever keep in mind that you are but the "borrowed glow" of the True Light, and that His treasure is in earthen vessels—the light is *within!*

February 16

". . . For thou hast a little strength, and hast kept my word, and hast not denied my name." (Rev. 3:8.)

AT a noon hour recently a minister was walking along Madison Square, New York, where a number of street meetings can always be found in session. He came across a group of extraordinary size, to which a speaker, mounted on a box, was airing his religious views. He was shouting at the top of his voice: *"There is no God! —and there never was a God! I dare anyone here to stand up on this box and prove that there's a God!"*

The speaker flung the taunt at the crowd: *"God hasn't a friend among you!"*

A fresh young voice rang out: *"YES, HE HAS!"* A young lad elbowing his way through the center of the throng was welcomed by his challenger and asked to state his proofs.

The young lad, throwing back his head and straightening his shoulders, began: *"This man here says that there ain't no God. He tells an untruth! I know there IS a God! He says that God hasn't a friend in this crowd. He tells an untruth! I am a friend of God! He says that no one can prove that there is a God. Again he tells an untruth, and I can prove it. God is in here right now,"* he said as he put his hand on his heart; *"HE LIVES! He lives in ME! I hear His voice saying to me right now, 'Don't let that man put such lies over on this crowd!'"*

It was truly a dramatic scene! In one solitary moment the leadership had passed from this blatant unbeliever to the boy of faith and vision! The infidel orator was unable to recapture his crowd.

Someone in the crowd started to sing the old familiar hymn "Nearer My God to Thee." The minister said, *"It swelled from lip to lip, until a mighty chorus rolled up against the great tower, and broke in a benediction upon every heart!"*

Youth is on the march! And these young friends of Jesus are coming to His defense now—openly and fearlessly—and are becoming His witnesses in this, *their* generation!

February 17

". . . Changed. . . ." (2 Cor. 3:18.)

I PRESUME everybody has known saints whose lives were just radiant. Joy beamed out of their eyes; joy bubbled over their lips; joy seemed to fairly run from their finger-tips. You could not come in contact with them without having a new light come into your own life. They were like electric batteries charged with joy.

If you look into the eyes of such radiantly happy persons—not those people who are sometimes on the mountain top, and sometimes in the valley, but those who are always radiantly happy—you will find that every one is a man or a woman who spends a great deal of time alone with God in prayer. God is the source of all joy, and if we come into contact with Him, His infinite joy comes into our lives.

Would you like to be a radiant Christian? You may be! Spend time in prayer. You cannot be a radiant Christian in any other way. Why is it that prayer in the name of Christ makes one radiantly happy? It is because prayer makes God real. *The gladdest thing upon earth is to have a real God!* I would rather give up anything I have in the world, or anything I ever may have, than give up my faith in God! You cannot have vital faith in God if you give all your time to the world and to secular affairs, to reading the newspapers and to reading literature, no matter how good it is. Unless you take time for fellowship with God, you cannot have a real God. If you do take time for prayer you will have a real, living God, and if you have a living God you will have a radiant life.

—*Dr. R. A. Torrey.*

Of all the lights you carry in your face,
Joy will reach the farthest out to sea.
—*H. W. Beecher.*

February 18

"Who is this that cometh ... perfumed. ...?"
(Song of Solomon 3: 6.)

IN Sargodha, India, there grows a shrub with exquisite perfume. Sometimes on summer evenings I had occasion to pass that way. Nothing in the surroundings was attractive, only barrenness and ugliness, mud walls that emitted heat, but when I would get a whiff of this plant's fragrance I would seem to be cooled and refreshed.

In Rumania there is a certain valley where nothing is grown but roses for the Vienna market, and the perfume of that valley in the time of the rose crop is such that if you go into it for a few minutes, wherever you go the rest of the day people know you have been there. You carry some of the fragrance of it away with you.

"One day a wanderer found a lump of clay so redolent of sweet perfume its odors scented all the room. From whence this wondrous perfume?—Say! Friend, if the secret I disclose, I have been dwelling with the rose. Sweet parable! And will not those who love to dwell with Sharon's rose distill sweet perfume all around, though low and mean themselves are found?"—*A Persian Fable.*

"Christ . . . hath given himself for us an offering and a sacrifice to God for a sweetsmelling savour."

This fragrance is for us to receive and pass on to others. God is ready to make manifest through us the savour of His knowledge in every place we go.

No matter how little natural winsomeness and attractiveness we may have, if we abide in the presence of our Lord, we shall manifest His beauty and His fragrance.

Mary, doubtless, anointed the Lord's feet quietly and inconspicuously, but the house was filled with the odour of the ointment.

February 19

"... He is altogether lovely. ..." (Song of Solomon 5:16.)

WHAT a glorious fact it is that there is one life that can be held up before the eyes of humanity as a *perfect pattern!* There were lips that never spoke unkindness, that never uttered an untruth; there were eyes that never looked aught but love and purity and bliss; there were arms that never closed against wretchedness or penitence; there was a bosom which never throbbed with sin, nor ever was excited by unholy impulse; there was a Man free from all undue selfishness, and whose life was spent in going about doing good.

There was One who loved all mankind, and who loved them more than Himself, and who gave Himself to die that they might live; there was One who went into the gates of death, that the gates of death might never hold us in; there was One who lay in the grave, with its dampness, its coldness, its chill, and its horror, and taught humanity how it might ascend above the grave; there was One who, though He walked on earth, had His conversation in heaven, who took away the curtain that hid immortality from view, and presented to us the Father God in all His glory and in all His love.

Such an One is the *standard* held up in the Church of Christ. The Church rallies round the Cross and gathers around Jesus; and it is because He is so attractive, and lovely, and glorious, that they are coming from the ends of the earth to see the salvation of God.
                                        —*Bishop Matthew Simpson.*

Majestic sweetness sits enthroned
  Upon the Saviour's brow;
His head with radiant glories crowned,
  His lips with grace o'erflow.

Since from His bounty I receive
  Such proofs of love divine,
Had I a thousand hearts to give,
  Lord, they should all be Thine. —*Thomas Hastings.*

February 20

". . . My speech shall distil as the dew . . ." (Deut. 32: 2.)

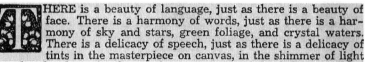

THERE is a beauty of language, just as there is a beauty of face. There is a harmony of words, just as there is a harmony of sky and stars, green foliage, and crystal waters. There is a delicacy of speech, just as there is a delicacy of tints in the masterpiece on canvas, in the shimmer of light on the dewdrop, in the semi-transparent petal of the woodland flower.

Beautiful nature is the robe of God, woven on the loom of His everlasting word.

The beautiful word, placed in the depths of mind, beautifies the language of life. Kind words, firm words, tender words, righteous words, loving words, draw on these elements of God, bringing them to bloom in human life, as the wick draws the oil and produces light.

The beautiful word makes beautiful faces, beautiful manners, beautiful lives.—*Selected.*

WATCH YOUR WORDS

Keep a watch on your words, my darlings,
For words are wonderful things;
They are sweet, like the bees' fresh honey,
Like the bees, they have terrible stings.

They can bless like the warm, glad sunshine,
And brighten a lonely life;
They can cut, in the strife of anger,
Like an open, two-edged knife.

May peace guard your lives, and ever
From the time of your early youth,
May the words that you daily utter
Be the words of beautiful truth.

—Selected.

Select your words as you would choice flowers for a friend. Be a model in the art of fine speech.

"Set a watch, O Lord, before my mouth; keep the door of my lips." (Psalm 141:3.)

"Let the words of my mouth, and the meditation of my heart, be acceptable in thy sight, O Lord, my strength, and my redeemer." (Psalm 19:14.)

February 21

". . . His praise shall continually be in my mouth."
(Psalm 34:1.)

"I heard a joyous strain—
A lark on a leafless bough
Sat singing in the rain."

HEARD him singing early in the morning. It was hardly light! I could not understand that song; it was fairly a lilt of joy. It had been a portentous night for me, full of dreams that did disturb me. Old things that I had hoped to forget, and new things that I had prayed could never come, trooped through my dreams like grinning little bare-faced imps. Certainly I was in no humor to sing. What could possess that fellow out yonder to be telling the whole township how joyous he was? He was perched on the rail fence by the spring run. He *was drenched.* It had rained in the night, and evidently he had been poorly housed. I pitied him. What comfort could he have had through that night bathed in the storm? He never thought of comfort. His song was not bought by any such duplicity. It was in his heart! Then I shook myself. *The shame that a lark has finer poise than a man!—Rev. G. A. Leichliter, M.A., B.D.*

"I heard a bird at break of day
Sing from the autumn trees
A song so musical and calm,
So full of certainties,
No man, I think, could listen long
Except upon his knees.
Yet this was but a simple bird
Alone among dead trees."

"Nothing can break you as long as you sing."

February 22

"Neither give place to the devil." (Eph. 4:27.)

E ARE never to leave a vacant place for the devil. He is always on the lookout for the empty moment, the unoccupied circumstance, in which he can obtain a foothold and begin his nefarious work. Our only safety is to fill everything with holy purpose and achievement; to fill it so full of God that there is no room left for the foe.

When we delay the performance of a duty we are giving place to the devil. When we say to the Lord, in answer to His command, "Suffer me first to . . ." we are offering the unfilled place to the devil. He loves the delays of Christians, their dilatoriness, their reluctance, their postponements and adjournments, because in the vacant hours he builds his own abode. If my brother has aught against me and I delay the rectification of the wrong, the wrong is aggravated and embittered, for the devil has used the delay to extend his evil dominion.

When we do our duty halfheartedly we offer the other half as a place for the devil. He loves the halfhearted, for they always provide him a home. They offer only a room or two to the Lord, and he takes the rest for himself. So that even our partial consecrations give him a foothold, and he uses it to extend his boundaries. A maimed discipleship always offers chances to the devil, and he leaps at the smallest chance. Give him an inch, he will begin his work as though he had a mile, and a mile he soon will have! Give him an empty port, and soon he will have a country. Only let him land, and he will never rest till his invasion is complete.—*J. H. J.*

Break up, oh, break up the font, my God, and stir the soul of me,
As I have seen Thee loose Thy winds and stir the mighty sea.
When calm is settling over my life, and listlessly I strive,
Tear loose the bonds that bind me, Lord, and shake my soul alive.
                                        —Dr. William L. Stidger.

February 23

"Thou therefore endure hardness, as a good soldier of Jesus Christ." (2 Tim. 2:3.)

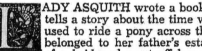LADY ASQUITH wrote a book called *Memoirs* in which she tells a story about the time when she was a little girl. She used to ride a pony across the wide expanse of fields that belonged to her father's estate. One day under the arch of a bridge she got off her pony and found a tramp sitting there. She asked him, "How do you decide which way to go?" He said, "I always go with the wind at my back." That is the way the vagabonds do; the vagabonds always want the wind at their backs. You put a kite up in the air and, if you could hear it, it would probably say, "Oh, let me go, I want to ride with the wind; I hate to be tied." But if you let the wind get at its back instead of in its face what will happen to the kite? Down it will go into the swamp! That is what happens to the things that always run with the wind. They never climb. But the string that you hold in your fingers, holding the kite's face to the wind, makes it rise, and it is the wind in your face that lifts you!

It is the wind in your face that brings the blood into your cheeks, running red and vigorous all through your body. Then life becomes strong, and you have power to do and dare. Stand up bravely facing the wind!

A SONG OF THE ROAD
Let me but walk with my face to the wind,
Keen though it be, and strong;
Let my way lead up the hill all the while,
Rough though the path, and long.
—*Irene Brock McElberen.*

February 24

"... *Quit you like men, be strong.*" (1 Cor. 16:13.)

GOOD TIMBER

The tree that never had to fight
For sun and sky and air and light,
That stood out in the open plain
And always got its share of rain,
Never became a forest king,
But lived and died a scrubby thing.

The man who never had to toil
To heaven from the common soil,
Who never had to win his share
Of sun and sky and light and air,
Never became a manly man,
But lived and died as he began.

Good timber does not grow in ease;
The stronger wind, the tougher trees;
The farther sky, the greater length;
The more the storm, the more the strength;
By sun and cold, by rain and snows,
In tree or man, good timber grows.

Where thickest stands the forest growth
We find the patriarchs of both;
And they hold converse with the stars
Whose broken branches show the scars
Of many winds and of much strife—
This is the common law of life.
—*Douglas Malloch.*

The cedar braves all storms and grows near the eternal snows, the Lord Himself filling it with a sap which keeps its heart warm and its boughs strong. "Lord, so let it be with me, I pray Thee!"

"Be like the pine on the hilltop, alone in the wind for God. There is a curious comfort in remembering that the Father depends upon His child not to give way. It is inspiring to be trusted with a hard thing. You never ask for summer breezes to blow upon your tree. It is enough that you are not *alone* upon the hill."

February 25

"Now unto him that is able to keep you from falling, and to present you faultless before the presence of his glory with exceeding joy." (Jude 24.)

DR. PAUL S. REES, young American evangelist, has used these apt illustrations:

"I grew up in Southern California, where one of the familiar trees is the pepper. Now a pepper tree may not be among the prettiest of which California can boast, but it is unquestionably one of the cleanest. Its small leaves exude a substance that makes it well-nigh impossible for dust and dirt to stick to them. Dust may fill the atmosphere about them, but it will not cling, thanks to a secret which the Creator has put within the tree itself. If that pepper tree could talk to God, it might be heard to say: 'Dear God, I do not ask that you take me where there is no dust; I only ask that you keep me from its soiling and bedraggling effect.' And God does it.

"Here is a lotus flower—easily one of the loveliest creations in the world of natural beauty. Its delicate hue and spotless texture make you gasp in admiration. But look at its setting! What a contrast! Muck and mire and scum are all around it. How can it be so chastely and exquisitely beautiful in a setting like that? That answer obviously is that it has a life within it that enables it to push its stem up through oozy muck and scummy water, and blossom, not because of the filth but in spite of it, with a splendor worthy of the onlooking angels. If flowers talk to God, as they must in their own way, then that lotus must be saying: 'Dear God, I do not ask that you plant me where there are no ill-smelling weeds or foul water; I only ask that you keep alive within me that vitality which lives where death abounds and blooms in beauty where ugliness runs riot.' And God hears that prayer!"

Chastity, whiter than new snow on a raven's back.—*Shakespeare.*

"If I ascend up into heaven, thou art there: if I make my bed in hell, behold, thou art there. If I take the wings of the morning, and dwell in the uttermost parts of the sea; Even there shall thy hand lead me, and thy right hand shall hold me. (Psalm 139: 8-10.)

"I pray not that thou shouldest take them out of the world, but that thou shouldest keep them from the evil." (John 17:15.)

February 26

". . . No man should be moved by these afflictions: . . . we are appointed thereunto." (1 Thess. 3:3.)

WE ALL like the sunshine, but the Arabs have a proverb that "all sunshine makes a desert," and it is a matter of common observation that the graces of Christian living are more often apparent in the cases of those who have passed through tribulation. God desires to get as rich crops as possible from the soil of our natures. There are certain plants of the Christian life, such as meekness, gentleness, kindness, and humility, which cannot come to perfection if the sun of prosperity always shines. The dark things in life become the ground-bed of everlasting flowers.

All the early life of Paderewski was a heart-breaking struggle.

Credit for the discovery of an antidote for one of the world's most deadly poisons, cyanide of potassium, goes to tall, blonde Dr. Matilda Brooks, research associate in biology at the University of California. Her treatment with methylene blue has also been successfully used to counteract poisoning from carbon monoxide.

As a child in Pittsburgh, Pennsylvania, young Matilda gave music lessons to the neighborhood children for twenty-five cents an hour to help keep the family budget from becoming too depleted, for her father had died when she was but a child, leaving the family in straitened circumstances. When it seemed that her schooling would have to end because of the family finances, Matilda obtained a job after school hours clerking in a near-by store just so she could earn enough money to pay her own school expenses.

"Your secret, giant oak? He only said,
'Long have I borne the blast, and suffered long,
Far as my branches are my roots outspread:
Learn to be patient ere thou canst be strong.'"

February 27

"Wherefore be ye not unwise, but understanding what the will of the Lord is." (Eph. 5:17.)

HOW TO ASCERTAIN THE WILL OF GOD

1. *Surrender your own will.*

I seek at the beginning to get my heart into such a state that it has no will of its own in regard to a given matter. Nine-tenths of the difficulties are overcome when our hearts are ready to do the *Lord's* will, whatever it may be. When one is truly in this state, it is usually but a little way to the knowledge of what His will is.

2. *Do not depend upon feelings.*

Having done this, I do not leave the result to feeling or simple impression. If I do so, I make myself liable to great delusions.

3. *Seek the Spirit's will through God's Word.*

I seek the will of the Spirit of God through, or in connection with, the Word of God. The Spirit and the Word must be combined. If I look to the Spirit alone without the Word, I lay myself open to great delusions also. If the Holy Ghost guides us at all, He will do it according to the Scriptures and never contrary to them.

4. *Note providential circumstances.*

Next I take into account providential circumstances. These often plainly indicate God's will in connection with His Word and Spirit.

5. *Pray.*

I ask God in prayer to reveal His will to me aright.

6. *Wait.*

Thus, through prayer to God, the study of the Word, and reflection, I come to a deliberate judgment according to the best of my ability and knowledge, and if my mind is thus at peace, and continues so after two or three more petitions, I proceed accordingly.

In trivial matters, and in transactions involving most important issues, I have found this method always effective.—*George Muller.*

February 28

". . . A light that shineth in a dark place, . . ." (2 Peter 1:19.)

 WAS sitting in the gloamin', an' a man passed the window. He was the lamplighter. He pushed his pole into the lamp and lighted it. Then he went to another and another. Now, I couldna' see him. But I knew where he was by the lights as they broke out doon the street, until he had left a beautiful avenue of light.

"Ye're a' lamplighters. They'll know where ye've been by the lights. Ye'll want your son to be a noble man. Let him say wi' pride when you've passed on: 'Ma faither lit that lamp.'

"The first burst of light that the world had was the lamp lit by Jesus, or rather, He was the light Himself. He said truly, 'I am the Light of the world.' Ye're in His succession. Be careful how ye bear yoursel's."—*Harry Lauder.*

TORCHBEARERS

How fares it, Torchbearer?
  Nay, do not stay me!
Swift be my course as the flight of an arrow!
Eager, exultant, I spring o'er the stubble,
Thread through the briers, and leap o'er the hollow;
Firm nerve, tense muscle, heart beating:
  Onward!
How should I pause, e'en to fling thee an answer?

How fares it, Torchbearer?
  Ah, do not stay me!
Parched is my mouth, and my throat may scarce murmur,
Eyes are half blinded with sunshine's hot glitter,
Brands half consumed from the torch drop upon me,
Quenching their fire in my blood heated boiling,
Scarcely less hot than the fierce falling embers!
Breath would scarce serve me to answer thy question.

How fares it, Torchbearer?
  Reeling, I falter,
Stumbling o'er hillocks that once I leaped over,
Flung by a tangle that once I had broken,
Careless, unheeding. The torch, half extinguished,
Fierce-darting pains through the hot hand that holds it;
Careless of all, if at last I may yield it
Into the hands of another good runner.

How fares it, Torchbearer?
  Well! now I fling me
Flat on the turf by the side of the highway.
So in one word be thy questioning answered.
Praise for my striving? Peace—I am weary;
Thou are unwinded; stand, then, and shading
Eyes with the hand, peer forward, and tell me
How fares the torch in the hands of yon runner?
Naught do I risk of my strength, gladly yielded,
So it be only the torch goeth onward.
                              —Arthur Chamberlain.

We are called to go here and there as lamplighters on dark roads.

On the flyleaf of the Bible of missionary warrior, Charles E. Cowman, are found these lines: "When I am dying, how glad I shall be that the lamp of my life has been blazed out for Thee!"

March 1

". . . Thus saith the Lord, hast thou seen all this great mul-
titude? behold, I will deliver it into thine hand this day; and
thou shalt know that I am the Lord. And Ahab said, By whom?
And he said, Thus saith the Lord, Even by the young men of the
princes of the provinces. Then he said, Who shall order the
battle? And he answered, Thou." (1 Kings 20:13, 14.)

"WHO?," asked the king. "Thou," replied the prophet. The youth were the chosen warriors. The young princes led the way, and although the odds against them were terrific, they won a marvelous victory. If God calls a youth to a work He will be with him in that work, and he will succeed no matter how formidable the obstacles.

Our youth to Thee we bring, O gracious Saviour, King:
Guide Thou our feet. Then all the coming years
Shall know no dismal fears;
And tho' it brings its tears, life will be sweet.

Our minds to Thee we bring, O glorious Christ, our King:
Help us to learn the truth that makes men free,
The truth that leads to Thee,
The truth that is to be, for which men yearn.

Our hearts to Thee we bring, O loving Jesus, King,
To crown Thee there, beside Thy blood-stained cross,
Life's pleasures turned to dross;
We too would know the loss that love must dare.

Our wills to Thee we bring, O mighty Christ, our King,
To make them Thine. We dare not choose our way,
Lest we should miss the day,
O hear each as we pray, "Thy will be mine."

Thus all to Thee we bring, O conq'ring Christ, our King,
For service true. We would help Thee to win
Our world from blight of sin,
Made strong without, within, Thy will to do.
                                        —*Mrs. Frank Siler.*

"And when the Philistine looked about, and saw David, he dis-
dained him: for he was but a youth, and ruddy, and of a fair
countenance. (I Samuel 17:42.)

". . . David prevailed over the Philistine with a sling and with
a stone, and smote the Philistine, and slew him; but there was no
sword in the hand of David." (I Samuel 17:50.)

March 2

". . . Faultless . . . with exceeding joy." (Jude 24.)

WHEN I was a young girl an intense passion for music was awakened within my soul. Father brought great joy into my life by presenting me with a beautiful organ. It would thrill me to the very fibre of my being as the days slipped by to be able to draw forth such wonderful harmony from my beloved instrument.

I used to sit at the organ in the early morning hours, just as the birds began to awaken, and through the open windows listen to their sweet little bird notes as they mingled with the melody of the organ, like a paean of praise to our Creator!

Then, one morning, quite suddenly, and at a time when I was preparing with girlish enthusiasm for my first concert appearance, one of the notes became faulty. How the discordant sound grated upon my sensitive ear! Father, sensing my grief, said: "Never mind, daughter, I will have the tuner come." Long hours the tuner worked on that faulty note before it again rang out all sweet and true with the others. And the concert was a success *because the tuner was successful!*

> Good Tuner, why
>   This ruthless, slow examination?
> Why, on that one poor note,
> Expend such careful concentration?
> Just pass it by.
> Now I will let my soul respond to Thee!
>   And see.
>
> But, no! Again, and yet again,
> With skilled determination,
> Rang out that meaningless reiteration.
> While, ever and anon, through the great
>   aisle's dim space,
> Echoed the reverent chord; the loud har-
>   monious phrase,
>
> Till day began to wane.
> And still, more patiently, the Tuner wrought
> With that one faulty note; until, with zest,
> All sweet and true, it answered like the rest.
>
> Then, as the haloed glories of the sunset
>   flamed and gleamed,
> Swift through the storied windows long
>   shafts of crimson streamed:

And we poor whispering wayfarers heard,
round about and o'er us,
The throbbing, thundering triumphs of the
Hallelujah Chorus!
        —"The Tuner in the Cathedral"—*Fay Inchfawn.*

March 3

"For all the promises of God in him are yea, and in him Amen, unto the glory of God by us." (2 Cor. 1:20.)

WHEN James Chalmers was a young, careless fellow he was led out of deep conviction and great depression on account of sin by this text: "The blood of Jesus Christ his Son cleanseth us from all sin."

It caught the eye of Captain Hedley Vicars when he was a daring leader in sin, sent him to toss all night on a sleepless bed, and enabled him to rise calmly in the morning, believing that it was true for him.

It was spoken by John Wesley to a highwayman who, in a wild and desolate region, had robbed him of his purse. Many years after, that man met him as he was leaving a church, and told him that that verse of Scripture was the means of a total change in his heart and life.

Is there any unsurrendered sin that makes you still vulnerable to the assaults of Satan? What is the besetting sin that prevents you from demonstrating daily your identity of nature with the Son of God? Give it up! It is the death-spot in your armor! Invulnerable you cannot be until you bring the *whole* life under the influence of that shielding Blood. Do that, and the very God of peace will sanctify you wholly, and your whole spirit and soul and body will be preserved blameless unto the coming of our Lord Jesus Christ.

        —*W. W. Moore in The Northfield.*

There is not a single half-promise, not a single promise of partial deliverance from sin in the Bible. "The blood of Jesus Christ his Son cleanseth us from *all* sin." (1 John 1:7.)

I commend to you a prayer—a prayer that you may pray alone on the hillside, pray as you kneel in your own room, pray in the darkness of the night, when sleep is denied, pray in the dawning of the morning:

        "Create in me a clean heart, O God."

O Saviour, bid me "go and sin no more,"
And keep me always 'neath the mighty flow
Of Thy perpetual fountain; I implore
That Thy perpetual cleansing I may fully know.
        —*Frances Ridley Havergal.*

March 4

"... They came and saw where he dwelt, and abode with him that day: . . ." (John 1:39.)

THEY HAVE BEEN WITH JESUS

"Yes, they are changed—
How kindly do they speak;
The crippled beggar stands erect
Since they have passed,
And surely, yonder blind man
Is gazing toward the mountain—seeing!"

So spoke the ones who scoffed
When those who had left all
To follow Him passed by.
These men had been with Jesus,
Had seen His mighty works
And heard His words.

So, too, may we be changed by Him
When earnestly we strive.
'Twas not for them alone
He broke the bread of Life,
Stilled storm-tossed wave,
And banished pain and sorrow.

Oh, may it be
That some who scorn, today
Are speaking thus of you—and me:
Some wonder has been wrought—
Where once she was so cold,
She now is kind!

And thankfully we say—
Though none but God may hear:
"Rejoice! Rejoice!
For He is guiding me—
I, too,
Have been with Jesus."

—Selected.

"Ancient of Days!" So much happens in a day! He is the Lord of it as of old.

"Go forth, then, ye ransomed ones, and remember that you bear through the world the image and superscription of Jesus Christ; in whatever company of men ye stand, forget not that His signature is upon you."

March 5

"But we all, with open face beholding as in a glass the glory
of the Lord, are changed into the same image from glory to
glory, even as by the Spirit of the Lord." (2 Cor. 3:18.)

DROP of water lay one day in a gutter, stained, soiled, polluted. Looking up into the blue of the sky it began to wish for purity, to long to be cleansed and made crystalline. Its sigh was heard, and it was quickly lifted up by the sun's gentle fingers—up out of the foul gutter, into the sweet air. Then higher and higher, until at length the gentle winds caught it and bore it away, away, and by and by it rested on a distant mountaintop, a flake of pure, white, beautiful snow! This is a little parable of what the grace of God does for every sinful life that longs and cries for purity.—*J. R. Miller, D.D.*

Every inmost aspiration is God's Angel undefiled,
And in every "O my Father" slumbers deep a "Here, my child."
                                    —*Jalal-ed-din-Rumi.*

"AND HE SAID UNTO HIM, FOLLOW ME"

"When Christ calls He also draws. 'Come!' says the sea to the river. 'Come!' says the magnet to the steel. 'Come!' says the spring to the sleeping life of the field and forest."—*C. Stanford.*

ANSWERING THE CALL

Beneath the cover of the sod
The lily heard the call of God;
Within its bulb so strangely sweet
Answering pulse began to beat.
The earth lay darkly damp and cold
And held the smell of grave and mould,
But never did the lily say,
"O who will roll the stone away?"
It heard the call, the call of God,
And up through prison house of sod
It came from burial place of gloom
To find its perfect life in bloom.
                                    —*Author Unknown.*

"Soar we now where Christ has led,
    Following our exalted Head;
Made like Him, like Him we rise;
    Ours the Cross, the Grave, the Skies."

March 6

". . . Keep thyself pure." (1 Tim. 5:22.)

IR JOSHUA REYNOLDS used to give a coat of white paint to all the canvas he used for his pictures before commencing to work. He said it gave luminousness and brilliance to the whole picture. That is a little parable for you. You are just beginning to paint a life picture. Let Jesus in to make the groundwork of your life white and pure."

"Take the flower that hangs in the morning, impearled with dew, arrayed as no queenly woman ever was arrayed in jewels. Once shake it, so that the beads roll off, and you may sprinkle water over it as carefully as you please, yet it can never again be made what it was when the dew fell silently upon it from heaven.

"On the frosty morning you may see the panes of glass covered with landscapes—mountains, lakes, trees, blended in a beautiful, fantastic picture. Now lay your hand upon the glass, and by the scratch of your finger, or by the warmth of your palm, all the delicate tracery will be obliterated! So there is in Youth a beauty and purity of character which, when once touched and defiled, can never be restored; a fringe more delicate than frost-work, and which, when torn and broken, will never be re-embroidered."

—*H. W. Beecher.*

"The crimson of the sunset; the azure of the ocean; the green of the valleys; the scarlet of the poppies; the silver of the dewdrop; the gold of the gorse: these are exquisitely beautiful—God paints in many colors, but He never paints so gorgeously as when He paints in *white!*"

March 7

"And at the entrance of the Dwelling in the Trysting tent, he placed the altar of burnt-offering." (Exod. 40:29, Trans.)

HERE is always an altar of sacrifice at the door that leads to enriching experience.

There is always an altar at the door. The student who would enter the temple of learning finds that he must place a sacrifice upon the altar at the door.

Albert Schweitzer, preacher, philosopher, musician, missionary, is an authority on Bach. He says in his autobiography that one day he was able to buy for fifty pounds the complete works of Bach from a wealthy woman who had tired of them. Without this good fortune he never could have mastered Bach, because the only time he could get for study was at night when all the libraries were closed. He became an authority on Bach; but he placed a sacrifice of sleep on the altar at the door.

The more a lover sacrifices, the more he loves. And the greater the sacrifices we make for God, the farther we penetrate into "the Dwelling in the Trysting tent." Perhaps that explains some of the sacrifices we are called upon to make. A door leading to a rich experience may lie just beyond!

—Selected.

> *"The heights by such men reached and kept,*
> *Were not attained by sudden flight,*
> *But they, while their companions slept,*
> *Were toiling upward in the night."*

March 8

". . . He left not himself without witness, . . ." (Acts 14:17.)

MISS HAVERGAL tells of her experience in the girls' school at Dusseldorf. She went there soon after she had become a Christian and had confessed Christ. Her heart was very warm with love for her Saviour, and she was eager to speak for Him. To her amazement, however, she soon learned that among the hundred girls in the school, she was the only Christian. Her first thought was one of dismay—she could not confess Christ in that great company of worldly, non-Christian companions. Her gentle sensitive heart shrank from a duty so difficult! Her second thought, however, was that *she could not refrain* from confessing Christ. *She* was the only one Christ had there, and she must be faithful! "This was very bracing," she writes. "I felt I must walk worthy of my calling for Christ's sake! It brought to me a new and strong desire to bear witness for my Master. It made me more watchful and earnest than ever before, for I knew that any slip in word or deed would bring discredit to my Lord and Master." She realized that she had in that school a mission to fulfill; that *she* was called to be Christ's witness there—His only witness!—and that she dare not fail.

The Christian life cannot be a subterfuge. It cannot be lived incognito! There must be *confession;* a bold and clarion-like avowal that henceforth I am a soldier of the Lord!

Give a positive testimony!

If you are a branded young man or a branded young woman, wear your marks as an insignia of honor.

God has put you where you are because He wants a witness just there.

> *"Just where you stand in the conflict*
> *That is your place."*

March 9

"If then ye were raised together with Christ, seek the things that are above. . ." (Col. 3:1, Trans.)

"It is always clear in the stratosphere!"

AUGUSTE PICCARD, the Swiss physicist, tells in *The National Geographic Magazine* of his flight into the stratosphere. There the sun is always shining. There there are no earth-born dust particles to interfere with visibility. It is an area of perfect and perpetual calm, far above the storms which rage on the surface of the earth. Professor Piccard imagines the trip of a business man from New York to Paris in one of the airships of the future. The vessel rises in a driving rain. It is intensely cold, and the wind is howling. The ship climbs steadily. "Shall we have a good passage?" the passenger asks the porter. "Undoubtedly," is the answer. "It is always clear in the stratosphere!"

There is a stratosphere of the soul—a place where vision is always clear, where the dust of earth does not penetrate. There are no storms in the soul's stratosphere, for there reigns "the peace of God, which passeth all understanding."

Let us keep the horizons clear!

"Keep thy soul's large windows free from wrong."
—*Mrs. Browning.*

> *Lift me, O God, above myself—*
> *Above my highest spheres,*
> *Above the thralling things of sense*
> *To clearer atmospheres.*
>
> *Lift me above the little things—*
> *My poor sufficiencies,*
> *My perverse will, my lack of zeal,*
> *My inefficiencies;*
>
> *Above the earth-born need that gropes,*
> *With foolish hankerings,*
> *About earth's cumbered lower slopes*
> *For earthly garnerings.*
>
> *Lift me, O God, above myself,*
> *Above these lesser things,*
> *Above my little gods of clay,*
> *And all their capturings.*
> —*John Oxenham.*

"The visions of God are seen only through the lens of a pure heart."

March 10

"Whereupon, O king Agrippa, I was not disobedient unto the heavenly vision." (Acts 26:19.)

A YOUNG GIRL'S VISION OF LIFE SERVICE

LL my fondest ambitions were bound up in doing something for the poor. What happy visions were mine as I arranged my doll's wardrobe or trundled my hoop—visions in which I saw myself surrounded by hungry people I was feeding with hot soup, ragged people I was dressing in warm jackets, very sad people I was comforting, and—for my mother's training about *goodness making gladness* had its effect at a very early age—very bad people I was helping to make good!

"They were wonderful daydreams, and the most wonderful feature about them was that they became dearer and more real as the years flew by, until they ceased to be daydreams at all, and I awoke to find they had all, one by one, come true."

—*Evangeline Booth.*

It was not that we made a choice, but that the choice made us.

What explains the life of Wesley, and Spurgeon, and Muller, and Luther, and Huss? Schools cannot explain them—thousands had the same advantage. Native ability cannot explain them—there were others more brilliant! God had a place in their plans, and their lives were lost in His will!

March 11

"I know thy works, and where thou dwellest, even where Satan's seat is: and thou holdest fast my name, and hast not denied my faith, . . ." (Rev. 2:13.)

HRIST preserves His own when they are placed in circumstances of peculiar temptation. "Thou holdest fast my name!" It is no light thing to lose our faith in God and in His Son Jesus Christ, for with that loss perishes the highest ideals and most energizing motives. "Hold it fast," says the Master; as a king holds fast his crown, for it is your glory; as a miser holds fast his gold, for it is your treasure; as a drowning man holds fast to the rope, for it is your life. Think it not impossible to retain your Christian faith because you live in an atmosphere of skepticism; holding fast your faith, Christ will hold you fast. "I have prayed for thee that thy faith fail not," says the Master; and His prayers are answered.

Amid the burning sands of the Sahara are bits of living green; in the snowy Alps a garden of flowers surprises the tourist. *Christ can preserve His own amid rampant wickedness.* Even in the devil's headquarters our Master can keep us undefiled.

"Now unto him that is able to keep you from falling, and to present you faultless before the presence of his glory with exceeding joy." (Jude 24.)

Put Christ in possession of your life and He will *keep* you.

March 12

"I beseech you therefore, brethren, by the mercies of God, that ye present your bodies a living sacrifice, . . ." (Rom. 12:1.)

BY the mercies of God." What does that mean? It is like this. One evening you are walking quietly home from your place of business. Suddenly the fire alarm rings out; your heart leaps with fear as the thought of home and loved ones flashes upon you. As you near home your worst fears are realized: your house is in flames. You rush thither and find that wife and the children have been saved, except one little one who is in the building. The next instant a brave fireman hurries past and dashing into the burning house, finds his way to the little one, carries her out through the flames and smoke, and puts her in your arms—safe. Weeks go by, and then one day this same brave man comes to you and showing his hands, says, "Behold my love and mercies to you. See these burned and blistered hands; see this scarred face, and these scorched feet. I am in need. I want help. I beseech you, by my mercies to your child, that you help me." There is nothing in the world you would not give to that man, even unto the half of your kingdom.

Even so, Jesus Christ, our loving Lord, stands here tonight. He stretches forth His hands, pierced with cruel nails for you and me. He points to the wound in His side, made by the blood-thirsty spear. He shows you the scars on His forehead, made by the crown of thorns. He says, "My child, behold My mercies to you. I saved you from the guilt of sin; I brought you from death unto life; I gave you the Spirit of God. Some day I will glorify your body and will make you to sit down with Me on My throne. My child, by *My mercies*, I beseech you." You say, "Lord, what do you want from me?" He answers, "I want yourself. I want *you* for My kingdom and My service. I beseech you, by My mercies to you, give your life to Me."

—*James McConkey.*

"What Thou hast given to me,
Here Lord, I bring to Thee,
Feet which must follow Thee,
Lips which must sing for Thee,
Limbs which must ache for Thee,
Ere they grow old."

March 13

"For God is not unrighteous to forget your work and labour of love, . . ." (Heb. 6:10.)

HE elders of a church in old Scotland remained for a chat with the minister at the close of a Sunday service. When they had gathered in the little session room, one of them, acting as spokesman, told the pastor that they wished him to resign; they felt that he was getting too old to fill the position acceptably. To prove their point they reviewed his work for the past year, during which time he added to the church just one new member, and that a boy.

With head bowed, the old parson strolled out into the churchyard after his visitors had left, and walked silently and thoughtfully among the graves. There was a tug at his coat sleeve, and looking around he saw the boy who had joined his church as a result of his efforts.

"Well, Robert," he asked, "what can I do for you?"

"If you please, sir, since I have been converted and joined the church I feel that I would like to be a missionary. I thought maybe you could help me to get ready."

What an encouragement to the aged minister! His work had not been *all* in vain! From his years of experience he dispensed counsel and guidance, which he was well fitted to give to youth.

Years later a meeting was being held in Exeter Hall, London. The great building was crowded to the doors. Robert Moffat, the well-known missionary from Africa, was to speak.

The elders of the little Scottish church had been ready to dismiss the old minister, since his only convert of the year had been a boy —just a boy! But this boy, Robert Moffat, had added a new chapter to the book of Acts. He had helped to open the continent of Africa to the gospel!

Faint not! faithful young minister. Your place of service may lie in some remote village, where you are ploughing your lonely furrow. Despise not the day of *small* things! There are heart-breaks of joy in God's plan. "Thou surpriseth him." (Psalm 21:3, Kay's Trans.)

The reward for your labour of love may be another great missionary like Robert Moffat.

David Livingstone was a faithful attendant of a small church in an obscure village in Scotland, but he wrote his life across Africa! Judson left his life written across the sands of India.

The work of modern missions was begun by young people, and has been carried throughout the years by *youth*. You may live to see the literal fulfillment of Isaiah 58:12: "And they that shall be of thee shall build the old waste places: thou shalt raise up the foundations of many generations; and thou shalt be called, The repairer of the breach, The restorer of paths to dwell in."

March 14

"...The place whereon thou standest is holy ground."
(Exod. 3:5.)

WHEN we picture God's call nearly all of us think of something dramatic, revolutionary, and startling. The scene on the road to Damascus at once comes to mind. We see the great light in the sky; we hear the voice from heaven; we picture the revolutionizing effect of it all upon the Apostle to the Gentiles. But we forget the great number of men to whom God's call came when they stood upon the holy ground of their everyday life and service. God's call came to Samuel as he ministered in the daily round of the temple; it came to David in the sheepfold; it came to some of the disciples as they were mending and casting their nets. In all these cases the call came to them as they stood upon the holy ground of their daily duties.

As of old, He calls His Gideon from the threshing floor, and His Amos from the sycamore fruit; His Moses from the flocks; His Matthew from the receipt of custom; His John from the priestly family; His Peter from the fishing net, and His Paul from the rabbi's school; so now He calls us from the farm and from the merchandise, from the shop and from the office, from the profession and from the trade, from the pulpit and from the servants' hall. He calls us in boyhood; He calls us in manhood; He calls us in old age. ALL have a mission to fulfill and all alike shall, if they do Christ's work, receive His reward.

"Among the things that this day brings
Will come to you a call,
The which, unless you're listening,
You may not hear at all;
Lest it be very soft and low,
Whate'er you do, where'er you go,
Be listening.

"When God shall come and say to you,
'Here is the thing that you must do,'
Be listening."

It is possible for a youth to go through life deaf to the sweetest sounds that ever fell over heaven's battlements. Our world is one vast whispering gallery, yet only those who listen hear the "still, small voice" of truth. Putting his ear down to the rocks, the listening geologist hears their story. Standing under the stars, the listening astronomer hears the music of the spheres. Listening to birds, Cuvier heard the song within the shell and found out the life history of all things that creep or swim or fly. That youth may have culture without college who gives heed to Channing's injunction to "Listen to stars and birds, to babes and sages."

March 15

"Thou wilt show me the path of life: in thy presence is fulness of joy; at thy right hand there are pleasures for evermore." (Psalm 16:11.)

DISCOVERY

They told me that His yoke was hard to bear,
And that the way of God was hard to go.
They said that I would find it only care
The path and purpose of my Lord to share,
A way beset with thorns no others know.
But no, it is a way of blessedness,
Flooded with song, and crowned with happiness.

They told me God was Vengeance, that His hand
Was hard upon His people, and His ear
Deaf to their prayers. They told me His command
Laid only pain and trouble on the land,
And that His children were but sons of fear.
But no, I found His throne a Father's chair,
And none who seeks denied a blessing there.
                                        —Clarence Edwin Flynn.

Tell the birds amidst the buds of spring not to sing; tell the waters welling from the depths not to flow; tell the happy child not to laugh and jump; tell the sun and stars not to shine; and when these have obeyed you, then tell the soul which has been baptized with the love of God that it must not speak of Him! It cannot but speak what it has seen and heard.

                                        —Dr. F. B. Meyer.

Bunyan's Pilgrim was at the cross when his burden of sin fell from his back. He leaped for joy, and three shining ones came to him, one saying, "Thy sins are forgiven thee." Another stripped him of his rags and clothed him with a new robe. The third set a mark on his forehead and gave him a book with a seal upon it.

"Christ could not be hid, for the blind and the lame
His love and His power would together proclaim;
The dumb would speak out and the deaf would recall
The name of that Jesus who healed them all."

Christ is not a disappointment!

"I never thought it could be thus, month after month to know
The river of Thy peace without one ripple in its flow;
Without one quiver in the trust, one flicker in the glow."

March 16

"Only take heed to thyself, . . . keep thy soul diligently, lest thou forget the things which thine eyes have seen, and lest they depart from thy heart all the days of thy life...."
(Deut. 4:9.)

WHAT a warning lesson we have in the life of David who had slain Goliath but was nearly slain himself long after by a famous giant, and had to be rescued from peril and shame by his men! Years of court life had gradually sapped his early vigour and simplicity, and when the "evil day" came, he was not able "to stand."

"Are you in danger? Tell your Lord. Are you tempted? Tell Him. Did you slip by the way and grieve Him? Tell Him. Never wait for the evening hour for confession and forgiveness. Pardon waits for your confession; make it immediately, wherever you are, in the train, in the office, on the street, amid the busy rush of the busy day, express your need in prayer. Practice the presence of God and speak to Him under stress and strain at every point whenever you feel you are burdened or in need."

I cannot snap my own chains or slay my own enemies. Thou knowest temptation, for Thou wast tempted. Thou knowest how to succour me in my hour of conflict. Thou canst save me from sinning, and save me when I have sinned. It is promised in Thy very name that Thou wilt do this, and I pray Thee let me this day verify the prophecy. Save me unto holiness of life, that the name of Jesus may be glorified in me abundantly!

"When temptation assails you, when the enemy pours in upon your soul, then be as the bird and seek the heights." "Flee as a bird to your mountain."

Who knows a mountain? One who has trod its cloud-swept summit alone with God!—*Ethel Romig Fuller.*

March 17

". . . Peter went up upon the house top to pray . . ."
(Acts 10:9.)

I BROKE MY TRYST WITH GOD

At such an hour on such a day
I had a tryst with God;
I was to put all things away
And keep that tryst with God.
But a friend of mine just happened in—
To go with him was sure no sin—
So I ran along, a friend to win,
But I broke my tryst with God.

My friends all know my word is good,
Yet I broke my tryst with God.
They know I'd keep my word if I could,
Yet I broke my tryst with God.
But somehow I felt when that day was done,
And my spirit sank with the setting sun
That I'd lost much more than I had won
By breaking my tryst with God.

O let us keep that meeting place—
The secret tryst with God.
At such a time He shows His face,
O holy tryst with God.
Never mind though friends and others call,
His love impels our best, our all;
Let us come alone, before Him fall
And keep our tryst with God.

—Selected.

The famous British general, Charles George Gordon, who died under such tragic circumstances in Khartoum, never allowed anything to hinder his morning hours alone with God. During his journey in the Sudan, for one hour each day there lay outside his tent a white handkerchief. The entire camp knew the significance of that small token, and it was sacredly respected by every man, whatever his color or creed. No message, however pressing, was carried in. Whatever the message was, whether of life or death, it had to remain until that guardian signal was removed. Every one knew that General Gordon was alone with God. That white handkerchief was the secret of his saintly, fearless, unselfish life. He was a man who lived in close communion with God.

Without prayer you will be weak as water in the presence of temptation; but by prayer you will become bold as a lion, and "the young lion and the dragon shalt thou trample under feet."

Always keep appointments with God, *exactly.* We must not suit our own convenience.

Be a lone watcher on the mountain height.

March 18

"*... Neither is this a work of one day or two...*" (Ezra 10:13.)

WATCHING the blacksmith, were you, son? Watching the way his work is done. Muscle is needed and also brain. Hammer and hammer, and hammer again, striking the blow, tirelessly true; fashioned at last the perfect shoe. Wasn't done quickly, lad, admit; persistence needed and strength and grit. That is the way we all must work (no use tiring nor trying to shirk). Not for an hour, not for a day; nor for a

week, nor month, nor year; just how long no one can say (keep on, laddie, success is near); hammer away, boy, hammer away."
—*Wilhelmina Stitch.*

The Swedish Nightingale, Jenny Lind, said, "The greater part of what I can do I have myself acquired by incredible labor in spite of astonishing difficulty."

Paderewski stated that, "Genius is three-quarters drudgery. I at one time practiced day by day, year after year, until I became almost insensible to sound—became a *machine*, as it were."

The world called Paderewski a genius, but Paderewski was a drudge before he became a genius.

Beethoven surprised the world with his musical ability before he had reached his teens.

Triumph and toil are twins.

March 19

"And if I go and prepare a place for you, I will come again, and receive you unto myself; that where I am, there ye may be also."
(John 14:3.)

"Blessed are they that do his commandments, that they may have right to the tree of life, and may enter in through the gates into the city." (Rev. 22:14.)

ONCE the great evangelist, Moody, said in his buoyant way: "Some day you will read in the papers that D. L. Moody of East Northfield, is dead. Don't you believe a word of it! At that moment I shall be more alive than I am now; I shall have gone up higher—that is all—out of this old clay tenement into a house that is immortal, a body that death cannot touch, that sin cannot taint, a body fashioned like unto His glorious body."

That is the way to meet present-day skepticism concerning immortality. When agnostics and infidels deny that blessed truth, "don't you believe a word of it." I have heard even Christians say, "Oh, I wish I could be sure of life after death!" *Sure?*—when our Lord rose from the dead! When He said that we are to rise even as He? When He declared that He is the resurrection and the life? To doubt the immortality of the soul is to doubt Jesus Christ.

Let us have the same staunchness of Moody's faith. Let us learn to say to the critics, "Don't you believe a word of it!"

Shortly before his departure he was heard saying: "Earth is receding, and Heaven is opening."

STEPPING ASHORE

Oh! think to step ashore,
And find it heaven;
To clasp a hand outstretched,
And find it God's hand!
To breathe new air,
And that, celestial air;
To feel refreshed,
And find it immortality;
Ah, think to step from storm and stress
To one unbroken calm:
To awake and find it Home.
                                    —*Robert E. Selle.*

Heaven—the Celestial City, never built with hands, nor hoary with the years of time, whose walls are salvation, and whose gates are praise—glories in having Jesus for its King, angels for its guards, saints for its citizens!

March 20

"For other foundation can no man lay than that is laid, which is Jesus Christ." (1 Cor. 3:11.)

MARTIN LUTHER preached the doctrine of Atoning Blood to slumbering Europe, and Europe awoke from the dead. Amid all his defences of Divine Sovereignty, *Calvin* never ignored or belittled the Atonement.
Cowper sang of it among the water lilies of the Ouse.
Spurgeon thundered this glorious doctrine of Christ crucified into the ears of peer and peasant with a voice like the sound of many waters.

John Bunyan made the Cross the starting-point to the Celestial City.
Moody's bells all chimed to the keynote of Calvary.

Napoleon, after conquering almost the whole of Europe, put his finger on the red spot on the map representing the British Isles, and said, "Were it not for that red spot, I'd conquer the world!" So says *Satan* about the place called Calvary, where Jesus Christ shed His Blood.

Every true preacher of the Gospel strings all his pearls on the Red Cord of the Atonement.—*Dr. T. L. Cuyler.*

"In the Cross of Christ I glory,
Tow'ring o'er the wrecks of time, . . ."

March 21

"These things have I written unto you that believe on the name of the Son of God; that ye may know that ye have eternal life, and that ye may believe on the name of the Son of God."
(1 John 5:13.)

THE fact of our salvation does not depend upon our own feelings. They are the least reliable of all things to rest upon, they are treacherous and not to be trusted. As surely as we rest upon these frauds—our feelings—the Lord will see fit to withdraw them, in order that we may learn to rest upon Him. Therefore stay your faith upon Christ, not upon your most hallowed feelings, but upon Christ Himself and His written promises. Whenever you are in doubt, perplexed, and unhappy, go at once to the Lord and His unfailing Word, and God's truth will disperse any mists of darkness which surround your soul.

Let us learn to lean more upon the fact and less upon our apprehension of it. We are to walk by faith and not by feelings.

"Believe! and the feeling
may come or may go,
Believe in the Word, that
was written to show
That all who believe their
salvation may know;
Believe and keep right on
believing."

By believing, we do not make anything true that was not true before. We simply bring ourselves into accord with what is and has always been the truth. There are some who say that that is true for us which finds us, or works in our case. But that only is true for us, when it finds us or works for us, which was true already in itself. There is an order, a divine order, . . . true, whatever we may think or deny, find or miss. Faith does not create this order. It realizes it. It is the loyal and loving acceptance of it. What we think and do is only a tardy response to the thought of God, and to what He has been ever doing for us.

—*Robert E. Speer.*

An old colored man who had a marvelous experience in grace was asked: "Daniel, why is it that you have so much peace and joy in religion?" "O Massa!" he replied, "I just fall flat on the exceeding great and precious promises, and I have all that is in them. Glory! Glory!" He who falls flat on the promises feels that all the riches embraced in them are his.—*Faith Papers.*

March 22

" . . . Thou hast holden me by my right hand." (Psalm 73:23.)

TRAVELER, following his guide amid the Alpine heights, reached a place where the path was narrowed by a jutting rock on one side and a deep precipice on the other. The guide passed around, and then holding on to the rock with one hand, extended the other out over the precipice for the traveler to step upon, and so pass around the jutting rock. He hesitated, but the guide called back saying, *"That hand has never lost a man."* The traveler stepped onto the hand and was soon safely past the danger.

> *"It isn't that I cling to Him*
>   *Or struggle to be blest;*
> *He simply takes my hand in His*
>   *And there I let it rest.*

> *"So I dread not any pathway,*
>   *Dare to sail on any sea,*
> *Since the handclasp of Another*
>   *Makes the journey safe for me."*

Hold Thou my hand, dear Lord,
   Hold Thou my hand!

March 23

"For everyone that asketh receiveth, and he that seeketh findeth; and to him that knocketh it shall be opened." (Luke 11:10.)

WHEN Napoleon's army was marching through the country, a good Christian woman, a widow with children, was somewhat fearful lest the soldiers should molest the home; and that night, around the family altar, she breathed her prayer, "Oh, God, build a wall around our home and protect us from the enemy." When the children retired they were heard asking one another, "What did mother mean asking God to build a wall around our home?" In the morning they knew, for a heavy wind and snow storm had come, and snowdrifts were all around the little home; the soldiers went by, not knowing that the house was there. That mother used God's promise. So may you, and then you will thank God for the answer.

> *" 'Daddy, teach me how to pray,'*
>   *Asks the little child down at my knee.*
> *Of all I can think, this is what I say,*
>   *'Trust God and ask, as you do of me.' "*

PRAYER

Prayer is so simple;
It is like quietly opening a door
And slipping into the very presence of God,
There in the stillness
To listen to His voice;
Perhaps to petition,
Or only to listen;
It matters not.
Just to be there
In His presence
Is prayer.

—*Selected.*

March 24

"*. . . All things work together for good to them that love God, . . .*" (Rom. 8:28.)

HOW many people are like birds with clipped wings! Life holds them enchained by some handicap. They feel they can never rise, and the temptation comes to settle down into despair or lassitude. But the spirit need not be earthbound. Its range is not restricted or its possibilities limited by physical handicap. Though he could not hear, Beethoven gave the world some of its finest music; Milton's blindness did not affect the noble range of his soul's vision. History has many instances of those who overcame handicaps because they lived in the spirit. Their souls were touched by an eternal flame, and any defect of body could not dim the light that was in them.

Sir Walter Scott is a brilliant example of grace and grit. He overcame lameness and misfortune, and instead of being crushed in spirit and defeated, he won out.

Charles P. Steinmetz, who rivaled Thomas A. Edison in his discoveries and inventions in the field of electrical enginering, was greatly deformed. He did most of his work half standing, half leaning upon a stool. However, he did not allow his handicap to embitter or discourage him. He knew he would have to fight his way. There was no personal popularity, no pleasant social contacts to speed him along. He tortured his brain into headaches and his eyes into burning balls of pain. Time after time he was defeated and undone, but Steinmetz kept climbing until he became the greatest electrical wizard of his time.

The march of progress is the conquering of impossibilities. The mountain that cannot be climbed may be tunneled.

March 25

"With thy meekness thou hast multiplied me."
(Psalm 18:35, margin.)

HE charm of a little child is its utter unconsciousness of self; and that is the charm of God-likeness. It is like the bloom on a peach, the dew-jewel on the morning lawn, or the stillness of the surface of a mountain pool."

Oh, we're too high. Lord Jesus, we implore Thee,
Make of us something like the low green moss,
That vaunteth not, a quiet thing before Thee,
Cool for Thy feet sore wounded on the Cross.
"Wings" by A. W. C.

Be like the dewdrop that finds a drooping rose and sinks down into its folds and loses itself but revives the weary flower. So be content to do good and bless the life that needs your benediction and be only remembered by what you have done.

"How I long to be centered in Thee—so completely centered in Thee that I do not realize it—none of self and all of Thee."
—*Oswald Chambers.*

March 26

"There came unto him a woman having an alabaster box of very precious ointment, and poured it on his head, as he sat at meat." (Matt. 26:7.)

ALL THAT I HAVE

HEN Queen Victoria first came to the British throne the whole of India was not under British rule, and it was only during her reign that Punjab became her possession. At that time the Maharajah was a mere boy. In order to show his allegiance to the Empress of India, he sent Queen Victoria the wonderful jewel known as the Koh-i-noor diamond. This magnificent offering was placed in the Tower of London, among the other carefully guarded crown jewels.

Some years later, when the Maharajah was a grown man, he paid a visit to England, and of course, went to Buckingham Palace to pay his respects to the Queen. He was taken to the state apartments, and after bowing to Her Majesty, he requested that he might be allowed to see the Koh-i-noor. Greatly wondering at his request, the Queen with her usual kindliness and courtesy gave orders that it should be brought under armed guard, and shown the Maharajah.

After a little time the priceless jewel was brought in and presented before the young Indian Prince. Very reverently he took it in his hands, and then walked over to the window where he examined it carefully. Then, while the onlookers gazed in wonder, he turned and knelt at the feet of the Queen, saying with great emotion in his voice: "Madam, I gave you this jewel when I was too young to know what I was doing. I want to give it again, in the fullness of my strength, with all my heart, and affection, and gratitude, now and forever, fully realizing all that I do."

> "May I have those pearls?" He questioned,
>   Knowing that I prized them so—
> "If you love Me, will you lay those
>   At My feet?" I answered, "No."
>
> But He looked so disappointed;
>   Then I cried, "O though it grieves,
> Take them, Master, take them, take them!
>   Yea, I love THEE 'more than these.'"
>
> Yes, He took my pearls, just cheap things
>   That could last but for a day,
> But He gave me back some REAL ONES—
>   PRICELESS! JOYS for aye—FOR AYE!
>   —Edith Mapes.

March 27

"The king's daughter is all glorious within: ..." (Psalm 45:13.)

> King's daughter!
> Wouldst thou be all fair,
> Without—within—
> Peerless and beautiful,
> A very queen?
> Know then:
> Not as men build into the Silent One—
> With clang and clamor,
> Traffic of rude voices,
> Clink of steel on stone,
> And din of hammer:
> Not so the temple of thy grace is reared.
> But, in the inmost shrine
> Must thou begin,
> And build with care

A Holy Place,
A place unseen,
Each stone a prayer.
Then, having built
Thy shrine, sweep bare
Of self and sin,
And all that might demean;
And, with endeavor,
Watching ever, praying ever,
Keep it fragrant—sweet, and clean;
So, by God's grace, it be a fit place,
His Christ shall enter and shall dwell therein.

Not as in earthly fane—where chase
Of steel on stone may strive to win
Some outward grace—
Thy temple face is chiseled from within.
                          —John Oxenham.

"... Her companions that follow her shall be brought unto thee. With gladness and rejoicing shall they be brought: they shall enter into the king's palace." (Psalm 45:14,15.)

"As pure as a pearl,
And as perfect—a noble and beautiful girl."
                          —Lord Lytton.

March 28

"And I was afraid, and went and hid thy talent in the earth: ... Take therefore the talent from him, ..." (Matt. 25:25, 28.)

IF a man should hang his arm in a sling and refuse to make any use of it, within a few months that arm would lose its strength and become useless. And it is thus with our talents for doing good; it is 'use or lose.' If you have ability to do something, do that something and you will be able with each succeeding day to do it better. But if you do not do it, you will perhaps attempt to do it some time, and find it impossible."
                          —J. B. Chapman.

It is told of the great violinist, Paganini, that he left his marvelous violin to his native city Genoa, but with instructions that no one was ever to play upon it. This was most unfortunate, for it is a peculiarity of wood that as long as it is handled and used, it wears but slightly, but as soon as it is laid aside or discarded, it begins to decay. Paganini's violin with its marvelous tones has become worm-eaten in its beautiful case and is worthless as a musical instrument.

THE FIDDLE AND THE BOW
"We did not choose our way of making,
Not sleeping ours to choose, or waking,
Not ours the starry stroke of sound
To choose or fly, though ours the wound.

"Though dead wood cry, 'How shall I dare it?'
And wood reply, 'I cannot bear it,'
Yet His alone to choose, whose fingers
Take the dead wood, and makes His singers."

"Let us allow Christ to speak through us. He desires this more than we do and for that reason prepared the instruments which He would not have remain unused and idle."—*Chrysostom.*

Hide not thy talent, but trade with it, and thou shalt bring in good interest to thy Master. Use or lose!

March 29

". . . O Daniel, servant of THE LIVING GOD, is thy God, whom thou servest continually, able to deliver thee? . . ."
(Daniel 6:20.)

OW many times we find this expression in the Scriptures, and yet it is just this very thing that we are so prone to lose sight of. We know it is written *"the living God"*; that He is now what He was three or four thousand years ago; that He has the same sovereign power, the same saving love towards those who love and serve Him as ever He had, and that He will do for us now what He did for others two, three, four thousand years ago, simply because He is *the living God,* the unchanging One! Oh, how we should confide in Him, therefore, and in our darkest moments never lose sight of the fact that He is still and ever will be *the living God!*

Be assured, if you walk with Him and look to Him and expect help from Him, He will never fail you. An older brother who has known the Lord for forty-four years writes for your encouragement that He has never failed him! In the greatest difficulties, in the heaviest trials, in the deepest poverty and necessities, He has never failed me; but because I was enabled by His grace to trust Him He has always appeared for my help. I delight in speaking well of His name.—*George Muller.*

"Who delivered us . . . doth deliver: in whom we trust that he will yet deliver us." (2 Cor. 1:10.)

March 30

"I am he that liveth, and was dead; and, behold, I am alive for evermore, Amen; . . ." (Rev. 1: 18.)

UTHER was once found, at a moment of peril and fear, when he had need to grasp unseen strength, sitting in an abstracted mood, tracing on the table with his finger the words, "Vivit! Vivit!" ("He lives! He lives!"). This is our hope for ourselves, and for His truth, and for mankind! Men come and go; leaders, teachers, thinkers speak and work for a season, and then fall silent and impotent. He abides! They die, but *He* lives! They are lights kindled, and therefore, sooner or later, quenched; but He is the true Light from which they draw all their brightness, and He shines for evermore.—*Alexander Maclaren.*

"One day I came to know Dr. John Douglas Adam," writes C. G. Trumbull. "I learned from him that what he counted his greatest spiritual asset was *his unvarying consciousness of the actual presence of Jesus.* Nothing bore him up so, he said, as the realization that Jesus was *always* with him in actual presence, and that this was so independent of his own feelings, independent of his deserts, and independent of his own notions as to how Jesus would manifest His presence.

"Moreover, he said that Christ was the home of his thoughts. Whenever his mind was free from other matters it would turn to Christ; and he would talk aloud to Christ when he was alone—on the street, anywhere—as easily and naturally as to a human friend. So real to him was Jesus' *actual presence."*

March 31

". . . And how shall they hear without a preacher?"
(Rom. 10:14.)

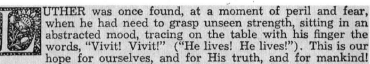

HIS story is told by Bishop Taylor. He had called at a village in Africa with his little missionary boat but was unable to leave a missionary with them. They were bitterly disappointed, and long entreated him to alter his purpose and leave a teacher, but it was beyond his power, and he sorrowfully left them. As he sailed up the river he saw them standing on the bank beckoning to him with eager entreaty.

Two days later he returned, sailing down the stream. As he passed the village, the natives were still standing on the banks waiting for him, and as they saw that he did not intend to land, they became wild in their gesticulations and cries, waving their arms, leaping high in the air, shouting and trying in every way to attract his attention. He felt the appeal in every fibre of his being.

but he could do nothing! He had no one to leave, and as he sailed down the river, his heart was broken with the sight.

When at length he passed out of sight of the village and was hidden by a projecting promontory from their view, he said he heard a great and bitter cry go up from these people, long and loud, until it pierced his very soul, and seemed to go away up to Heaven as a protest to God against the cruelty of man. It was the lamentation of the heathen after God. We shall hear that cry! It will come up in our ears once more in the judgment day. God help us to be able to stand in that awful hour and say: "I am pure from the blood of all men."

> *"Tell all the world there is sight for its blindness;*
> *Balm for its healing, a song for its dumb.*
> *Blood for its cleansing and life for its dying;*
> *Tell them of JESUS and bid them to come."*

Prayer: "Keep the sense of Thy call in me vivid and fresh."

April 1

"He delivereth me from mine enemies: yea, thou liftest me up above those that rise up against me: . . ." (Psalm 18:48.)

"Set your affections on things above, not on things of the earth." (Col. 3:2.)

ALTITUDE

"It's safer flying high," declared the pilot;
  We climbed another thousand feet or so;
"The higher up we are, the better landing,
  Emergency airports ahead, below."

"It's safer flying high"—sometimes it echoes
  When conscience indicates the need of care,
When tempted to some base or fleshly interest,
  And sin presents itself in colors fair.

The sky way is the highway for the victor,
  For those who wish to live among the few
So evident in life as in air travel—
  The farther from the earth, the fuller view.

The hills of difficulty are no longer,
  The mountains of despair are ironed smooth;
When high and looking down upon your problems,
  The deep and darker valley seems a groove.

No fogs will blur the lines of demarcation,
  And make the black of wrong a blended gray,
When you are living in the open sunshine,
  Where altitude will brighten all your way.

"It's safer flying high," says the apostle,
The world beneath, and God's own blue above;
Remember, Christ is seated in the heavenlies,
And you are with Him there—climax of love!

How worthless then the world, how dull its glory,
When you live high, and far enough away
To get a sense of values, wise and proper;
Then why not live your altitude today?

                                        —*Dr. Will H. Houghton.*
                            (Used by permission of the author.)

April 2

". . . If there be a prophet among you, I the Lord will make
myself known unto him, . . ." (Numbers 12:6.)

THE desperate need of the hour, both for the home base
and fields afar, is for youth of ability and consecration.
Some say "There is no place for me." They are mistaken.
There is need for young people with vision, purpose, and
a deep love for God and His message!

"There is a niche in God's own temple;
It is thine,
And the Hand that shapes thee for it
Is Divine."

Thank God that you have youth and determine that by His help
you will make good use of every privilege and blessing which the
year may bring. The hours of time which have been allotted to you
will soon slip away. Determine that you will do things while you
are still young, and begin right now to accomplish them. Will you
pause to hear God speaking as the poet said:

"Youth, O youth, can I reach you?
Can I speak and make you hear?
Can I open your eyes to see Me,
Can My presence draw you near?
Is there a prophet among you,
One with a heart to know:
I will flash My secrets on him,
He shall watch My glory grow.
For I, the God, the Father,
The Quest, and the final Goal,
Still search for a prophet among you
To speak My word in his soul."

O! youth, awake! Answer the call. Be brave soldiers of Christ.
Go forward in full armor. Crush Satan's work, and victory will be

yours. The day is fast approaching when you will see the starlights in their glory. Then give your health, wealth, and life to win souls for Christ! Oh, may you not blush on that day!

—*Sadhu Sundar Singh.*

April 3

"If ye then, being evil, know how to give good gifts unto your children: how much more shall your heavenly Father give the Holy Spirit to them that ask him?" (Luke 11:13.)

I WAS standing on the wall of a great lock. Outside was a huge lake vessel about to enter. At my feet lay the empty lock—waiting. For what? Waiting to be filled. Away beyond lay great Lake Superior with its limitless abundance of supply, also waiting. Waiting for what? Waiting for something to be done at the lock ere the great lake could pour in its fullness. In a moment it was done. The lock-keeper reached out his hand and touched a steel lever. A little wicket gate sprang open under the magic touch. At once the water in the lock began to boil and seethe. As it seethed I saw it rapidly creeping up the walls of the lock. In a few moments the lock was full. The great gates swung open, and the huge ship floated into the lock now filled to the brim with the fullness inpoured from the waiting lake without.

Is not this a picture of a great truth about the Holy Spirit? Here are God's children, like that empty lock, waiting to be filled. And, as that great inland sea outside the lock was willing and waiting to pour its abundance into the lock, so here is God willing to pour His fullness of life into the lives of His children. But he is *waiting!*

For what? Waiting, as the lake waited, *for something to be done by us.* Waiting for us to reach forth and touch that tiny wicket gate of consecration through which His abundant life shall flow and fill.

Is it hard to move? Does the rust of worldliness corrode it? Do the weeds and ivy-vines of selfishness cling about and choke it? Is the will stubborn, and slow to yield? Yet God is waiting for it. And once it is done, He reveals Himself in fullness of life even as He has promised; even as He has been all the time willing and ready to do. For all the barriers and hindrances have been upon our side, not upon His. They are the barriers not of His unwillingness, but of our unyieldedness. And do you say you got all of Christ when you were saved? Doubtless you did, but the point in issue here is not whether you got all of Christ, but *did Christ get all of you?"*

—*James McConkey.*

Give your life to God, and God will fill your life.

April 4

"... There was silence, and I heard a voice, saying, ..."
(Job 4:16.)

IT is said of Ole Bull, the master violinist of Norway, that he was found one day sitting out upon a rock by the sea. He was asked, "Why are you here?"

"Listening," he answered, "to the surge and fall of the breakers, that I may catch the music of the sea."

Are *you* ever listening to the far notes of divine grace that you may reproduce all upon the wondrous instrument—the life that the Father has given?

OMNIPRESENT

I found God in the dawning
In the crimson flight of night,
In the notes of the birds at matins,
In the sun-burst glory light.

I found Him in a garden,
In the dew-drenched columbine,
In the shy and modest clinging
Of the morning-glory vine.

I found Him in the patches
Of the white clouds floating high,
That touched with animation
The majestic vault of sky.

I found Him in a roadway,
Through a quiet countryside,
And on a lake at sunset,
Where the golden ripples ride.

At last in purple twilight,
In the cooling, fragrant air,
I heard God's presence whisper—
I knew that He was there.

—*Frank G. Weaver.*

If we make a great silence in the heart, we shall hear God speak.

Tread in solitude thy pathway,
Quiet heart and undismayed.
Thou shalt know things strange, mysterious,
Which to thee no voice has said.

April 5

"... I know whom I have trusted, ..." (2 Tim. 1:12, Trans.)

GOD loves an *uttermost confidence in Himself*—to be *wholly trusted!* This is the sublimest of all the characteristics of a true Christian—the basis of all character.

Is there anything that pleases you more than to be trusted—to have even a little child look up into your face, and put out its hand to meet yours, and come to you confidingly? By so much as God is better than you are, by so much more does He love to be trusted.

There is a Hand stretched out to you; a Hand with a wound in the palm of it. Reach out the hand of your faith to clasp it, and cling to it, for "without faith it is impossible to please God."
—*Henry Van Dyke.*

Reach up as far as you can, and God will reach down all the rest of the way.—Bishop Vincent.

> *Not what, but WHOM I do believe!*
> *That, in my darkest hour of need,*
> *Hath comfort that no mortal creed*
> *To mortal man may give.*
> *Not what, but WHOM!*
> *For Christ is more than all the creeds,*
> *And His full life of gentle deeds*
> *Shall all the creeds outlive.*
> *Not what I do believe, but WHOM!*
> *WHO walks beside me in the gloom?*
> *WHO shares the burden wearisome?*
> *WHO all the dim way doth illume,*
> *And bids me look beyond the tomb*
> *The larger life to live?*
> *Not what I do believe, BUT WHOM!*
> *Not what,*
> *But WHOM!*
> —*John Oxenham.*

I have always felt so sorry in that walk to Emmaus the disciples had not said to Jesus, "We still trust"; instead of *"We trusted."* Let us never put our faith, as these disciples did, in a past tense —*"We trusted."* But let us ever say, *"I am trusting."*

"'Tis so sweet to trust in Jesus!"

April 6

*". . . Every branch that beareth fruit, he purgeth it, that it
may bring forth more fruit."* (John 15:2.)

WHEN the violin-makers of the Middle Ages wished to form
a perfect instrument, they caused the selected tree to be
felled at a particular period of its growth. The wood was
then planed and cut into small pieces. These were exposed
to the heat of the sun and to the winter's storms; then they
were bent, rubbed, polished, and finally fastened together with in-
comparable skill.

If the wood could have found tongue, doubtless it would have
begged to grow in the forest, to rustle its branches, and to bear its
fruit as its companions were left to do, becoming at last a part of
sodden earth. But it was this harsh treatment that made out of
common boards the Stradivari violin, whose music still charms the
world.

> *God of the gallant trees*
> *Give to us fortitude;*
> *Give as Thou givest to them*
> *Valorous hardihood!*
> *We are the trees of Thy planting, O God,*
> *We are the trees of Thy wood.*
>
> *Now let the life-sap run*
> *Clean through our every vein,*
> *Perfect what Thou hast begun*
> *God of the sun and rain.*
> *Thou who dost measure the weight of the wind,*
> *Fit us for stress and strain.*
> —*Amy Wilson Carmichael.*

Be weather-worn timber!

April 7

*"Study to shew thyself approved unto God, a workman that
needeth not to be ashamed, rightly dividing the word of truth."*
(2 Tim. 2:15.)

JESUS CHRIST is the heart of the Bible. He is the *Shiloh*
in Genesis; the *I AM* in Exodus; the *Star and Sceptre* in
Numbers; the *Rock* in Deuteronomy; the *Captain of the
Lord's Host* in Joshua; and the *Redeemer* in Job. He is
David's *Lord and Shepherd* in the Psalms; in the Song of
Songs He is the *Beloved;* in Isaiah He is the *Wonderful,* the *Coun-
sellor,* the *Mighty God,* the *Everlasting Father,* and the *Prince of
Peace.* In Jeremiah He is the *Lord our Righteousness;* in Daniel

He is the *Messiah;* in Zechariah He is the *Branch,* in Haggai He is the *Desire of all Nations;* in Malachi He is the *Messenger of the Covenant* and the *Sun of Righteousness;* in the Book of Revelation He is the *Alpha* and the *Omega,* and also the *Morning Star.*

> *I supposed I knew my Bible,*
>   *Reading piecemeal, hit or miss,*
> *Now a bit of John or Matthew,*
>   *Now a snatch of Genesis,*
> *Certain chapters of Isaiah,*
>   *Certain Psalms (the twenty-third!)*
> *Twelfth of Romans, first of Proverbs—*
>   *Yes, I thought I knew the Word!*
> *But I found that thorough reading*
>   *Was a different thing to do,*
> *And the way was unfamiliar*
>   *When I read the Bible through.*
>
> *You who like to play at Bible,*
>   *Dip and dabble here and there,*
> *Just before you kneel, aweary,*
>   *And yawn through a hurried prayer,*
> *You who treat the crown of writings*
>   *As you treat no other book—*
> *Just a paragraph disjointed,*
>   *Just a crude, impatient look—*
> *Try a worthier procedure,*
>   *Try a broad and steady view;*
> *You will kneel in very rapture,*
>   *When you read the Bible through!*
>
> —*Selected.*

Mark your Bible. It will emblazon glorious truths. Well-springs of inspiration will stand out like electric signs in the night.

Said Dr. Frank Crane: "Commit something to memory every day. Thus train the waters of the great Reservoir of wisdom to irrigate your daily life."

Today may I discover riches which have hitherto been hidden from me!

"All scripture is given by inspiration of God, and is profitable for doctrine, for reproof, for correction, for instruction in righteousness: That the man of God may be perfect, throughly furnished unto all good works."   (2 Timothy 3: 16, 17.)

April 8

*"But they that wait upon the Lord shall renew their strength;
they shall mount up with wings as eagles; they shall run, and
not be weary; and they shall walk, and not faint."* (Isa. 40:31.)

THERE was a hero once who, when an overwhelming force
was in full pursuit, and all his followers were urging him
to a more rapid flight, coolly dismounted to repair a flaw in
his horse's harness. While busied with the broken buckle,
the distant cloud swept down in nearer thunder; but just
as the prancing hoofs and eager spears were ready to dash upon
him, the flaw was mended, and like a swooping falcon he had vanished from their view. The broken buckle would have left him on
the field a dismounted and inglorious prisoner; the timely delay,
sent him in safety back to his bustling companions.

There is in daily life the same unfortunate precipitance and the
same profitable delay. The youth who from his prayerless awakening bounces into the hours of the day, however good his talents and
great his diligence, is only galloping upon a steed harnessed with
a broken buckle, and must not marvel if, in his hottest haste or most
hazardous leap, he be left inglorious in the dust; and though it may
occasion some little delay beforehand, his neighbor is wiser who
sets all in order before the march begins.

We cannot rush through a chapter of the Bible and come out of
it laden with the Word. That is the reward of patient and leisurely
movement. Dr. Joseph Parker advised a young minister never to
"gallop" through the Scriptures. "Go slowly, and look around."

What do motorists see of the wayside flowers when they are
racing along at fifty or sixty miles an hour? And what do they
hear of the song of birds, and what do they see of the movements of
the sky, graceful things which only venture out when everything
is quiet and still? The beauty of the Word is the reward which is
given to the soul which moves with reverent and unhasty steps.
If we rush along we shall miss it!

April 9

"... Lovest thou me more than these?" (John 21:15.)

IT is "things" that hinder a clear vision of Christ in many
lives. A tiny steel splinter in the eye of a friend robbed
him of half his vision for the balance of his life. "Things"
keep many from lives of obedience. "Things" may rob us
of God's best—things present and things to come, little
things and big things, real things and imaginary things. Beautiful
lives have been wrecked by mere "things." "Things"—just "things"
—will find some unprepared when Jesus comes. Again and

again our attention is held by "things," attractive, beautiful wonderful! Sweet but subtle voices speak: "They are yours! Take them!"
But a faithful Voice whose identity cannot be mistaken by the child
of God, says, "Things, or Christ?" And we are called upon to make
another choice. We have answered the question, "Barabbas, or Jesus?" And now comes another which leads to a second crisis,
"Things, or Christ—a real, indwelling, living Christ, actuating the
life and filling it with holy joy!"

"I count all things but loss," said St. Paul.

Paul, are you not mistaken? It is necessary for you to give up
only what is harmful, distasteful, or sinful!

"What things were gain to me, those I counted loss for Christ."

But you would certainly make a difference; some things are really
worthwhile, and Christians are not to lose these!

"What things were gain to me, those I counted loss for Christ."

But listen, Paul, I speak of things that are truly advantageous.

"What things were gain . . ."

But Paul, leave us a few things! Why should we be deprived? Is
not your way too narrow? Modify your testimony somewhat, for
we are young, and yours is a hard way! Do you insist that we may
not have even a few things, the very best things?

"Yea doubtless, and I count all things but loss for the excellency
of the knowledge of Christ Jesus my Lord: for whom I have suffered the loss of all things . . . that I may win Christ."

There is no easier pathway to God's best. The price is small, the
gain is great. We give up our own little contracted life and receive
in return a rich, full, overflowing, triumphant, victorious, and abundant life.

> He ventured all: the loss of place, and power, and love of kin—
> O bitter loss! O loneliness and pain!
> He gained the Christ! Who would not dare the loss
> Such priceless bliss to win?
> Christ for today, and each tomorrow—Christ!
>
> —J. Mannington Dexter.

"Then Peter began to say unto him, Lo, we have left all,
and have followed thee. And Jesus answered and said, Verily
I say unto you, There is no man that hath left house, or brethren, or sisters, or father, or mother, or wife, or children, or
lands, for my sake, and the gospel's, But he shall receive an
hundredfold now in this time, houses, and brethren, and sisters,
and mothers, and children, and lands, with persecutions; and in
the world to come eternal life." (Mark 10:28-30.)

April 10

". . . A vessel unto honor, sanctified, and meet for the master's use, and prepared unto every good work." (2 Tim. 2:21.)

JOHN WESLEY, a classical scholar gifted with a virile mind, gave himself fully to God and consecrated all his powers to His service. Although possessed of a scholar's love for books, he spent most of his life in the saddle and in the active duties of a most strenuous life. With a passionate love for art, especially for music and architecture, he turned away from their charms to blow the gospel trumpet with all his might. With a more-than-ordinary longing for the sweets and comforts of human love, he arose above disappointments which would have crushed ordinary men, forgot his "inly-bleeding heart" (his own expression), and gave himself unreservedly to the work of binding up the brokenhearted. Visiting the beautiful grounds of an English nobleman, he said, "I, too, have a ravish for these things—but there is another world!" John Wesley followed a Homeless Stranger —the Stranger of Galilee.

> *If Thou dost need a hand today*
> *To clasp another hand on life's rough way;*
> *Take mine, dear Lord, take mine.*
> *If Thou art needing feet to tread*
> *In paths where sin to woe is wed;*
> *Use mine, dear Lord, use mine.*
> *If thou art needing lips today*
> *For words that help and heal, to say;*
> *Fill mine, dear Lord, fill mine.*
> *If Thou art needing eyes to see*
> *When souls begin to stray from Thee;*
> *Fit mine, dear Lord, fit mine.*
> *But cleanse, dear Lord, and purify,*
> *And then each talent sanctify;*
> *Of mine, dear Lord, of mine.*
>
> *—Mary E. Kendrew.*

"The placing of the Cross on Simeon's shoulders glorified his whole career."—*F. N. Boreham* in *The Ivory Spires.*

"I speak of my severe labors for the Gospel. I am ready even to die in the same cause. If I am required to pour out my life-blood as a libation over the sacrificial offering of your faith, I rejoice myself and I congratulate you all therein. Yea, in like manner I ask you also to rejoice and congratulate me.
(Phil. 2:17, 18, Trans.)

April 11

"They looked unto him, and were radiant." (Psalm 34:5, R.V.)

WHEN the great missionary, Adoniram Judson, was home on furlough, he passed through Stonington, Connecticut. In those days the Stonington Line was the principal route between New England and New York, and the boys of the town often played about the wharves in the evening in the hope of catching a glimpse of some famous man. Two trains connected with the boat—an accommodation and an express.

One evening, when the accommodation came in, one of the boys noticed a man whose appearance excited his curiosity and wonder. Never before had he seen such a light on any human face. Presently it dawned on him that the man was the famous missionary whose picture he had once seen. He ran up the street to the minister's to ask if he could be the man. The minister hurried back with him. Yes, the boy was right. But the minister, absorbed in conversation with the missionary, forgot all about the boy who had brought him the news. The boy, silent, eager, unable to tear himself away, stood by and watched the wonderful face, the face like a benediction.

Many years afterward, that boy, Henry Clay Trumbull, became a famous minister himself, and wrote a book of memories in which was a chapter entitled, "What a Boy Saw in the Face of Adoniram Judson." Doctor Trumbull, too, has passed into the presence of the Master whom he served, but the light in the missionary's face still shines down the years. Friends to whom Doctor Trumbull told the story tell it to others, and the printed pages—who can tell to how many lives they have carried their message?

The shining face is no mystery. Centuries ago the Psalmist knew the secret and wrote, "They looked unto him and were radiant." It comes to those whose faces are always turned toward Him, as a flower turns toward the light. It was said at the time of the Boxer rebellion that Chinese Christians could not be disguised—the light in their faces betrayed them. The pity of it, that every Christian may not be known by the shining of his face!

—The Youth's Companion.

Is Christ in us? Be ours the glorious dower
To show the Saviour shining in our face,
And through our eyes forth-putting His sweet power
To help the weak and wayward with His grace;

Oh, let no sin in us these windows dim,
Through which the world might catch some glimpse of Him.
—R. Milton.

April 12

"...I count all things but loss for the excellency of the knowledge of Christ Jesus my Lord: for whom I have suffered the loss of all things, ... that I may win Christ." (Phil. 3:8.)

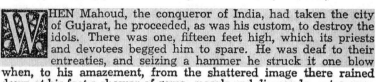

WHEN Mahoud, the conqueror of India, had taken the city of Gujarat, he proceeded, as was his custom, to destroy the idols. There was one, fifteen feet high, which its priests and devotees begged him to spare. He was deaf to their entreaties, and seizing a hammer he struck it one blow when, to his amazement, from the shattered image there rained down at his feet a shower of gems—pearls and diamonds—a treasure of fabulous value, which had been hidden within it! Had he spared the idol, he would have lost all this wealth. Let us not spare *our* idols. It is to our interest to demolish them. If we shatter them, there will rain about our hearts the very treasures of heaven, the gifts and graces of the Holy Spirit; but if we spare our idols, we miss the riches unsearchable. If you do not crown Him Lord *of all*, you do not crown Him Lord *at all*.

—*John MacNeil.*

> The dearest idol I have known,
> Whate'er that idol be,
> Help me to tear it from Thy throne,
> And worship only Thee.

—*William Cowper.*

April 13

"... Henceforth ... unto him, ..." (2 Cor. 5:15.)

IN THE cemetery of an English town there is a tombstone which attracts the attention of many visitors. It marks the grave where the celebrated Swedish singer, Jenny Lind, known as the Swedish Nightingale, was buried, and upon the stone is the text, "I know that my Redeemer liveth."

Jenny Lind was born in 1820. When only seventeen she came from her native land, and her lovely voice took the concert-loving people by storm. The good Queen Victoria often was found in her audience and signally honored "the slim girl with a marvelous voice," as she was called, by throwing to her a bouquet of flowers. From the crowned heads of Europe Jenny Lind received honor, and gifts were showered upon her from all sides. Wealth poured in, but all her success did not make her proud or exacting, as is so often the case, and she humbly wrote to a friend in later years, "My unceasing prayer is that what I gave to my fellows may continue to live on through eternity and that the Giver of the gift and not the creature to whom He lent it may be acknowledged."

A certain writer has remarked, "Nothing is more astonishing about the career of Jenny Lind than its comparative shortness. She sang in the English opera for only two years and retired practically in five years after her first appearance in London, though she appeared occasionally during the next few years, but chiefly for charities."

To many it would seem strange circumstances which led a young girl to abandon such a promising career and retire to the quietness of an English country home. On one occasion she sat on the sea-shore, reading a Bible, when one who greatly admired her beautiful voice saw her and asked, "How is it, madam, that you abandoned the stage at the very height of your success?" Jenny Lind gave the following reason: "When every day it made me think less of this"—laying her hand upon the open Bible, "what else could I do?" What a beautiful answer and how convincing! It was the knowledge that this precious Book had brought her—the knowledge of a Saviour's love which led her to abandon what the world counts of such value —riches, honor and popularity.

One of her great successes was in the oratorios in which she sang with deepest feeling "The Messiah," and doubtless the words of it meant more to her than human voice could express. She knew the Lord Jesus as her Redeemer, the One who loved her and gave Himself for her, and that love constrained her to withdraw from the stage and henceforth live "unto Him who died and rose again."

> *Crown Him with many crowns,*
> *The Lamb upon the throne;*
> *Hark, how the heavenly anthem drowns*
> *All music but His own:*
> *Awake, my soul, and sing*
> *Of Him who died for thee,*
> *And hail Him as the matchless King*
> *Through all eternity.*
> *—Sir George J. Elvey.*

"May I not covet the world's greatness if it cost me the crown of life!"   *—Dr. Jowett.*

"And they sung a new song, . . . Saying with a loud voice, Worthy is the Lamb that was slain to receive power, and riches, and wisdom, and strength, and honour, and glory, and blessing."   (Rev. 5:9, 12.)

April 14

"The Lord knoweth how to deliver the godly out of temptations, . . ." (2 Peter 2:9.)

TEMPTATION happens to the purest; but it fascinates and imperils only as it finds a welcome in the soul itself.

No temptation becomes sin until it is tolerated or welcomed. Sin consists in yielding to temptation. So long as temptation finds no sympathy within, no sin enters, and the soul remains unharmed, no matter how long or severe the fiery trial may prove.

The bushmaster in South America is the most terrible of all serpents: it is not only highly venomous, it also grows to be of great length, and it is very aggressive. For its venom there seems absolutely no antidote. He who has the misfortune to be bitten by it seldom lives longer than twenty minutes; all of his blood is turned to a frightful corruption. Yet the creature is most beautiful—a sort of a living rainbow, every color being beautifully shown with superb iridescence as it glides and shimmers in the sunlight—a meet symbol of evil transfigured in the imagination and passions of faithless souls! Temptation will attract you at your weakest spot.

Beware of selling your birthright for a mess of pottage!

> *"And when our hands should bar the gate*
> *We parley with the foe."*

In the hour when temptations assail us may we be ready to accompany the Master to the old olive tree in the Garden and then on to Calvary's hill!

> *Go to dark Gethsemane*
> *Ye that feel the tempter's power:*
> *Your Redeemer's conflict see;*
> *Watch with Him one bitter hour:*
> *Turn not from His grief away*
> *Learn of Jesus Christ to pray.*
> *—Richard Redfield.*

"There hath no temptation taken you but such as is common to man: but God is faithful who will not suffer you to be tempted above that ye are able; but will with the temptation also make a way of escape, that ye may be able to bear it." (1 Cor. 10: 13.)

April 15

"For ye are bought with a price: therefore glorify God in your body, and in your spirit, which are God's." (1 Cor. 6:20.)

JAPANESE lady called to see the head mistress of a mission school. "Do you take only beautiful girls in your school?" she inquired.

"Why, no! We welcome *all* girls," was the reply.

"But I have noticed that all your girls are beautiful," the woman exclaimed.

"Well, we teach them to love our Saviour, Jesus Christ, and He gives them a look of holy beauty," replied the missionary.

"I myself am a Buddhist, and I do not desire my daughter to become a Christian. Yet I should like her to attend your school to get that look on her face," was the reply.

> *I want that adorning Divine*
> *Thou only, my God, canst bestow;*
> *I want in these beautiful garments to shine*
> *Which mark out Thy household below.*
>
> *I want to be marked for Thine own,*
> *Thy seal on my forehead to wear,*
> *And have that 'new name' on the mystic*
> *   white stone*
> *Which none but Thyself can declare.*
> —Charlotte Elliott.

Here is a plain strip of canvas. Before it stands the master painter. "Do you see the golden sunset?" he asks. "Trust yourself to me and I will paint its glory in your face." And the canvas says, "I am coarse in texture. I am scant in size. I do not see how you can fill me with the glory of that sunset sky." And the master says, "Yield, and you shall see."

April 16

". . . I will never leave thee, nor forsake thee." (Heb. 13:5.)

THE LITTLE BLACK DOG

> *I wonder if Christ had a little black dog,*
> *   All curly and woolly like mine;*
> *With two silky ears and a nose round and wet,*
> *   And two eyes, brown and tender, that shine.*
>
> *I'm sure if He had, that little black dog*
> *   Knew right from the first He was God;*
> *That he needed no proof that Christ was divine,*
> *   But just worshiped the ground He trod.*

I'm afraid that He hadn't because I have read
How He prayed in the garden alone;
For all of His friends and disciples had fled—
Even Peter, the one called a stone.

And, oh, I am sure that little black dog,
With a heart so tender and warm,
Would never have left Him to suffer alone,
But creeping right under His arm,

Would have licked the dear fingers, in agony clasped;
And counting all favors but loss,
When they took Him away would have trotted behind,
And followed Him to the cross!
—Elizabeth Gardner Reynolds.

Oh, that we may not fail Him when love comes to that testing point!

April 17

"And I will pray the Father, and he shall give you another Comforter, that he may abide with you for ever." (John 14:16.)

THERE is a guide in the deserts of Arabia who is said never to lose his way. They call him "The Dove Man." He carries in his breast a homing pigeon with a very fine cord attached from the pigeon to one of his arms. When in any doubt as to which path to take, the guide throws the bird in the air. The pigeon quickly strains at the cord to fly in the direction of home and so leads his master unerringly. They call that guide "The Dove Man." The Holy Spirit, the heavenly Dove, is willing and able to lead us if we will only allow Him to do so.

Awake to the Presence that is always in the fully surrendered life!

"The Holy Spirit is our indwelling Partner."—*Dr. J. H. Jowett.*

A beautiful story is told by the Norwegian author, Ibsen. It is a story of newly weds. One winter evening they were out on a hike through the mountains. The snow lay deep, and the villagers warned them of the dangers of an avalanche. But these two in their new-found love thought naught of danger, only laughed at the warnings. Waving a farewell to the villagers they shouted back the cry, "There is no precipice too steep for two."

Jesus, these eyes have never seen
That radiant form of Thine;
The veil of sense hangs dark between
Thy blessed face and mine.

I see Thee not, I hear Thee not,
Yet Thou art oft with me;
And earth has ne'er so dear a spot
As where I meet with Thee.

—*Dr. Ray Palmer.*

Unseen but not unknown!

A Boston student once came to Phillips Brooks greatly troubled in mind. "Bishop Brooks," he asked, "is conscious personal fellowship with Jesus Christ a part of Christianity?" The great preacher was silent a moment, and then with impressive earnestness he replied: "Conscious personal fellowship with Jesus *is* Christianity."

April 18

"*...If a son, then an heir,...*" (Gal. 4: 7.)

A DYING judge said to his pastor, "Do you know enough about law to understand what is meant by joint tenancy?" "No," was the reply, "I know nothing about law; I know a little about grace, and that has satisfied me."

"Well," he said, "if you and I were joint tenants on a farm I could not say to you, 'That is your hill of corn, and this is mine; that is your blade of grass, and this is mine,' but we would share alike in everything on the place. I have just been lying here and thinking with unspeakable joy that Christ Jesus has nothing apart from me; that everything He has is mine, and that we will share alike through all eternity."—*Selected.*

Oh, how sweet a sight it is to see a cross betwixt Christ and us, to hear our Redeemer say, at every sigh, and every blow and every loss of a believer, "Half Mine!" —*Samuel Rutherford.*

"From whence shall *we* buy bread?" The Master said "WE!"

WE TWO

"*I cannot do it alone;*
The waves run fast and high,
And the fogs close chill around,
And the light goes out in the sky;
But I know that We Two shall win—
in the end:
—*Jesus and I.*

"*I cannot row it myself—*
The boat on the raging sea—
But beside me sits Another,
Who pulls or steers—with me;
And I know that We Two shall come
safe into port,
—*His child and He.*

"Coward and wayward and weak,
I change with the changing sky;
Today, so eager and brave,
· Tomorrow, not caring to try:
But He never gives in; so We Two
shall win!
— *Jesus and I.*

"Strong and tender and true,
Crucified once for me;
Ne'er will He change, I know,
Whatever I may be.
But all He says I must do—
Ever from sin to keep free;
We shall finish our course, and reach
Home at last!
— *His child and He."*

An old Negro's prayer: "O Lord, help me to remember that nothin' is goin' to happen to me today that You and me together can't handle."

April 19

"Unto you therefore which believe he is precious: . . ."
(1 Peter 2: 7.)

CHRIST'S presence is everything. John Brown, of Haddington, said he would not exchange the learning of one hour's fellowship with Christ for all the liberal learning in ten thousand universities during ten thousand years, even though angels were to be his teachers. Phillips Brooks was once crossing the Atlantic and a young man, a fellow-passenger, having an intense desire for an interview with him, went to his cabin door and knocked gently. As no answer was received he quietly opened the door, to find the great saint of God prostrate upon the floor, his hands raised to heaven and his lips moving in prayer. These were the words which he heard: "O Lord Jesus, Thou hast filled my life with peace and gladness. To look into Thy face is earth's most exquisite joy."

Turn your eyes upon Jesus,
Look full in His wonderful Face,
And the things of earth will grow strangely dim,
In the light of His glory and grace.
— *Helen Howarth Lemmel.*

"He brought me to the banqueting house, and his banner over me was love." (Song of Solomon 2:4.)

April 20

"Ye are the light of the world. . . . let your light so shine, . . ."
(Matt. 5: 14, 16.)

THE keeper of a lighthouse at Calais was boasting of the brightness of his lantern, which could be seen ten leagues at sea. A visitor said to him, "What if one of the lights should chance to go out?" "Never! Impossible!" he cried, horrified at the thought. "Sir," said he, pointing to the ocean, "yonder, where nothing can be seen, there are ships going out to all parts of the world. If tonight one of my burners went out, within six months would come a letter, perhaps from India, perhaps from America, perhaps from some place I never heard of, saying, on such a night, at such an hour, the light of Calais burned dim, the watchman neglected his post and vessels were in danger! Ah, sir, sometimes in the dark nights, in stormy weather, I look out to sea and feel as if the eyes of the whole world were looking at my light. Go out? Burn dim? Never!"

> *Brightly beams our Father's mercy,*
> *From His lighthouse evermore*
> *But to us He gives the keeping*
> *Of the lights along the shore.*
>
> *Dark the night of sin has settled,*
> *Loud the angry billows roar;*
> *Eager eyes are watching, longing,*
> *For the lights along the shore.*
>
> *Trim your feeble lamp, my brother:*
> *Some poor sailor tempest tossed,*
> *Trying now to make the harbor,*
> *In the darkness may be lost.*
>
> *Let the lower lights be burning!*
> *Send a gleam across the wave!*
> *Some poor fainting, struggling seaman*
> *You may rescue, you may save.*
>
> *Hymnal.*

"For ye were sometimes darkness, but now are ye light in the Lord: walk as children of light: . . . " (Eph. 5: 8.)

> *"Lord, keep me shining for Thee,*
> *Oh, keep me shining for Thee;*
> *In a world wrapt in night,*
> *Keep me pure, keep me white;*
> *Lord, keep me shining for Thee!*
> *—Chalvar A. Gabriel.*

April 21

"... In thy presence is fulness of joy; at thy right hand there are pleasures for evermore." (Psalm 16: 11.)

CHIMING CHRISTIANS

AT the time when clocks were first being made to chime, the following words in a window—"Clocks converted to chiming"—caught the writer's eye.

"Conversion to chiming" is precisely what many need nowadays. In the midst of gloom and worry what a call there is for bright Christians who can advertise the grace of God which is able to dispel all sorrow and care!

Many are converted who yet are far from "chiming," and they require the change which can fill their lives with a music never dying, ever singing. Chimes are striking constantly—often every quarter of an hour, always every hour. Are we not often silent instead of chiming Christians?

> *Oh, the sheer joy of it!*
> *Living with Thee,*
> *God of the Universe,*
> *Lord of a tree,*
> *Maker of mountains,*
> *Lover of me.*
>
> *Oh, the sheer joy of it!*
> *Working with God,*
> *Running His errands,*
> *Waiting His nod,*
> *Building His heaven*
> *On common sod.*
> —Bishop Ralph S. Cushman.

No half-measures for you. Follow heroically in Christ's very footsteps.

My utmost for His highest.

As flowers carry dewdrops, trembling on the edges of the petals, and ready to fall at the first waft of wind or brush of bird, so the heart should carry its beaded words of thanksgiving, and at the first breath of heavenly favor, let down the shower perfumed with the heart's gratitude.   —H. W. Beecher.

April 22

"And he that taketh not his cross, and followeth after me, is not worthy of me." (Matt. 10:38.)

THERE is no way to Easter but by Calvary. Before you finally determine what you are going to do with your life, be sure you have all the facts before you. And look! The Cross that looks like a colossal failure is but the open door that opens straight out into triumph for a loyal heart. Dare you take the recruit's oath of allegiance, the vow the young soldier took before the battalion he was joining, that all he had—his very life—was not his any longer, but the emperor's, and that he would be true to him till death?

"Yet stay! Are you quite certain that you understand? That recruit's vow took him into strange places; many a long vigil, many a breathless jeopardy. It meant weariness and wounds and perhaps a life tossed away with disdain rather than break or yield. 'Dare you drink of the cup that I shall drink of?' asks the Master. Dare you? Look into its depths again! Grace and forgiveness are there, most surely there! Yes, but far more! There is self-sacrifice, you understand, and loyalty, and determination that you are going to live in this new way. And dare you? Do you answer, looking straight into Christ's eyes, 'I say I will, I do; and please God, I shall stand to it!'

"Why, then, the grub is changing to a butterfly! For you Easter has dawned; in you the new life has indeed begun. A thing that was once only you has risen to a radiant splendor, with Christ's character, Christ's heart, Christ's very ways!"

—*The Hero in Thy Soul,* by Arthur John Gossip.

Jesus Christ never hides the scars when He seeks for loyalty. He never promises ease to those whom He invites to companionship. The normal solvent for this world is not rosewater, but good red blood, warm and vital.

> *"Is there no other way, O God,*
> *Except through sorrow, pain, and loss,*
> *To stamp Christ's image on my soul?*
> *No other way except the Cross?"*
>
> *And then a voice stills all my soul,*
> *As stilled the waves on Galilee:*
> *"Canst thou not bear the furnace heat,*
> *If 'mid the flames I walk with thee?"*

April 23

*"Wherefore Jesus also, that he might sanctify the people with
his own blood, suffered without the gate."* (Heb. 13:12.)

PILATE'S WIFE AT GOLGOTHA

ROCLA," Pilate cried as she entered the great hall, "where
have you been? I have been mad with fear for you. With
the street full of frenzied crowds and this intolerable
eclipse happening just now! I have had twenty soldiers
out searching."

"I couldn't tell you before I left, Pontius," his wife answered, "for
you would not have permitted it. And I had to do it. It was the
least thing I could do, for I must share with you the weight of this
guilt. You sentenced Him to death. I could only stay beside Him
as he died. I have been at Golgotha. There were other women. He
often looked toward us. I wish He could have known who I was
—understood that I was suffering with Him those awful hours.

"Just before He died he raised His head. The darkness was lifting
and we could see the glory on it. And He spoke clearly and strongly
so that every one heard. 'Father,' He said, 'into thy hands I commend my spirit.'

"At that ghastly time, when He was passing through the excrucia-
tion of such a death, He could look up into the face of His God and
call Him Father! Pontius, don't you see what that must mean?
A Father in Heaven! Not able to save his children from all pain,
not even sometimes from tragedy, when all the threads of His world
are so intertangled. But still their Father! Supporting them by
His love! And suffering with them in the extremities of their lives!

"O, Pontius, there at the foot of that unspeakable cross of agony
I found Him! I found my God. I seemed all at once to see the great
Heart of the universe through Jesus' eyes."

—*Agnes S. Turnbull,* in *Far Above Rubies.*

> *Thy unblemished body on the tree*
> *Was bared and broken to atone*
> *For me, for me*
> *Thy little one.*

—*Christina Rossetti.*

In a Negro-spiritual chorus book the following searching lines
are found:

> *"Were you there when they crucified my Lord?*
> *Were you there when they nailed Him to the Tree?*
> *Sometimes it causes me to tremble, tremble!*
> *Were you there when they crucified my Lord?"*

April 24

"... He stedfastly set his face to go to Jerusalem." (Luke 9:51.)

THE firmness of His look expresses the *Resolve to Take the Rough Road.* He made the choice that changed the world! "Don't be put out by anything," was Captain MacWhirris' advice to his mate as the ship struggled in the crash of the elements. "Keep her facing it. They may say what they like, but the heaviest seas run with the wind. Facing it—always facing it—that's the way to get through. You are a young sailor. Face it. That's enough for any man."

The Captain of our salvation faced the stormy tempest of Jerusalem, Gethsemane, Golgotha. He is our great pattern of endurance and triumph. By His example and Spirit timid men are made brave, and shrinking men grow strong, and they who otherwise would run away become rooted to their task. They look the whole world in the face and fear no foe nor hostile circumstance.

—*John Macbeath, M.A.*

> *"Girt with the fragile armor of youth,*
> *Child, you must ride into endless wars;*
> *With the sword of protest, the buckler of truth,*
> *And a banner of love to sweep the stars."*

No wind serves him who has no destined port.

> *"The life of drift never reaches harbors;*
> *It reaches the quicksands and the reef."*

April 25

"The Lord shall count, when he writeth up the people, that this man was born there." (Psalm 87:6.)

IN New York City there is in process of construction one of the most beautiful and imposing religious structures in the world. In that beautiful sanctuary there have been placed nineteen heroic figures, one for each of the nineteen centuries of Christian history. Each figure is that of one of the great heroes of the race—some flaming soul that has burned itself out for humanity. A block of unchiseled marble stands in the twentieth place; prophetic of the faith of the builders that this century shall also produce a hero worthy of a place among these immortals.

As yet the world does not see that hero upon the horizon, but the century is still young and God is not dead! We await his arrival!

"Who knoweth whether thou art come to the kingdom for such a time as this?"

The hero is not fed on sweets,
Daily his own heart he eats;
Chambers of the great are jails,
And headwinds right for royal sails.
                                    —*Emerson.*

No man can accomplish that which benefits the ages and not suf-fer. Discoverers do not reap the fruit of what they discover. Re-formers are pelted and beaten. Men who think in advance of their time are persecuted. They who lead the flock must fight the wolf.
                                    —*Henry Ward Beecher.*

What! shall one monk, scarcely known be-
*   yond his cell,*
Front Rome's far-reaching bolts, and scorn
*   her frown?*
Brave Luther answered, "Yes." That thun-
*   der's swell*
Rocked Europe, and discharmed the triple
*   crown.*   —*Lowell.*

April 26

"From henceforth let no man trouble me: for I bear in my body the marks of the Lord Jesus." (Gal. 6:17.)

"But he was wounded for our transgressions, he was bruised for our iniquities: the chastisement of our peace was upon him; and with his stripes we are healed." (Isa. 53: 5.)

GARIBALDI, the great Italian reformer of a past genera-tion, in a fiery speech urged some thousands of Italy's young men to fight for the freedom of their homeland. One timid young fellow approached him, asking, "If I fight, sir, what will be my reward?" Swift as a lightning flash came the uncompromising answer: "Wounds, scars, bruises, and perhaps death. But remember that through your bruises Italy will be free."

Hast thou no scar?
No hidden scar on foot, or side, or hand?
I hear thee sung as mighty in the land,
*   I hear them hail thy bright ascendant star,*
Hast thou no scar?

Hast thou no wound?
Yet I was wounded by the archers, spent,
Leaned me against a tree to die; and rent
*   By ravening wolves that compassed me, I swooned;*
Hast thou no wound?

No wound? No scar?
Yet, as the Master shall the servant be,
And pierced are the feet that follow Me;
  But thine are whole; can he have followed far
  Who hath no wound nor scar?

—A. W. C.

April 27

"... When thou shalt make his soul an offering for sin, ...
He shall see of the travail of his soul, and shall be satisfied: ..." (Isa. 53: 10, 11.)

JESUS CHRIST, PERFECT GOD AND PERFECT MAN

IT IS true that He emptied Himself. He laid aside the outward appearance of Deity. His Godhead was veiled. But it was there! Again and again His Godhead showed itself. As man, He slept in the boat. As God, He calmed the waves. As man, He wept. As God, He cried, "Lazarus, come forth!" As man, He was laid in the tomb—as God, He arose!
—A. E. Hughes.

Calvary has no date. "The Lamb slain from the foundation of the world."

"Oh, the love that drew salvation's plan,
  Oh, the grace that brought it down to man,
  Oh, the mighty gulf that God did span
    At Calvary!

"Mercy there was great, and grace was free,
  Pardon there was multiplied to me,
  There my burdened soul found liberty,
    At Calvary!"

"Calvary stills all questions."

"The Cross spells two stories: one in black—ugly black—the story of sin. Sin carpentered the Cross, and wove the thorns, and drove the nails—*our* sin! And a story too, in red—bright-flowing red—the story of LOVE, HIS LOVE that yielded to the Cross and nails and shame for us! And only the passion of His love burning within will make us hate sin, as only HIS BLOOD can wash it out.
"The hill of the Cross is the highest hill on earth in its significance. There hate's worst and love's best met."

"AND LOVE WON."
—Dr. S. D. Gordon.

April 28

"I have trodden the winepress alone. . . ." (Isa. 63: 3.)

JESUS on the Cross, the center figure, and on either side of Him is a thief. Where were the Twelve, the faithful dozen who had the inestimable privilege of walking with Jesus and of being trained by Him—where were they? Judas betrayed Him; Peter denied Him; Thomas doubted Him; and they all forsook Him and fled.

NEW CALVARY

So one by one they turned away from Him,
Until He stood alone on Pilate's floor;
A tired young Man, yet stalwart, straight, and slim,
Whose heart was broken, yet whose visage bore
Such depths of peace the rulers paused, afraid,
And murmured, "Tell the sin this Man has done."
(In all Jerusalem none came to aid.)
The cry rang back, "He says He is God's Son!"

He says He is God's Son . . . Oh, where were they,
The halt, the deaf, the blind He had made well?
Why did they not come running swift to say,
"We are His proof!" They had so much to tell!
I censure them—and yet because of me
Christ kneels alone sometimes in Calvary.
                       —Helen Welshimer.

Let us go back to Calvary, fall down at His feet, look up into His face, and seek to understand His heart till such a love for Him shall be kindled as shall gather up and focus all the forces of our lives into a burning and shining flame!

April 29

". . . As it began to dawn toward the first day of the week, came Mary Magdalene and the other Mary to see the sepulchre."
                             (Matt. 28: 1.)

THE FIRST DAWN

THE Garden of the Sepulchre lay hushed beneath the light —of day's first glimmer . . . wet and gleaming with the dews of night—when suddenly upon the wind a little sound was borne—and God's own Son came walking in the beauty of the Dawn.
Every little bird poured out its rapture on the air; every blossom trembled in an ecstasy of prayer . . . Every Spring leaf danced for

Joy on every startled tree—in that first glad glorious Dawn of
Christianity."   —*Patience Strong.*

BEHOLD THE DAWN

Behold the dawn! When Jesus rose, triumphant o'er the last of foes,
When angels rolled away the stone, the living Lord came to His
*   own.*
Behold the dawn! Amid the flowers, the Master walked those
*   morning hours;*
With His disciples kept His tryst, revealed to them the living Christ.

Behold the dawn! With morning's breath, He rose victorious over
*   death;*
From fear He set His people free, and brought them immortality.
Awake and give Him worthy praise, as ever down the ageless days
Rings out a song, to greet the sun, a song of life forever won.
                                    —*H. Alexander Matthews.*

EASTER HOPE

A new dawn broke with the sweet glory of spring, the music of
bird song, the fragrance of lilies, and in the first rays of that morning light, troubled women found an open tomb. A messenger in
white spoke the most glorious word ever uttered to mankind: "He
is not here! He is risen!"

"Because I live ye shall live also." We shall have our Easter
morn, by the same divine power. Of us, too, it shall be said, "He is
not here!" This is our faith; this is the great hope of Easter morning.

"Where is Kanderstag?" a traveler in Switzerland asked a lad
along the road. "I do not know where Kanderstag is," replied the
lad, "but there's the road that leads to it." I do not know where
Life Hereafter is, but Easter Dawn is the road that leads to it.
                                    —*Bruce S. Wright.*

April 30

"He is not here: for he is risen, as he said. . . ." (Matt. 28: 6.)

"BUT HE ROSE AGAIN"

 WAS going down a street in Chicago, when in a window
I saw a very beautiful picture of the crucifixion. As I
gazed spellbound at the vividly pictured story, I suddenly
became conscious that at my side stood a street urchin.
He, too, was gazing, and his tense expression made me
know that "The Crucifixion" had really gripped his little soul.
Touching him on the shoulder, I said, "Sonny, what does it mean?"
"Doncha know?" he asked, his face full of marvel at my ignorance.
"That there man is Jesus, and them others is Roman soldiers, and

the woman that's cryin' is His mother, and," he added, "they killed Him."

I was loathe to leave that window, but I could not tarry always at the world's tragedy, so I turned and walked quietly down the street. In a moment I heard pattering footsteps at my heels, and there stood my little street urchin. "Say, mister," he breathlessly announced, I fergot to tell yer, *He rose again!"*   —*Selected.*

"The sign of our faith is an empty Cross, an empty tomb—'He is not here: for he is risen!'"

REDEMPTION

A Mother and her Child;
A wondrous Boy,
A dead man raised to life;
A few poor fishermen,
An Upper Room,
A feast, a garden and a judgment hall.

A crown of thorns, a scourge,
A bitter Cross;
A great stone rolled away
And tears;
A springtime morning
And an empty tomb;
A Feast, a Blessing and a Risen Christ.
                    —*Mary Winter Ware.*

"Oh, let me live as if He died
But yestertide;
And I myself had seen and touched
His pierced side."

May 1

"Search me, O God, and know my heart: try me, and know my thoughts: And see if there be any wicked way in me, and lead me in the way everlasting." (Psalm 139: 23, 24.)

JOHN RUSKIN, in his *Ethics of the Dust,* answers the question, *"What can mud become when God takes it in hand?"* He replies, "Well, what is mud? First of all, mud is clay and sand, and usually soot and a little water." Then he says, "When God takes it in hand He transforms the clay into a sapphire, for a sapphire is just that; and the sand into an opal, for that is the analysis of an opal; and the soot into a diamond, for a diamond is just carbon which has been transformed by God; and the soiled water into a bright snow crystal, for that is what the crystals are when God takes the water up into the heaven and sends it back again."

Let God have your life. He can do more with it than you can.
—D. L. Moody.

DIAMONDS

Diamonds are only chunks of coal
  That stuck to their jobs, you see;
If they'd petered out, as most of us do,
  Where would the diamonds be?
It isn't the fact of making a start,
  It's the sticking that counts. I'll say,
It's the fellow that knows not the meaning of fall,
  But hammers and hammers away.
Whenever you think you've come to the end,
  And you're beaten as bad as can be,
Remember that diamonds are chunks of coal,
  That stuck to their jobs, you see.

—Virginia Call.

May 2

"Now thanks be to God who leadeth us forth in the train of His triumph. . . ." (2 Cor. 2: 14, Trans.)

 TRAVELER through the Rockies once noted in the deep snow what seemed to be a trail of a solitary soldier leading up the gullies and passes. Wondering how a man alone could undertake such a journey on foot, he turned to the Indian guide and inquired. The guide answered: "The trail which you see is not that of a solitary soldier; it is that of a whole tribe of braves of my nation, who are on the warpath against our foes; before went our mighty Chief with tomahawk and bow and his gorgeous war paint, the eagle feathers nodding over his head. He made the trail. After him came the warriors in single file, each one stepping exactly in the footprints of the Chief. This track looks like a solitary track of a perishing wanderer, but it is the trail of a nation of warriors and braves stepping in the footprints of their Chief, and where they go, victory follows." Youthful crusaders, do you see that narrow track leading up to Calvary? Do you see the bloody footprints of our great Chief? That trail means victory. It alone leads to a crown and a throne. Before goes the Chief. Behind Him follow the serried ranks of the brave soldiers of God. Victory ever follows, has ever followed, will ever follow the youth who steps in that track, for the old rugged Cross is the attraction.

"The Son of God goes forth to war,
  A kingly crown to gain;
His blood-red banner streams afar,
  Who follows in His train?"

May 3

". . . There came a woman having an alabaster box of oint-ment of spikenard very precious; and she brake the box, and poured it on his head." (Mark 14: 3.)

O WHAT purpose is this waste? Yet it had no fragrance till it was broken; the hour of its triumph was the hour of its tragedy; and it filled ALL the house in the act of its impoverishment.

The Rabbis relate that King Solomon's greatest treasure was a vase containing the Elixir of Life, a medicine so powerful that anyone taking even the smallest amount would live forever. Accordingly, people from time to time would send to beg a little of the famous elixir, but the king would always refuse. His friends, when they became old, or ill, would beseech him to grant them, if it were only ever so tiny, a taste, but he would always excuse himself saying that if he gave it to one, all would be asking for it, and there would be none left for himself. At last he lay on his own deathbed and sent for his still unopened vase, thinking that he would take its contents and live forever. It was brought and opened, but in it was nothing. The elixir had vanished because it was not used; whereas had it been distributed freely, it would have increased more and more.   —*McVeigh Harrison.*

"Not in husbanding our strength, but in yielding it in service; not in burying our talents, but in administering them; not in hoarding our seed in the barn, but in scattering it; not in following an earthly human policy, but in surrendering ourselves to the will of God, do we find the pathway to fruitfulness."

May 4

"Come now, and let us reason together, saith the Lord: though your sins be as scarlet, they shall be as white as snow; though they be red like crimson, they shall be as wool."
(Isa. 1: 8.)

NE day when Dr. F. B. Meyer was speaking he paused in the middle of his address. Stooping down, he picked up from the floor an old discarded violin string which had been flung away by one of the players in the orchestra.

Holding it up, he said, "There shall never any more music come out of *this;* but contrariwise, though your *life* be broken and your heart full of sin, God can bring harmony out of them again."

That is what the transforming power of grace does to broken human lives!

Many a man is a harp with many a broken string: imperfect, defective; but if he will yield to the influences of the Holy Spirit, God can bring forth heavenly music from his soul. From an outcast of the highways he can become a guest at the marriage feast of the Lamb.

One of the greatest triumphs of the famous Italian violinist, Paganini, was on an instrument with a *single string.*

> *He shambled awkward on the stage, the while*
> *Across the waiting audience swept a smile,*
> *With clumsy touch, when first he drew the bow*
> *He snapped a string. The audience tittered low.*
> *Another stroke! Off flies another string!*
> *With laughter now the circling galleries ring.*
> *Once more! The third string breaks its quivering strands,*
> *And hisses greet the player as he stands.*
> *He stands—while his genius, unbereft,*
> *Is calm—one string and Paganini left.*
> *He plays. The one string's daring notes uprise*
> *Against the storm as if they sought the skies.*
> *A silence falls; then awe; the people bow,*
> *And they who erst had hissed are weeping now;*
> *And when the last note, trembling, died away,*
> *Some shouted, "Bravo!" some had learned to pray.*
>
> —*Selected.*

May 5

". . . According as he hath promised, . . ." (Exod. 12: 25.)

DR. ANDREW MURRAY, the great devotional teacher of the past century, said, "When you get a promise from God it is worth just as much as fulfillment. A promise brings you into direct contact with God. Honor Him by trusting the promise and obeying Him." *Worth just as much as fulfillment!* Do we grasp that truth often? Are we not frequently in the state of *trying* to believe, instead of realizing that these promises bring us into contact with God? *"God's promise is as good as His presence."* To believe and accept the promise of God is not to engage in some mental gymnastics where we reach down into our imaginations and begin a process of auto-suggestion, or produce a notional faith in which we argue with ourselves in an endeavor to believe God. It is absolute confidence in and reliance upon God through His Word.

By a naked faith in a naked promise I do not mean *a bare assent* that God is faithful, and that such a promise in the Book of God *may* be fulfilled in me, but a *bold, hearty, steady venturing* of my soul, body, and spirit upon the truth of the promise with an appropriating act.

"When once His word is past,
When He hath said, 'I will,'
The thing shall come at last;
God keeps His promise still."

"And God said . . . and it was so." (Genesis 1: 9.)

May 6

". . . I am come that they might have life, and that they might have it more abundantly." (John 10: 10.)

 THRILL with expectancy; with my Father's plan, with the world's clarion call for lives, and with my soul aflame with willingness; therefore—
Everything great and worthwhile in interesting experience and the great unfolding of my life and character are up ahead. I am determined to live a radiant, victorious, overcoming life. It is coming. I am jubilant. I shall press on, for I know God leads, and life holds blessings untold.

Father, I am *assured.* I leap from crag to crag up and on. For life to the full is mine.   —*Quests and Conquests.*

CHALLENGE TO YOUTH

Be strong, O Youth, be strong!
Yield not thy life to the low desire
Nor falter at the tempter's cast;
Trust in thy God, He will inspire
And give thee strength in every blast.
Be strong, O Youth, be strong!

Be brave, O Youth, be brave!
The thoughtless throng will scoff and slight,
And sometimes friends may pass thee by;
The inner Voice will show the right
And hold thee for thy purpose high,
Be brave, O Youth, be brave!

Arise, O Youth, arise!
The cry of those in need today
Is heard most clear from far and near;
The summons heed, the call obey;
Consider not thy life too dear.
Arise, O Youth, arise!

Press on, O Youth, press on!
Join hands with those who dare ascend,
With courage strong, surmount the crest;
And when the battle's strife shall end
Attain with joy the victor's rest.
Press on, O Youth, press on!   —*Selected.*

"And youth must strike for goals afar which old men dare not try."

May 7

"Looking unto Jesus the author and finisher of our faith."
(Heb. 12: 2.)

DO not look to yourselves! Do not be occupied with self. In beholding the picture of your own soul, you can but continue to reproduce yourself. Look to Jesus, and beholding Him you will be changed from glory to glory. In us there is nothing good, but in Him is the whole glory and holiness of God!

In former years I was often desperately discouraged by the thought, "Why all the admonitions in Scripture to live a holy life, pleasing to God, if it is not possible to attain it?" I could not solve the problem of the disparity between personal experience and the ideal given us by God, and I was almost driven to desperation. Somehow, somewhere, I thought it must surely be possible to satisfy the Biblical requirements of God. Then God enlightened me, first, in the year nineteen hundred, through our little brother Oetzbach, in whom I saw God dwelt; he led a life of childlike harmony with His will, and received deliverance from a reproaching conscience and from the works of the flesh. I then saw that there was a holiness to be found in the gospel, in which the inner conflict ceased, and it was for me to find the key. The Lord led me by many paths, but He never allowed me to lose sight of this goal—this holiness that is possible in Christ. When we turn our eyes away from ourselves and fix them in faith on Him—then He gives us His righteousness, not only imputed righteousness, but also the power to live righteous lives in Him.
                              —*Sister Eva of Friedenshort.*

"Whereby are given unto us exceeding great and precious promises: that by these ye might be partakers of the divine nature, having escaped the corruption that is in the world through lust."
                              (2 Peter 1: 4.)

May 8

"... Be ye separate ..." (2 Cor. 6: 17.)

E all dread to be separated from companions and friends. It is hard to see them stand aloof and drop away, leaving us to take a course by ourselves. The young girl finds it hard to refuse the evening at the theater, and to stay alone at home when her gay companions have gone off in high spirits. The young city clerk finds it hard to refuse to join the "sweepstake," which is being arranged on the occasion of some annual race. . . . And yet, if we really wish to be only for God, it is inevitable that there should be many a link snapped; many a companionship forsaken; many a habit and conventionalism dropped; just as a savage must gradually and necessarily abjure most of his past, ere he can be admitted into the society and friendship of his European teacher. . . . Let this be understood, that, when once our spirit has dared to take up that life of consecration to the will of God to which we are called, there break upon it visions, voices, comfortable words, of which the heart could have formed no previous idea. For brass He brings gold, and for iron, silver, and for wood, brass, and for stone, iron. . . . The sun is no more needed for the day, nor the moon for the night, because the Lord has become the everlasting light of the surrendered and separate heart.   *—Dr. F. B. Meyer.*

> *"I've tried the broken cisterns, Lord,*
> *But, ah, the waters failed,*
> *E'en as I stooped to drink they fled,*
> *And mocked me as I wailed,*
> *'Now none but Christ can satisfy.'"*

Jesus never enters a life to make it poorer.

"When God is pleased to bless men He loves, His hands have other gifts than silver and gold."—*Ian Maclaren.*

May 9

"Surely he shall deliver thee from the snare of the fowler ..."
(Psalm 91: 3.)

HE noblest souls are the most tempted. The devil is a sportsman and likes big game. He makes the deadliest assaults on the richest natures, the finest minds, the noblest spirits.   *—John L. Lawrence.*

> *Lord! the fowler lays his net*
> *In Thine evening hour;*
> *When our souls are full of sleep—*

Void of full power . . .
Look! The wild fowl sees him not
As he lays it lower!

Creeping round the water's edge
In the dusk of day;
Drops his net, just out of sight,
Weighted lightly!—Stay!
You can see him at his work . . .
Fly to God—and pray!

Like the wild birds; knowing not
Nets lie underneath!
Gliding near the water's edge—
"Fowler's snare" beneath—
Little feet, caught in the net:
Souls lie, near to death.

But the promise still rings clear:
"He delivers thee,"
From the snare, however great
He will set thee free.
"Pluck my feet out of the net!"
He delivers me.

When Thou dost deliver, Lord,
From the fowler's snare,
Then—the glory is all Thine,
Thou madest us aware,
And though it was stealthy-laid,
We saw it was there!

       —L. M. Warner.

May 10

"Wash me throughly . . . cleanse me . . ." (Psalm 51: 2.)

WHEN I opened the door of the church," recently wrote a young pastor, "I heard a flutter of wings, and looking in, saw a brightly-colored bird fly across the room over the pews and dash against the window pane. It seemed dazed at first, but soon righted itself and made another dash across the room for a window on the other side. It made repeated attempts, growing almost frantic in its efforts to fly through the glass, and never seeming to learn that there may be hindrances to passage that cannot be seen by the eye.

"At last it fell exhausted. I picked up the beautiful trembling creature and stroked its feathers gently, musing the while on an expression that had come into mind as I watched the strange procedure—"*Invisible Barriers.*" As I stood thus it seemed to me that I was the church and that the Saviour was seeking entrance into my heart and life. To all appearances the way was open for Christ to come in; yet He had not come in the fullness I had longed for; I wondered why it was so. Now, I knew that it was the invisible barriers of my inner life that only He and I could know about—invisible to all others—and these barriers within my soul were the closed door to the Saviour's presence and power.

"I realized now the meaning and the consequences of certain things. The thoughts that I had allowed myself to think many times —the Saviour could not come in and share those with me. There were plans and hopes that were not for the glory of God or the advancement of His Kingdom—the Saviour could not come in and share those with me. There were many pictures hung upon the walls of my memory, ones that I left hanging there—the Saviour could not come into my soul until those were taken down. There were selfishness and worldliness; there were pride and jealousy; there was a condition that could be called "self-centered" instead of "God-centered"—the Saviour could not come in to live and work in me while such things held sway within. There were wrong emotions in the deep-down intents of my heart, the mire underneath what was apparently the pure, clear-flowing stream of life above—the Saviour could not come in while that condition was there. And there was lack of faith; failure to trust when the way was rough or the work apparently impossible—could the Saviour trust me when I did not trust Him? Could He believe in me when I did not believe in Him? Could we be partners in this great life of the Kingdom when I was not co-operating more fully than I was?

"More than all of these, there was the *stubborn will* that would not submit. How strange it all seemed to me now as I stroked the bird and repeated again the words, "*Invisible Barriers.*"

"Flinging open the door of the church, I set the bird free to fly off into the sky where it longed so much to go. Turning back, I faced the Master, pleading that He would help me and show me how to fling wide open all those invisible doors that I had closed against Him and let Him come in to live with me and work with me and I with Him."—*A Young Minister's Testimony.*

"*Just as I am—Thy love unknown*
Has broken every barrier down—
Now, to be Thine, yea, Thine alone,
O Lamb of God, I come."

"Him that cometh to me I will in no wise cast out" (John 6: 37).

May 11

*"Ye have not chosen me, but I have chosen you, and ordained
you, that ye should go and bring forth fruit . . ."* (John 15: 16.)

IN the hour of David's anointing it dawned upon him that
his was a selected life—that he was set apart for an unusual destiny. What thought is greater than this to a soul
that is noble!—*C. C. Hall.*

"Pearls and diamonds, emeralds and rubies have to be
sought and found. They are not lying about as pebbles. Great men
were once boys and must be searched for and found. David must
be discovered, and it is Samuel's crown of honor that it was he who
did it. He found the boy and gave him his chance, and second only
in honor to the great man is the man who discovers the great man
who is yet untried and unheralded, and sets him on the way to
greatness."—*Robert W. Rogers.*

God's wondrous plan—beyond our comprehension—
To make of mortal man, companion for the King!
"According to the power" that worketh in our being,
The mighty power of God, the change must bring.

Before the world was born, God's plan was started;
"To be holy, without blemish," we were chosen then in Him;
When Jesus died, and rose again in triumph,
He made the plan complete, He died to save from sin.

The Spirit came—by faith I see the mystic union—
The soul of man united to his God in love!
Redeemed, he stands before the Throne in holy adoration,
Redeemed on earth, but home at last in heaven above.
                                        —*V. E. H.*

May 12

*"Commit thy way unto the Lord; trust also in him; and he
shall bring it to pass."* (Psalm 37:5.)

YOU cannot live the Christian life unless you meet the Captain every day. The day is the only period of time marked
out for us, as it lies between the two black curtains of the
night. Every day meet the Captain. Have a space in that
day for the interview, a place where you can easily gain
access to His presence!

"Crown Him as your Captain
In temptation's hour,
Let His will enfold you
In its light and power."

Our great Captain sometimes seems to lose a battle, but He never loses the war!

> *I am not the master of my fate;*
> *That lies in wiser, abler hands;*
> *And I am captain of my soul*
> *Only if He beside me stands.*
>
> *He alone knows the quiet lanes*
> *Through which my little bark must steer;*
> *The rocks and shoals to me unknown*
> *To that keen eye are plain and clear.*
>
> *Black though the night be, as the pit,*
> *Unlighted by a single star,*
> *Steadfast He guides me on; to Him*
> *Alike the light and darkness are.*
>
> *Wild blasts upon my vessel sweep,*
> *From my weak grasp the wheel would tear,*
> *I feel beside my hands His hands,*
> *Master of sky and sea and air.*
>
> *I cannot plot my onward way;*
> *He holds all things in His control,*
> *Jesus, the Master of my fate,*
> *Pilot and Captain of my soul.*

—*Selected.*

May 13

"Commit thy way unto the Lord; trust also in him; and he worketh." (Psalm 37:5, Trans.)

LET GO AND LET GOD

IT is one thing to be willing to take the Lord, to intend to take the Lord, to be trying to take the Lord for the blessing you need; but it is quite another thing to *take* the Lord and count it done; this is committal. It is to drop your letter into the post-office box, and not hold onto it by the corner, but let it go and leave the responsibility of its delivery with the authorities.

Many people are simply trying but not trusting, and there is no more help in that than in the faint efforts of the poor little kitten which had fallen into a well, and was in the process of being rescued. The farmer had heard its pitiful cries and noticed that it had climbed out of the water and was hanging onto a ledge in the brick work. He gently dropped a bucket down beneath it and tried to induce it to drop in, but the kitten simply reached out its little paws and then drew them back timorously, and cried and cried again in its helplessness and despair. This was all in vain. The kitten could not be rescued until it would let go the ledge and commit itself to the bucket. The struggle lasted a long while until at last, tired and ready to fall, it ventured; there was a little plunge, and the farmer knew by the added weight that the refugee was safely caught, and it was a small matter now to land his burden on solid ground.

Exactly so we hesitate and struggle, until at last, tired, we just let go, and then it is easy for God to do anything for us. The prayer of faith is a transaction which you must settle at a definite moment, and ever after count it settled.

> As helpless as a child who clings
>   Fast to his father's arm,
> And casts his weakness on the strength
>   That keeps him safe from harm.
>
> So I, my Father, cling to Thee,
>   And thus I every hour
> Would link my earthly feebleness
>   To Thy almighty power.   —Selected.

May 14

"Wherewithal shall a young man cleanse his way? by taking heed thereto according to thy word." (Psalm 119:9.)

 INNAEUS once said of the unfolding of a blossom: "I saw God in His glory pass near me, and bowed my head in worship."

I SAW GOD WASH THE WORLD

> I saw God wash the world last night
>   With his sweet showers on high;
> And then when morning came
>   I saw Him hang it out to dry.
> He washed each tiny blade of grass
>   And every trembling tree;
> He flung His showers against the hills
>   And swept the billowy sea.
> The white rose is a cleaner white;
>   The red a richer red
> Since God washed every fragrant face
>   And put them all to bed.
> There's not a bird; there's not a bee

> *That wings along the way,*
> *But is a cleaner bird or bee*
> *Than it was yesterday.*
> *I saw God wash the world last night;*
> *Ah, would He had washed me*
> *As clean of all my dust and dirt*
> *As that old white birch tree!*
>   —Dr. W. L. Stidger.

"But if we walk in the light, as he is in the light, we have fellowship one with another, and the blood of Jesus Christ his Son cleanseth us from all sin." (1 John 1: 7.)

May 15

"Go to the ant, . . . consider her ways, and be wise."
                  (Prov. 6: 6.)

"GO to the ant." Tammerlane used to relate to his friends an anecdote of his early life. "I once was forced to take shelter from my enemies in a ruined building, where I sat alone many hours," he said. "Desiring to divert my mind from my hopeless condition, I fixed my eyes on an ant that was carrying a grain of corn larger than itself up a high wall. I numbered the efforts it made to accomplish this object. The grain fell sixty-nine times to the ground; but the insect *persevered*, and the *seventieth* time it reached the top! This sight gave me courage at the moment, and I never forgot the lesson."—*The King's Business.*

Rubenstein, the great musician, once said, "If I omit practice one day, I notice it; if two days, my friends notice it; if three days, the public notices it." It is the old doctrine, *"Practice makes perfect."* We must continue believing, continue praying, continue doing His will. Suppose along any line of art, one should cease practicing—we know what the result would be. If we would only use the same quality of common sense in our religion that we use in our everyday life, we should go on to perfection.

The motto of David Livingstone was in these words, "I determined never to stop until I had come to the end and achieved my purpose." By unfaltering persistence and faith in God he conquered.

> *"Silently sat the artist alone,*
> *Carving a Christ from the ivory bone;*
> *Little by little, with toil and pain*
> *He won his way through the sightless grain,*
> *That held and yet hid the thing he sought,*
> *Till the work stood up like a growing thought."*

May 16

"... So that I cannot come down: ..." (Neh. 6:3.)

THINGS WE CAN'T AFFORD

We can't afford to win the gain that means another's loss;
We can't afford to miss the crown by stumbling at the cross.
We can't afford the heedless jest that robs us of a friend;
We can't afford the laugh that finds in bitter tears an end.
We can't afford the feast today that brings tomorrow's fast;
We can't afford the race that comes to tragedy at last.
We can't afford to play with fire, or tempt a serpent's bite;
We can't afford to think that sin brings any true delight.
We can't afford with serious heed to treat the cynic's sneer;
We can't afford to wise men's words to turn a careless ear.
We can't afford for hate to give like hatred in return;
We can't afford to feed a flame and make it fiercer burn.
We can't afford to lose the soul for this world's fleeting breath;
We can't afford to barter life in mad exchange for death.
But blind to good are we apart from THEE, all-seeing Lord;
Oh, grant us light that we may know the things we can't afford!
                                        —*Author Unknown.*

There are many things in which one gains and the other loses; but if it is essential to any transaction that only one side gain, the thing is not of God.—*George MacDonald.*

May 17

"... Neither count I my life dear unto myself, so that I might finish my course with joy, and the ministry, which I have received of the Lord Jesus, to testify the gospel of the grace of God." (Acts 20:24.)

CHARLES KINGSLEY was a young college student, a Christian. Graduation day was drawing near—a time in his life when a definite decision for his future must be made. Leaving the campus, he went to the seashore to be quite alone, to think, to pray, to seek God's will. Seriously and deeply he thought of his relationship to God, the brevity of life, his relationship to his fellow-man. All day long he sat looking out over the vast blue in deep meditation. In the hush of the evening he thought he heard a Voice saying, "For thee I gave my life. Is the price of utter surrender to Me too great to pay?"

There on the sands of the seashore and under the starlit heavens he made the supreme dedication of his lovely young life. His will was merged in the will of God, and he could truly say,

*"I have lost myself in Jesus
I am sinking into God."*

From that memorable night when he lost his life he was clothed
with mystic strength, and his own life was enriched a thousand—
yea, a millionfold! Many years have passed since that time. He
has gone to his mansion on high, but the stream still flows on and
on—never ceasing, never ending. Through him it reached the burnt
sands and desert wastes, and thousands drank of the life-giving
stream; their thirst was quenched, their souls revived, and they,
too, lived in Him. Was the price too great to pay?

The truly *great* are the God-possessed!

May 18

"... This mystery ... Christ in you, the hope of glory."
(Col. 1: 27.)

HAS life any meaning? Is it all "just a battle of ants 'neath
the glare of a million, million of suns?" asks one. Nay!
Every man's life is a plan of God. God has purposed something unsurpassingly wonderful for those who are prepared to seek Him and take Him at His word. You do not
know what the Lord can do for you until you put yourself and your
all into His hand.

THE LISTENING EAR
*Methought I heard One calling "Child!"
And I replied,
    "My Lord!"*

—George Herbert.

*"You ask me how I gave my heart to Christ?
I do not know.
I had a longing for Him in my soul
So long ago.
I found earth's flowers would fade and die,
I longed for something that would satisfy;
And then—and then—somehow I seemed to dare
To lift my broken heart to Him in prayer.
I do not know—
I cannot tell you how;
I only know
He is my Saviour now."*

*I know not how that Calvary's cross
    A world of sin could free;
I only know its matchless love
    Has brought God's love to me.*

—H. W. Farrington.

May 19

"Take us the foxes, the little foxes, that spoil the vine: for our vines have tender grapes." (Song of Sol. 2:15.)

AN eagle carrying a serpent in its talons to its nest on the mountains was bitten to the heart and fell to the ground. Have you seen a young man or woman fall away from God? Do you know the cause of their fall? The neglect of prayer, that stealthy indulgence in the intoxicating cup, that licentiousness and profligacy unseen of man, that secret tampering with unbelief and error, was the serpent at the heart that brought the eagle down.—*Theodora L. Cuyler.*

If we wish to bask perpetually in the sunshine of God's love, the problems of sin must be firmly dealt with, and all love of it must cease. For it is literally true that there is more evil in one drop of sin than in a whole sea of affliction.

Christian youth, beware how thou thinkest lightly of sin! Take heed lest thou fall little by little. Sin, a little thing? Is it not a poison? Who knows its deadliness? Sin, a little thing? Do not the foxes spoil the grapes? Doth not the tiny coral insect build a rock which wrecks a navy? Sin, a little thing? It girded the Redeemer's head with thorns, and pierced His heart! Could you weigh the least sin in the scales of eternity, you would fly from it as from a serpent. Look upon all sin as that which crucified the Saviour, and you will see it to be "exceeding sinful."—*C. H. S.*

He who keeps off the ice will not slip.

"Be not entangled;
Let nothing entangle your free limbs!"

To invite Satan is easy, to dismiss him is hard.
—*An Indian Saying.*

May 20

"... None of us liveth to himself, ..." (Rom. 14: 8.)
"... And he that winneth souls is wise." (Prov. 11: 30.)

MY CHUM

He stood at the crossroads all alone,
  With the sunrise in his face;
He had no fear for the path unknown;
  He was set for a manly race.
But the road stretched east, and the road stretched west;
There was no one to tell him which way was the best;

So my chum turned wrong and went down, down, down,
Till he lost the race and the victor's crown
And fell at last in an ugly snare,
Because no one stood at the crossroads there.

Another chum on another day
  At the selfsame crossroads stood;
He paused a moment to choose the way
  That would stretch to the greater good.
And the road stretched east, and the road stretched west;
But I was there to show him the best;
So my chum turned right and went on and on,
Till he won the race and the victor's crown;
He came at last to the mansions fair,
Because I stood at the crossroads there.

Since then I have raised a daily prayer
That I be kept faithful standing there.
To warn the runners as they come,
And save my own or another's chum.

                                        —*Author Unknown.*

May I cultivate a heart-throb of constant interest in my fellow-strugglers, and "live in the house by the side of the road and be a friend to man!"

> *"Lord crucified, give me a heart like Thine,*
> *Teach me to love the dying souls of men,*
> *And keep my heart in closest touch with Thee,*
> *And give me love, pure Calvary love,*
> *To bring the lost to Thee."*

May 21

". . . I will set him in safety . . ." (Psalm 12: 5.)

"WHO IS HE THAT OVERCOMETH?"

SOMETIMES it is highly expedient to retreat from an exposed position. Wellington is reported to have said that "the best general is he who knows best how to conduct a retreat." Certainly such strategy is often as desirable as it is honorable in working out the moral life; the best thing we can do is to withdraw abruptly from dangerous places, persons, and practices. Plutarch tells of a general who fled from the field of battle, afterwards excusing himself that he "did not run away, but embraced an advantage that lay behind him." Such tactics usually savor of cowardice in regard to the temptations of life. However, it is often the height of wisdom to run away. Joseph did. "Deliver me, O Lord, from mine enemies: I flee unto Thee to hide me." In the late war some soldiers suffered because thy would not "take cover." Let us shelter ourselves in God's holy Word, as the Master did; take cover at the throne of grace; arm ourselves with the whole armor of light; and the crown of life is ours.—*Selected.*

Avoiding temptation is next in importance to resisting temptation. For the lust of the eye is fearfully apt to begin the lust of the flesh. We read this in Matthew Henry's commentary the other day: "Do not approach the forbidden tree unless you want to eat forbidden fruit." It reminded us of old Thomas Fuller's quaint saying, "If you do not wish to trade with the devil, keep out of his shop."

—*A. J. Gordon.*

May 22

"Ye are our epistle written in our hearts, known and read of all men." (2 Cor. 3:2.)

THE MOST VALUABLE LIFE

AFTER all, the lives that do the most for the world are the steady, quiet lives. They are like stars; they just stay in their appointed places and shine with the light God has given them. Meteors shoot brilliantly across the sky, and we exclaim and wonder, but long after they have vanished the stars shine on to guide us."

I need not shout my faith:
Thrice eloquent are quiet trees,
And the green listening sod;
Hushed are the stars, whose power is never spent,
The hills are mute: yet how they speak of God.
—*Charles Hanson Towne.*

It is not necessarily the busiest, who are ever on the rush after some visible work; it is the lives like stars, which simply pour down upon us the calm light of their bright and faithful being, out of which we gather the deepest calm and courage. It is good to know that no man or woman can be strong, gentle, good, without somebody being helped and comforted by the very existence of that goodness.—*Phillips Brooks.*

"The rose needs no tongue to tell its fragrance; the flower to speak its beauty. The best arguments for Christianity are the Christians themselves."

Calmness is the seal of strength.

May 23

". . . Gather up the fragments that remain, that nothing be lost." (John 6:12.)

ETERNAL issues hang upon fragments of time. There is a proverb which says, "He that gathereth in summer is a wise son." Youth is a summer. It is time for gathering knowledge. It is time for the formation of habits, for the knitting of the thews and sinews of character. Youth who improve their opportunities, who are diligent in the "summer-gathering for winter's need," will come up to the responsibilities of their later years prepared to accept them and meet them with honor.

Those who would shine as God's fairest children must have no wasted years. They must harvest time. All the prizes of life are taken by those who are earliest in the field. The man who excels in the world of music is he who from childhood has yielded to the wizardry of minstrelsy. The man who figures prominently in the world of letters is he whose brain was disciplined in his schooldays; he who excels in godliness is he who in the springtime of his career was obedient to the heavenly vision.

Early on God's altar in youth's springtime we can master the music of the Everlasting City, learn the dialect of the King's country, graduate in divine wisdom, become proficient in spiritual knowledge, adepts in the things of grace. A youth-time diligently improved prepares one for whatever may come in the stern days and mature years. Let not a fragment of the precious gift of life be wasted!

> *"A noble life is not a blaze*
> *Of sudden glory won,*
> *But just an adding up of days*
> *In which strong work is done."*

We all have some leisure moments. We have ten, twenty, sixty minutes during which no urgent duty demands our attention. Such moments are most numerous in youth. How shall they be used? Not aimlessly! Time is too valuable for that. Do we appreciate the full significance of the words written upon the dial of All Saints, Oxford: "The hours perish, and are laid to our charge!"

. Your life work is recorded—every detail, every phase; an unseen pen is writing out the story of your days.

May 24

"Whosoever therefore shall humble himself as this little child, the same is greatest in the kingdom of heaven." (Matt. 18:4.)

IN my college days there was a boy in the class above me whom we called Tom. He was quiet and somewhat reserved, but was able, scholarly, and withal popular among the boys. We all thought he would make good when he went out into the world. Graduation day came and with it the breaking of college ties and the parting of college friends. Thirty-five years rolled by. Then one day I heard that our college mate, whose full name was Thomas Woodrow Wilson, was to speak in this city. I went down to the great hall to hear him. There I found a splendid audience of four thousand Christian men gathered to hear his message upon a great moral and religious theme. It was a magnificent address and captivated the audience by its eloquence and literary finish. At its close I went up and greeted him, and we had a pleasant chat about the old college days. He went back to the White House, and I wended my way down to a little two-room office on the tenth floor of a city skyscraper. I sat there thinking of my old college friend. He was at the zenith of his fame. The eyes not only of the country, but of all the world were centered upon him. My own life was quiet, obscure, hidden away in a little corner from whence I was sending out over the world simple devotional messages from the Lord. Yet do you know, that as I looked into my own heart, I could not find one atom of envy toward my distinguished fellow-collegian, nor of covetousness for his high position. Do you ask why? Simply because I had found the humble place to which my lot was cast to be God's holy ground of service, and that was the joy of all life to me.—*James McConkey.*

Cherish in your thoughts and incarnate in your life this wonderful admonition of Hudson Taylor:

"Be God's man;
In God's place;
Doing God's work;
In God's way."

In Caius College, Cambridge, there are three gateways in succession: The first is called Humilitatis; the next, Virtutis; the third (which opens toward the Senate House), Honoris. Not in vain did our forefathers make these emblems of an undergraduate's progress; and happy would it be if every youth entered by the gate of humility, to pass through the gate of Christian virtue, that he might come forth in the highest sense to that of honor.

—*R. F. Walker.*

May 25

"But covet earnestly the best . . ." (1 Cor. 12: 31.)

"Like the straightness of the pine tree
Let me upright be!"

BE THE BEST

If you can't be a pine
  on the top of the hill,
Be a scrub in the valley—but be
The best little scrub
  by the side of the rill:
Be a bush if you can't be a tree.

If you can't be a bush,
  be a bit of the grass,
Doing something for somebody's sake;
If you can't be a muskie,
  then just be a bass—
But the liveliest bass in the lake!

We can't all be captains,
  some have to be crew,
There's something for all of us here,
There's big work and little
  for people to do,
And the task we must do is the near.

If you can't be the highway,
  then just be a trail,
If you can't be the sun, be a star;
It isn't by size that you
  win or you fail—
Be the best of whatever you are!
           —Douglas Malloch.

If you cannot be a lighthouse, be a candle.
           —D. L. Moody.

"And he gave some, apostles; and some, prophets; and some, evangelists; and some, pastors and teachers; For the perfecting of the saints, for the work of the ministry, for the edifying of the body of Christ." (Eph. 4: 11, 12.)

May 26

"Who knoweth not in all these—[the beasts, and they shall teach thee, and the fowls of the air, and they shall tell thee: Or speak to the earth, and it shall teach thee: and the fishes of the sea shall declare unto thee (v. 9)] that the hand of the Lord hath wrought this?" (Job 12: 7-9.)

"FATHER," said Thomas, looking up from his studies, "how do you know that there is a God?"

"Why do you ask that question?" asked the father; "do you doubt the existence of God?"

"Well," replied the boy, "I heard one of the professors say that we could not be sure there is a God. Is there any way to really know?"

"Do you remember, my boy, the other day that you were laughing about Robinson Crusoe's dismay at discovering that there were other persons on the island beside himself? How did he discover them? Did he see them? No; he saw one track of a bare foot in the sand, and he knew that it could not be his own. He knew that whoever made it could not be far off, for the tide had not reached it. All these things he knew to be true, although he had not seen a human being; and the knowledge was all gained from a mark in the sand.

"If one print of a bare foot in the sand is absolute proof of the existence and presence of a human being, what are we to suppose when we see 'the prints of the Master's shoes,' as Bunyan calls it, covering the whole wide world? We see on mountain and valley the prints of the fingers of God. We see a million plants, and flowers, and trees, that only God could make grow. We see all the rivers and the springs of the world fed from the sky. We see a great universe, perfectly made and ordered, from the tiniest speck to the greatest of all the worlds. What do all these things mean— these millions upon millions of footprints on the clay of the world? They mean God, living, present, ruling and loving! They mean God, and nothing else!"

THE AWAKING

I lay me down on the ground
By the newly furrowed row,
Where the plow had recently torn
The earth asunder.
A doubting Thomas I.
Carelessly my hand fell into the earth,
And I felt its quickening pulse.
The rain beat upon my face;
Darkness surrounded me,
I knew no more of doubt or wonder
But slept.

The night passed—
The dawn came—
Dear God. . . .
That I should doubt Thy existence.
When I see a yellow sprout
Of grass today
Where only yesterday I saw
A barren field.

—Elizabeth Clotile Burns.

May 27

". . . Gather up the fragments . . ." (John 6: 12.)

IN the workshop of a great Italian artist was a poor little lad whose duty it was to clean up the floor and tidy up the rooms after the day's work was finished. He was a quiet little fellow and always did his work well. That was all the great artist knew about him. One day he came to his master and asked timidly, "Please, master; may I have for my very own the bits of glass you throw upon the floor?"

"Why, yes, my boy," said the artist; "the bits are good for nothing. Do as you please with them."

Day after day the lad might have been seen studying the broken pieces found on the floor—laying some aside, throwing others away. And this he did year after year, for he was still the artist's servant in the workshop.

One day his master entered a storeroom but little used, and in looking about, came upon a piece of work *carefully* hidden behind the rubbish. He brought it to the light and to his surprise found it a noble work of art nearly finished! He gazed at it in speechless astonishment. "What great artist could have hidden his work in my studio!" he cried, and he called his servant to him. "What is this?" cried the artist. "Tell me what great artist has hidden his masterpiece here?"

"Oh, master," faltered the astonished lad; "it is only my own poor work. You know you said I might have the broken bits you threw away."

The artist-soul had wrought this wonderful result! Not the broken bits of a kaleidoscope, but a masterpiece under the hand of God!

"Oh! be zealous in thy youth;
Fill every day with noble toils;
Fight for the victories of Truth,
And deck thee with her deathless spoils."

May 28

"... For our profit ..." (Heb. 12: 10.)

IN one of Ralph Connor's books he tells a story of Gwen. Gwen was a wild, willful lassie and one who had always been accustomed to having her own way. Then one day she met with a terrible accident which crippled her for life. She became very rebellious, and in the murmuring state she was visited by the "Sky Pilot," as the missionary among the mountaineers was termed.

He told her the parable of the canyon. "At first there were no canyons, but only the broad, open prairie. One day the Master of the Prairie, walking over His great lawns where were only grasses, asked the Prairie, 'Where are your flowers?' and the Prairie said, 'Master, I have no seeds.'

"Then He spoke to the birds, and they carried seeds of every kind of flower and strewed them far and wide, and soon the prairie bloomed with crocuses and roses and buffalo beans and the yellow crowfoot and the wild sunflowers and the red lilies all summer long. Then the Master came and was well pleased; but He missed the flowers He loved best of all, and He said to the Prairie: 'Where are the clematis and the columbine, the sweet violets and windflowers, and all the ferns and flowering shrubs?'

"And again He spoke to the birds, and again they carried all the seeds and scattered them far and wide. But, again, when the Master came He could not find the flowers He loved best of all, and He said, 'Where are those, my sweetest flowers?'

"And the Prairie cried sorrowfully, 'Oh, Master, I cannot keep the flowers, for the winds sweep fiercely, and the sun beats upon my breast, and they wither up and fly away.'

"Then the Master spoke to the Lightning, and with one swift blow the Lightning cleft the Prairie to the heart. And the Prairie rocked and groaned in agony, and for many a day moaned bitterly over the black, jagged, gaping wound.

"But the river poured its waters through the cleft, and carried down deep black mould, and once more the birds carried seeds and strewed them in the canyon. After a long time the rough rocks were decked out with soft mosses and trailing vines, and all the nooks were hung with clematis and columbine, and great elms lifted their huge tops high up into the sunlight, and down about their feet clustered the low cedars and balsams, and everywhere the violets and windflower and maidenhair grew and bloomed, till the canyon became the Master's favorite place for rest and peace and joy."

Then the "Sky Pilot" read to her: "The fruit—I'll read 'flowers'—of the Spirit are love, joy, peace, longsuffering, gentleness—and some of these grow only in the canyon."

"Which are the canyon flowers?" asked Gwen softly, and the

Pilot answered: "Gentleness, meekness, longsuffering; but though the others—love, joy, peace—bloom in the open, yet never with so rich a bloom and so sweet a perfume as in the canyon."

For a long time Gwen lay quite still, and then said wistfully, while her lips trembled: "There are no flowers in my canyon, but only ragged rocks."

"Some day they will bloom, Gwen dear; the Master will find them, and we, too, shall see them."

Beloved, when *you* come to your canyon, remember!

May 29

"...From the womb of the morning: thou hast the dew of thy youth." (Psalm 110:3.)

CHILD of the morning, fresh and strong and beautiful with the dew of thy youth, on whose brow there are no marks of Cain, in whose heart there are no stains; purpose in your heart not to defile yourself. Be the young man without blemish, and you can stand before all the wise men of Babylon unafraid. You can walk through the fiery furnace of earth's devices against you and come through unharmed. You can stand before kings and not cower. You can be thrown on the lonely isle of Patmos, and heaven will open to you. You can see through prison bars a crown of righteousness that the world cannot take away. You can be placed in a dungeon, but your songs in the night will break prison doors. Ah, the unanswerableness of purity! Ah, the silence and beauty and peace of the soul that dwells apart in the world, and yet above the world!

—*The Life Beautiful.*

> *Keep pure thy soul!*
> *Then shalt thou take the whole of delight;*
> *Then without a pang*
> *Thine shall be all beauty whereof the poet sang—*
> *The perfume, and the pageant, the melody,*
>   *the mirth of the golden day, and the*
>   *starry night:*
> *Of heaven and of earth.*
> *Oh, keep pure thy soul!*

—*Gilder.*

"But of him are ye in Christ Jesus, who of God is made unto us wisdom, and righteousness, . . ." (I Cor. 1:30.)

> *Jesus, Thy blood and righteousness*
> *My beauty are, my glorious dress;*
> *'Midst flaming worlds, in these arrayed,*
> *With joy shall I lift up my head.*

—*John Wesley.*

May 30

"... I am an ambassador in bonds: that therein I may speak boldly, as I ought to speak." (Eph. 6:20.)

I AM a marked man, marked with the marks of the Master. I am a slave—a slave to righteousness, and not to sin; a slave to honesty, and not to deception; a slave to purity, and not to vice; a slave to liberty, and not to license; a slave of the kingdom, and not of the crowd; a slave to faith, and not to fear; and, best of all, a slave to the Master, and not to Mammon. As a slave, I must make haste and be about my Master's business. —*Wesley G. Huber.*

> *"I would not halve my service,*
> *His only it must be!*
> *I love, I love my Master,*
> *I will not go out free!"*

> *"I will not work my soul to save,*
> *For that the Lord has done,*
> *But I will work like any slave*
> *From love to God's dear Son."*

May 31

"For as the heavens are higher than the earth, so are my ways higher than your ways, and my thoughts than your thoughts."
(Isa. 55:9.)

A VERY interesting book has lately appeared, entitled *The Life and Letters of James A. Garfield.* Consider for a moment the *boyhood* of that man. His widowed mother, with a splendid independence of spirit, would not go to live with her kin after her husband's death. Although she had a little brood of children to care for and to bring up, and her ideals for their education were high, she stayed on the little farm, and those youngsters did a man's part for the family. James had always wanted to go to sea, and the nearest thing he could do in that line was to get a job as driver on a canal boat. One cold night he was suddenly thrown into the canal by accident. He could not swim. It was midnight. Nobody heard his cries for help. He managed to get his hands on a rope which was attached to the boat but as he pulled on it to draw himself aboard, the rope kept coming toward him in his hands, and it appeared as if he would not be able to save himself. At the very desperate peak of his need the rope tightened and held. It had kinked and caught in a crevice, and he drew himself aboard. There he sat in the midnight alone in his wet clothes doing some serious thinking, and the net result of that thinking was that he felt in his heart that he had been saved, as he believed, *by God* for the sake of his mother and for something better than "canaling," as he put it. So he went home, and as he looked in the window he saw his mother praying. She was praying for him! That was the beginning of his pursuit of a higher education. When he entered school he had six cents in his pocket, and at the first church service he attended after he entered school he placed the six cents in the collection box "for luck" and made up his mind he would see what he could do absolutely on his own. He obtained board and lodging with mending for $1.06¼ per week. Notice the quarter of a cent. There is a world of meaning in that fraction. Those were simple days. Motives were simple, purposes were simple, principles were simple, and goals were clear. That is the type of person which Mr. Coolidge calls "self-owned."

If the Weaver of our life's pattern chooses another plan than the one we thought to use, is He not wiser than we?

—*Chapel Talks.*

June-1

". . . Go quickly, and tell . . ." (Matt. 28: 7.)

I AWOKE this morning with a sob," said Bishop Hendrix at a great missionary convention, "thinking about the millions of little children who do not know that the Father's face is turned toward them. The agonizing thought was occasioned last night by my small son, whose little bed is close to mine. In the night he reached out his chubby hand saying, 'Daddy, hold baby's hand.' I can remember the thrill of it as I reached out my hand to his little bed and took firm hold of that little chubby hand! Then he put his other hand out and said, 'Daddy, hold *both* baby's hands.' Then I did not go to sleep! There broke against my heart like the sob of an ocean tide the cry of the millions of this earth who do not know that their Father's face is turned toward them like my face was turned toward that little lad."

> *"Sudden, before my inward open vision,*
> *Millions of faces crowded up to view,*
> *Sad eyes that said: 'For us is no provision,*
> *Give us your Saviour, too.'*
>
> *"'Give us,' they cry, 'your cup of consolation;*
> *Never to our outreaching hands 'tis passed;*
> *We long for the Desire of every nation,*
> *And, oh, we die so fast!'"*

One morning a Hindu mother went out to the banks of the Ganges, leading in either hand her two children. A missionary saw her going to the banks of the river, and he knew what she was going there for. He looked into her eyes with all the pleading of fatherhood and tried to persuade her not to do it; not to give up one of these little children. Then he looked at the faces of the two children. One of them was as perfect a baby as any mother ever held close to her heart in America or anywhere; the other was blind and lame and crippled. The missionary went away, knowing he could not persuade that woman to break from the thought of centuries in a single hour's pleading. He came back to that spot and saw the Hindu mother still standing by the river bank, her heart breaking! One child was missing. As the missionary drew near he discovered that the perfect child was gone; the mother had kept the little blind and lame one for herself. As he looked into the eyes of that mother, he said to her, "Woman, if you had to give one, why didn't you give this little lame and blind one and keep the perfect one for yourself?" She said, "O sir, I do not know what kind of God you have in America, but I know that out here in India our god expects us to give him our very best."

June 2

". . . Abraham . . . went out, not knowing whither he went."
(Heb. 11: 8.)

ABRAHAM only knew that he was following the Guide who was leading him.

This lesson is needed by all. We want our guidance as far in advance as possible instead of being content to walk with God a step at a time. Yet this is at once faith's severest test and highest development. Most of our mistakes in guidance come from our wanting to see beyond the next turn in the road, or the next bend in the river.

Each of us carries a lantern of his own. Our lanterns make but tiny circles of light, but it is enough. We must move ahead to be able to see ahead. As we move, the circle of light moves with us. The lantern throws light only one step at a time, but as we take that step the light is thrown forward enough to show us the next step beyond.

"I thank God for the tracklessness of the desert," said a devout child of God. It is a beautiful picture. The traveler who rises in the morning to traverse the great desert looks out upon a trackless waste. There is not a trace of a signboard or beaten path. There is but one thing for him to do. That is to follow his guide, step by step, through all the weary journey of the day, over the untrodden waste. Such is the perfect walk of the child of God who has learned to trust Him.

"Seek not to mark thy road by human wisdom. Thy feet would never find His pathway so."

"Sometimes—a mist on the road;
Sometimes—a radiant way;
Sometimes—a wearisome load;
Sometimes—a light-hearted day;
* But always—Thy hand in mine.*

"Sometimes—a journey with friends;
Sometimes—a march alone;
Sometimes—a rest when day ends;
Sometimes—a weary walk home;
* But always—Thyself divine."*

June 3

"Wilt thou not from this time cry unto me, My father, thou art the guide of my youth?" (Jer. 3: 4.)

Why do I drift on a storm-tossed sea,
With neither compass, nor star, nor chart,
When, as I drift, God's own plan for me
Waits at the door of my slow-trusting heart?

Down from the heavens it drops like a scroll,
Each day a bit will the Master unroll,
Each day a mite of the veil will He lift.
Why do I falter? Why wander and drift?

Drifting, while God's at the helm to steer;
Groping, when God lays the course so clear;
Swerving, though straight into port I might sail;
Wrecking, when heaven lies just within hail.

Help me, O God, in the plan to believe;
Help me my fragment each day to receive.
Oh, that my will may with Thine have no strife!
God-yielded wills find the God-planned life.
*   —James McConkey.*

Allow God to carry out His plans for you without anxiety or interference.

There's a throne above the world. There's a Man on the throne. He has a plan for things down here during this time of turmoil and strife. His Spirit is down here to get that plan done. He needs each one of us. He puts His hand on each Christian life and says, "Separate yourself from all else for the bit I need you to do." His hand is on *you*. Are you doing it? *Anything else classes as failure.*

—*The Bent Knee Time.*

June 4

". . . Shall I yet again go out to battle . . . or shall I cease?"
(Judges 20: 28.)

ERTAIN officers approached Napoleon to recommend a young captain for promotion. Napoleon asked them: "Why do you suggest this man?" Their answer was that through unusual courage and cleverness he had won a signal victory several days before. "Good," said Napoleon, "but what did he do the next day?" That was the last that was ever heard of the young man.

There are two kinds of people in the world—those who show an occasional outburst of brilliancy and those who can be depended upon to do their best every day in the year—in other words, the flashers and the plodders. The backbone of a Christian civilization is its dependable people. These are the ones who can always be counted on for a steady stream of influence and service no matter what happens anywhere.

—*Religious Telescope.*

A boy taunted for failing in a prolonged attempt to answer a hard question said, "I would rather try and fail than do as you did —sit still and do nothing."

"Failure after long perseverance," wrote George Eliot, "is much grander than never to have a striving good enough to be called a failure."

Consecrated perseverance conquers!

You may do miracles by persevering.—*Robert Burns.*

> *Courage! What if the snows are deep,*
> *And what if the hills are long and steep,*
> *And the days are short, and the nights are long,*
> *And the good are weak, and the bad are strong!*
> *Courage! The snow is a field of play,*
> *And the longest hill has a well-worn way,*
> *There are songs that shorten the longest night,*
> *There's a Day when wrong shall be ruled by right,*
> *So courage! Courage! 'Tis never so far*
> *From a plodded path to a shining star.*
> —*Writer Unknown.*

June 5

"I must work the works of him that sent me, while it is day; the night cometh, when no man can work." (John 9: 4.)

TOMORROW

He was going to be all that a mortal could be—
    Tomorrow;
No one should be kinder nor braver than he—
    Tomorrow;
  A friend who was troubled and weary he knew
  Who'd be glad of a lift and who needed it, too;
On him he would call and see what he could do—
    Tomorrow.

Each morning he stacked up the letters he'd write—
    Tomorrow;
And he thought of the folks he would fill with delight—
    Tomorrow;
  It was too bad, indeed, he was busy today,
  And hadn't a minute to stop on his way;
"More time I'll have to give others," he'd say—
    "Tomorrow."

The greatest of workers this man would have been—
    Tomorrow;
The world would have known him had he ever seen—
    Tomorrow;
  But the fact is he died, and he faded from view,
  And all that he left here when living was through
Was a mountain of things he intended to do—
    Tomorrow.

        —Anonymous.

Today is better than tomorrow.

"My friend, have you heard of the town of YAWN,
On the banks of the river SLOW?
Where grows the WAIT-A-WHILE flower fair,
And the SOMETHING-OR-OTHER scents the air,
And the soft GO-EASIES grow.
It lies in the valley of WHAT'S-THE-USE,
In the province of LET-IT-SLIDE:
That tired feeling is native there,
It's the home of the listless I-DON'T-CARE,
Where the PUT-IT-OFFS abide."

Make the attainments of yesterday the starting point of today.

June 6

". . . Choose you this day whom ye will serve; . . ."
(Joshua 24: 15.)

WE CANNOT travel east and west at the same time. We cannot in the same moment clothe appropriately for the Arctic regions and the tropics. We must make our choice and ignore either the one or the other. We cannot be both refined and the vulgar. We cannot be pure and impure. We cannot move horizontally and vertically in the same movement, onward in the companionship of the world, and upward in the companionship of the Lord.

We too commonly believe that we can have two masters, and that it is possible to render service to both. We split up our life, and divide our inheritance. We give a portion to Mammon and a portion to God. I have seen a shopkeeper selling his goods on the Sabbath, and paying his respects to the Lord by retaining one shutter on the window! That one-shutter expedient is very common in other concerns besides Sunday trading. A woman lives a worldly life and wears a crucifix. A man makes money as he pleases but never misses the sacrament. The home never hears the sound of worship, but the family Bible is always on the table by the window. "No man can serve two masters." The Lord demands our all.

Abraham Lincoln once pointed out that no nation could endure half slave and half free. This truth applies to individuals no less than to nations.

He who pursues two hares will catch neither. —*Indian Proverb.*

June 7

"...David...served his own generation by the will of God."
(Acts 13: 36.)

LIVINGSTONE

To lift the sombre fringes of the night,
To open lands long darkened to the Light,
To heal grim wounds, to give the blind new sight,
  Right mightily wrought he.

Forth to the fight he fared,
High things and great he dared,
He thought of all men but himself.
  Himself he never spared.

He greatly loved—
He greatly lived—
And died right and mightily.

Like Him he served, he walked life's troublous ways,
With heart undaunted, and with calm, high face;
And gemmed each day with deeds of sweetest grace,
Full lovingly wrought he.

Like Him he served, he would not turn aside;
Nor home nor friends could his true heart divide;
He served his master, and naught else beside,
Right faithfully wrought he.

He passed like light across the darkened land,
And dying, left behind him this command,
"The door is open! So let it ever stand!"
Full mightily wrought he.

—Selected.

"God has always had His man ready to turn the scale of events in crucial moments and to fit that one into His eternal purposes. God has a program, and there are no breaks in His plan."

There is no choice;
We cannot say, "This will I do, or that."
A hand is stretched to us from out the dark,
Which grasping without question, we are led
Where there is work THAT WE MUST DO FOR GOD.

—Lowell.

June 8

"I being in the way, the Lord led me." (Gen. 24: 27.)

THE Bible has the answer to all the problems of life. In Genesis 24 we have the story of Abraham sending to his native land for his eldest and most trusted servant to obtain a wife for Isaac. Isaac himself must not go lest he fail to return to the inheritance promised to Abraham and his descendants.

The servant made his errand a matter of prayer. And why not? Surely God is interested in this important step, the choosing of one's life companion. After he saw Rebekah there was a period when "the man wondering at her held his peace, to wit whether the Lord had made his journey prosperous or not." If young people would pause to make inquiry as to the Lord's will before they made advances, much unhappiness would be avoided.

Rebekah was a virgin. She had kept herself clean and pure, and hence, was worthy of a good man like Isaac. She could look forward with confidence to a happy wedded life. She was kind. She not only gave the stranger a drink but ran to draw water for his camels. When she, with her family, was persuaded that "the thing proceedeth from the Lord," she said, "I will go." She prepared to marry, not as an experiment but meaning to cling to Isaac as long as they both should live. For her, marriage was a divine institution, and she was entering into a life contract. When she first saw Isaac she alighted from the camel and took a veil and covered herself. Isaac brought this modest, pure young woman into "his mother Sarah's tent, and took Rebekah, and she became his wife; and he loved her."

So Isaac secured his wife. God's favor and blessing enriched their lives. Our lives, too, can be divinely planned. May we prayerfully commit ourselves to the will of God.

—R. Barclay Warren.

If anyone wants a happy home let him find a life companion who loves the Lord.

June 9

"...But in every thing by prayer and supplication with thanksgiving let your requests be made known unto God."
(Phil. 4:6.)

AN UNFAILING REMEDY

HAYDN once was in the company of other noted artists when one of them asked how, after a period of great exertion, one might recover inner strength quickest. Different methods were suggested, but when Haydn was asked what methods he followed, he said: 'In my home I have a small chapel. When I feel wearied because of my work, I go there and pray. This remedy has never failed me.'

"Experience tells us that Haydn was right. In believing prayer to God we tap the source of *all* strength."

If you do not feed your soul, it will die.

MY RENDEZVOUS WITH GOD

I have a rendezvous with God,
Where spirit doth with spirit meet;
Where He enfolds me in His love,
While I anoint His blessed feet:
I have a rendezvous with God—
Detain me not from its retreat.
For there He clasps me by the hand,

And there I see Him face to face;
I tell Him all my vexing cares,
   He whispers of sufficient grace;
I have a rendezvous with God,
   A holy, happy meeting-place;
No earthly thing dare enter there
   To mar the fellowship we share.

The turmoil of the daily life,
   The burdens of the mind and heart,
Cannot dismay, must not distract
   My soul from meeting God apart!
For I've a rendezvous with God,
   And well I know that at that hour,
Abounding grace, more faith, new power
   For all these needs He doth impart.

World-vision of His harvest field,
   Supernal strength, its work to do,
In that blest hour with God alone
   Within my heart He doth renew:
With Christ's constraining love for souls
   With joy the labor to imbue.

Lord, keep me to this love-tryst true—
Let me not fail our rendezvous!

Anne M. Waite.

"The reinforcements gathered in the quiet season turn the tide of battle."—*G. A. Buttrick.*

June 10

". . . I am purposed . . ." (Psalm 17: 3.)

I HAVE half a mind to do it," we sometimes say. What a curious thing is half a mind! Where are the great pictures it has painted, the books it has written, the palaces it has built? Where are the mountains it has scaled, the battles it has won, the continents it has discovered? What is done with half a mind no one cares to look upon; the sickly and abortive efforts are soon and best forgotten. But when we make up our minds, determine once for all, take a stand, put our hearts into a thing, it means a great deal in any line of life. There is a strange depth of power within us if only we will call upon it.

"I see what I want, and I do it," said one of our great painters. Such language is most becoming on our lips who believe in God and in His grace, which can more than fulfill all our desires.

—*William Watkinson, D. D.*

"If I am but a raindrop in a shower, I will seek to be at least a perfect drop; if but a leaf in a whole June, I will seek at least to be a perfect leaf."—"This one thing I do."—"Seek to excel!"

"A lost battle is a battle one believes lost. There are three courses: you can retire, stand fast, or attack. I forbid the first. You can take your choice of the other two."
—*Sir George Astor* in his *Life of Marshal Foch.*

Over the spot on which Captain Scott and his band met death in that little tent of thin canvas after their heroic attempt to find the South Pole, there stands a cross bearing these words:

"To strive, to seek, to find, and not to yield!"

June 11

"Then said Jesus ... I am the door: by me if any man enter in, he shall be saved, and shall go in and out, and find pasture."
(John 10:7, 9.)

THE YOUNG MAN OF NAZARETH

The young man out of Nazareth
Was good to see—
  I felt a breath
Awaken, dew-fresh, like a breeze
Astir among the olive trees,
The grace of youth flowered in His speech—
Into my heart. I followed His
Brave, eager words with a strange reach,
Half-wondering why, until the rim
Of the gray mountain ridge was white
With stars—
  Men told strange tales of sight
Come to a beggar, one born blind—
I do not know, Some say they find
Those still who think it was a king
They killed. And never anything
Has brought such quiet to my bed
As thinking of the things he said:
A kingdom simple as a child—
Its king a servant—
  Though He smiled
A lion looked out of His eye.
His brave, young heart brake like a cry.
If time came back, and He as then,
I could but follow Him again.
     —Author Unknown.

"Thou young man Christ, we worship Thee. We feel our need beyond ourselves to supply. We want the Rock on which to plant our feet. The slippery places where the climbing tides make ooze have proven too slippery for our feet. We clamor for the Rock. Thou art very God. Thou hast taken pains to get close to us and bid us be the might for which Thou hast created us. Thou Hero Christ, Thou Manly Christ, Thou Father Christ, Thou Christ of noon, when battle and toil are fierce as the impassioned ocean, take our lives in Thy strong hand and shape them into holiness and beauty. Make the meaning of the incarnation of God apparent to our need by Jesus Christ. Amen!"

—Bishop Quayle, in The Climb to God.

June 12

"Beloved, now are we the sons of God, and it doth not yet appear what we shall be: but we know that, when he shall appear, we shall be like him; . . ." (1 John 3: 2.)

THIS is the great day which you young people have reached; the greatness of it lies not in that which is behind you but more truly in that which is before. Your success will be measured when the story is all finished, not by what you have done or enjoyed, or had, but *by what you have become.* All great becoming grows out of ideals, large purposes, far horizons, visions that seem impossible of achievement, heights that are on the far rim of the horizon and seem too steep and lofty for your feet. Perhaps they are too steep for your feet *yet,* but they constitute your goals, and strength always grows with the use of the powers we have. They who lift up their eyes to lofty summits that are afar off find the end of their journey in high places where the sky is nearer, and all the roadways of the earth are clearer, and the sense of achievement and of growth offers them great and beautiful and abiding rewards.

—Selected.

Shall our lives be lived in chasing short-lived butterflies of pleasure or in going into a wilderness to recover lost sheep?

> *To every man there openeth*
> *A way and ways and a way.*
> *And the high souls choose the high way,*
> *And the low souls take the low,*
> *And in between on the misty flats*
> *The rest drift to and fro.*
> *So to every soul there openeth*
> *The high way and the low,*
> *And every man decideth*
> *Which way his soul shall go.—John Oxenham.*

June 13

"... The kingdom of God ... is like a grain of mustard seed, which, when it is sown in the earth, is less than all the seeds that be in the earth: But when it is sown, it groweth up, and becometh greater than all herbs, and shooteth out great branches so that the fowls of the air may lodge under the shadow of it." (Mark 4:30, 31, 32.)

"IS NOT this the carpenter's son?" Moses was the son of a poor slave Levite; Gideon was a thresher; David was a shepherd boy; Euripides was the son of a fruiterer; Virgil, of a baker; Horace, of a freed slave; Tamerlane, of a shepherd; Ben Jonson, of a mason; Shakespeare, of a butcher. Melancthon, the great theologian of the Reformation, was an armorer; Luther was the child of a poor miner; Fuller was a farm servant; Carey, the originator of the plan of translating the Bible into the language of the millions of Hindustan, was a shoemaker; Morrison, who translated the Bible into the Chinese language, was a last-maker; Dr. Milne was a herd-boy; Adam Clarke was the child of Irish cotters.

Who would have expected that Goliath's antagonist would emerge from the quiet pastures? "Genius hatches her offspring in strange places." Very humble homes are the birthplaces of mighty emancipators.

There was a little farm at St. Ives, and the farmer lived a quiet and unsensational life. But the affairs of the nation became more and more confused and threatening. Monarchial power despoiled the people's liberties, and tyranny became rampant. And out from the little farm strode Oliver Cromwell, the ordained of God, to emancipate his country.

There was an obscure rectory at Epworth. The activities in the little rectory were just the quiet practices of simple homes in countless parts of England. And England was becoming brutalized because its religious life was demoralized. The church was asleep, and the devil was wide awake! And forth from the humble rectory strode John Wesley, the appointed champion of the Lord to enthuse, to purify, and to sweeten the life of the people.

On what quiet farm is the coming deliverer now laboring? Who knows?

—Dr. J. H. Jowett.

June 14

*". . . Joseph, being seventeen years old, . . . dreamed a dream
. . . And Pharaoh said unto his servants, Can we find such a
one as this is, a man in whom the Spirit of God is? And Pharaoh said unto Joseph, Forasmuch as God hath shewed thee
all this, there is none so discreet and wise as thou art: Thou
shalt be over my house, and according unto thy word shall
all my people be ruled: only in the throne will I be greater
than thou. And Pharaoh said unto Joseph, See, I have set thee
over all the land of Egypt."*

(Gen. 37:2, 5; 41:38-41.)

WHEN the records which men have written are read, it will
be found that *young* men have ruled the world. The oldest literatures have this recorded. The patriarchs un-
folded the careers of boys into the conquest of old age.
Kingdoms and empires rode upon the shoulders of young
men; and their voices of enthusiasm and hope have sounded
through many a blackhearted midnight to trumpet the dawn. To
courses that dropped they have come and added the raptures of
hope; to enterprises that were sickening and faint they have
brought the bounding power of new enthusiasm. To the dead they
have brought life. Everything from the foundation of the world has
been crying for young blood . . . . Age and experience put themselves upon dying pillows made by young hands; into young palms
and upon young ears falls the meaning of the past. And thus has
God written the natural dignity of a young man's life in the
eternal statute book of the universe."

—Dr. Frank W. Gunsaulus in A Fleece of Gold.

> YOUTH!
> . . . Cut a path into
> The heaven of glory
> Leaving a track of light for men
> to wonder at.
>
> *—Wm. Blake.*

A short life which fulfills its mission is a success. "That life is
long which answers life's great end."—*Young.*

It is better to *live* thirty years, than *exist* seventy!

> A short life in the saddle, Lord,
> Not long life by the fire.
> *—Louise Imogene Guiney.*

June 15

"Blessed are the peacemakers: for they shall be called the children of God." (Matt. 5:9.)

A PARABLE OF THE FANNER BEES

IT WAS a glorious night of midsummer—a moon at full and a host of stars. The old bee garden was bathed in soft crystalline light—and ever so light a breeze lisped in the treetops. At the door of one of the hives we came to a halt. There arose from the hive a sibilant...persistent...not unlike the sound of sea waves...advancing...retreating.

"They are fanner bees," whispered the old beekeeper. "It's their job to keep the hive sweet and fresh. They're standing with their heads lowered, turned toward the center of the hive. Their wings are moving so rapidly that if you could see them you would think you were looking at a gray mist. They are drawing the bad air through one side of the entrance, whilst the pure air is sucked in on the other side."

Standing there close to nature, listening to the bee fanners, I felt close to one of nature's wonders—the mystery of the hive life. Presently the old bee-keeper stooped to the hive, holding a lighted candle in his hand. Instantly the light was extinguished by the strong air current, those infinitesimal bee wings moving in unison, making a draft so strong that the candle light was instantly quenched. Think of it!

As we stood there in the starlit garden the old preacher said, "The fanners—drawing out the bad air, letting in the fresh. Isn't that how people who call themselves Christians ought to act?" If we had enough fanners, if they were as keen on their jobs as those bees are on theirs, wouldn't the great hive of the world grow sweet and fresh?

—Selected.

"Year after year, with a glad content,
In and out of our home one went—
In and out;
Ever for us the skies were clear,
His heart carried the care and fear,
The care and doubt."

"Now thanks be unto God, which ... maketh manifest the savour of his knowledge by us in every place. For we are unto God a sweet savour of Christ, in them that are saved, and in them that perish." (2 Cor. 2:14, 15.)

June 16

*"... If ye will obey my voice indeed, and keep my covenant,
then ye shall be a peculiar treasure unto me above all people:
..." (Exod. 19:5.)*

WHAT a mighty man of God was Samson! Consecrated to God in infancy, separated unto God in his upbringing as a Nazarite. Nothing seemed successfully to oppose this man. But there came a day of the violation of the life-long separation, the destroying of that which made him differ from other men; a day when he became as other men, no longer standing out as the Lord's own possession. In that day he became weak, powerless, and an object of ridicule.

Whenever a young man or woman steps over the line of separation into the world, his strength goes. The moment a Christian forgets he is God's peculiar possession, and allies himself with the world, he is on the road to ineffectiveness.

—W. W. Martin.

Lord, show me the thing that stands in the way,
The stone that is under the wheel,
Reveal the idol to be cast down,
Lord, hear me as I kneel.

And, Lord, if I have not the strength to cut off
The part that offendeth me,
Nor have I the courage to overthrow
The thing I love more than Thee:

Oh, cripple the limb with a touch of Thy hand!
To bear it give me grace,
And when I awake tomorrow morn
May the idol be on its face.

But more than this I would ask, O Lord,
Grind it to powder fine,
Then fill up my heart with Thy wondrous love,
Making my face to shine. Amen.

—Author Unknown.

"Set apart for Jesus!
Is not this enough,
Though the desert prospect
Open wild and rough?
Set apart for His delight,
Chosen for His holy pleasure,
Sealed to be His special treasure:
Could we choose a nobler joy?
And would we if we might?"

June 17

"If ye then be risen with Christ, seek those things which are above, where Christ sitteth on the right hand of God."

(Col. 3:1.)

AN officer in the American Flying Corps says: "I was out over the ocean alone, and I saw in the distance, coming rapidly toward me, a storm that was blacker than midnight; the inky clouds seemed to be coming on with lightning rapidity. I knew I could not reach shore ahead of the storm. I looked down to the ocean to see if I could go underneath the cloud and perhaps alight on the sea, but the ocean was already boiling with fury. Knowing that the only thing to do was to rise above it, I turned my frail craft straight up toward the sky, and I let her mount 1,000, 2,000, 2,500, 3,000, 3,500 feet, and then the storm struck me. It was a hurricane, a cyclone, and a typhoon all in one! The sky became as black as midnight. I never saw blackness like that. I could not see a thing. Rain came in torrents, the snow began to fly, the hail struck like bullets. I was 4,000 feet up in the air. I knew there was only one thing to do, and that was to keep on climbing. So I climbed to 6,500 feet; then suddenly I was swept out into sunlight and glory such as I had never seen in this world before. The clouds were all below me. The sapphire sky was bending low above me in amazing splendor. It seemed the glory of another world; I immediately began to repeat Scripture to myself, and in the heavens above the clouds I worshiped God."

We have not lived the highest, we have not pursued the best; we have gone after the butterflies instead of trying to fly with the eagles; we have learned the lesson of the snail rather than the lesson of high-mountain-climbing into the skies. May God have mercy on us!—*The Climb to God.*

God made us to soar like eagles, but we are content to scratch like sparrows.

June 18

". . . O thou of little faith, wherefore didst thou doubt?"

(Matt. 14:31.)

CAN YOU DOUBT?

Can you sit on top of a hill in spring,
And watch the birds sailing by on the wing,
And see the clouds drifting on in the sky,
And doubt there's a God who dwells on high?

Can you watch the rainbow span the blue,
Or tread the grass full of morning dew,

Or sit by the seaside and hear the waves,
And doubt there's a God who lovingly saves?

Can you watch the butterfly flit through the air,
And see the flowers blooming fragrant and fair,
Or watch the trees reaching ever above,
And doubt there's a God of wisdom and love?

Oh! dear ones!
As sure as the sun tints the west,
And the birds of the air go home to their nest,
As sure as the butterflies, birds, and bees
Flit and wander 'mid flowers and trees;
As sure as the rainbow spans the sky
There's a God who reigns forever on high,
Who will all of our joys and sorrows share,
And will over us watch with infinite care,
Our divine Redeemer; in that great above,
He watches, and waits with eternal love.
—Esther E. Rowe.

We are likely to sit down under the greening tree and never catch the miracle which turns winter branch and trunk into a bower of perfumed blossom and transfigured leafage. Blessed be God for the wonder of things!

June 19

". . . Ascribe ye greatness unto our God." (Deut. 32:3.)

LOOK through the telescope on a starry night at the millions upon millions of stars and planets whirling through space— myriads of systems in which the little earth is but a single grain of sand in a sandstorm! Yet the One who is responsible for the amazing energy and orderliness of all that dazzling universe is God—a powerful, intelligent God at work!

Peer into a microscope at a cross section of a blade of grass or bit of an insect's wing. All is as orderly as the movements of the planets and stars in the infinite spaces, yet incredibly intricate and exquisite. And the source of the tiniest forms of life that swarm unseen in billions under one's feet in the grass, or through the woods or along a country road, is God—the God of all life everywhere! The living God is not merely a pious phrase; He is the mighty force at work in the universe! Psalm 104; Matthew 10:29.

One asked a sign from God; and day by day the sun arose in pearl; in scarlet set; each night the stars appeared in bright array;

each morn the thirsty grass with dew was wet; the corn failed not
in harvest, nor the vine—
And yet he saw no sign!
　　　—*Anonymous* from *The Girls' Every Day Book.*

This God is *"our own God."* (Psalm 67: 6.)

June 20

"They looked unto him and were radiant: . . ."
　　　　　　　　　　　　　　　　(Psalm 34:5, R. V.)

THINK for a moment about faces of God's saints!—what
wonderful faces *He* has developed! A doubting college
student who had heard and seen A. J. Gordon is said to
have exclaimed: "That man's *face* would convert me to
a belief in Christ!" Phillips Brooks was once heralded as
"the man with the face like God." Paton, Taylor, Drummond, won
the students a generation ago by their very faces before they uttered a word. The face is, after all, a reflection as well as the re-
vealer of the soul within. The gods we worship write their names
on our faces!

> How lovely are the faces of
> 　The men who talk with God—
> Lit with an inner sureness of
> 　The path their feet have trod;
> How gentle is the manner of
> 　A man who walks with Him!
> No strength can overcome him, and
> 　No cloud his courage dim.
> Keen are the hands and feet—ah, yes—
> 　Of those who wait His will,
> And clear as crystal mirrors are
> 　The hearts His love can fill.
>
> Some lives are drear from doubt and fear
> 　While others merely plod;
> But lovely faces mark the men
> 　Who walk and talk with God.
> 　—*Marked for His Own.*—*Pauline Prosser-Thompson.*

> *"O! to be like thee, blessed Redeemer,*
> 　*This is my constant longing and prayer;*
> 　*Gladly I'll forfeit all of earth's treasures,*
> 　*Jesus, thy perfect likeness to wear."*

"Stamp thine own image deep on my heart!"

June 21

"... Keep thyself pure." (1 Tim. 5: 22.)

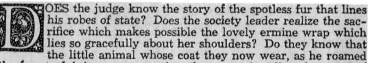

DOES the judge know the story of the spotless fur that lines his robes of state? Does the society leader realize the sacrifice which makes possible the lovely ermine wrap which lies so gracefully about her shoulders? Do they know that the little animal whose coat they now wear, as he roamed the forest of Asia was as proud as they—aye, inordinately proud of his beautiful snowy coat? And we do not wonder, for it is the most beautiful fur to be found in all the markets of the world!

Such pride does the little carnivore take in his spotless coat that nothing is permitted to soil it in the slightest degree. Hunters are well acquainted with this fact and take very unsportsmanlike advantage of this knowledge. No traps are set for him. No, indeed! Instead, they seek out his home—a tree stump, or rocky cleft, and then—be it said to their everlasting shame—they daub filth within and around the entrance. As the dogs are loosed and the chase begins, the little animal naturally turns to his one place of refuge. Reaching it, rather than enter such a place of uncleanness, he turns to face the yelping dogs.

Better to be stained by blood than sully his white coat!

Only a white coat, little ermine, but how your act condemns us! *"Made in the image and likeness of God," with minds and immortal spirits;* and yet, how often, in order to obtain something we desire, our character is sacrificed on the altars of worldly pleasure, greed, selfishness!

Everything is lost when purity is gone—purity, which has been called the *soul of character.* Keep thyself pure: *every thought, every word,* every deed, *even the motive behind the deed—all, ermine-pure!*

> *I ask this gift of Thee—*
> *A life all lily-fair;*
> *And fragrant as the place*
> *Where seraphs are.*
>
> —Mrs. H. Bradley.

THE DAUGHTERS OF THE KING

"Princesses still, in ermine, white, like wool,
  Cleansed by the King's own touch from spot or stain;
Emptied of self; of His own life so full,
  That, overflowing on a world in pain,
  They bless and serve, and by their service reign."

Chastity is the ermine of a woman's soul.—*Queen Elizabeth.*

June 22

". . . God forbid that I should glory, save in the cross of our Lord Jesus Christ." (Gal. 6: 14.)

CROSS-CENTERED CHRISTIANITY FOR YOUTH

YOUTH need to be on their guard lest they enter upon a way of life which claims to be Christian but ignores the Cross or moves it out of the center. That is only pseudo-Christianity, though it may masquerade under the deceptive costume of Christian profession and of Christian phraseology. Subtle references to great names, to the modern trend of thought, to the results of science are being employed to inveigle youth into the acceptance of this false way of life.

Youth must never forget that the Cross introduced Christianity to the world, and that the Cross planted Christianity in the world. True Christianity will forever be centered in the Cross. Wherever the Cross is lifted out, there remains only a pagan religion. Wherever the Cross is moved out of the center, there is left only a distorted interpretation of Christianity, which in reality repudiates Christianity.

The Cross represents a fact in God's dealing with man. That fact is that Jesus Christ, Himself God and Man, through His death on the Cross, has intervened in behalf of man, settled all his sin accounts, and provided him with a capital investment of divine grace.

Christianity is centered in that fact. Only when youth realize the significance of that fact and apply it to themselves by penitently accepting Christ crucified as their personal Saviour, will they know what Christianity means. Then the Cross will become central in their own lives.

Youth who are gripped by a Cross-centered Christianity will be inspired thereby to make the Cross touch all of life. Business, politics, professional life, science, art, social relations, yea—every realm of life ought to feel the mighty impact of the uplift of Christ crucified! Youth with the Cross central in their own lives will be challenged to give themselves sacrificially for Christ so as to make the Cross central in human society.

The Cross-centered Christianity, or no Christianity at all, is the alternative for youth. —S. A. B.

General Gordon, who was neither an "old woman" nor a "soft man," but a hero of the highest order, expressed his faith in his favorite verse as follows:

> "We read Thee best in Him who came
> To bear for us the Cross and shame;
> Sent by the Father from on high,
> Our life to live, our death to die."

June 23

"His coming is certain as the dawn." (Hosea 6: 3, Arabic.)

REMEMBER well when God was pleased to open my heart to this great truth that the Lord Jesus is coming again, and that He may come *at any time!* What was the effect? I had not a great many books, but it sent me to see if I could give a good account of all I had, and also of the contents of my wardrobe. The result was that some of the books disappeared before long, and some of the clothing, too. It was an immense spiritual blessing to me. When I come home from China and can make time to go through the house from attic to basement with my dear wife, to review our things in the light of His speedy return, we always find it a helpful spiritual exercise to see what we can do without. It is profitable to remember that we are stewards who have to give account of everything that we retain, and unless we can give a good reason for the retention, shall we not be ashamed when the Master comes? Since He may come any day, is it not well to be ready every day? I do not know any thought that has been made a greater blessing to me through life than this."   —*J. Hudson Taylor.*

HIS RETURN

He is coming! He is coming!
  We can almost hear the sound
Of His footsteps at the threshold,
  And our hearts with gladness bound.
All around us men are seeking,
  Turning blind eyes to the light,
Longing, fearing, not yet daring
  To escape from sin's dark night,
Yet the message is so simple,
  "I will surely come again."
'Tis the glad news of the Gospel,
  Ringing sweetly through earth's pain.
When He comes may I be ready,
  Watching, praying, working still,
Though He tarry, may I daily
  Learn more perfectly His will.

—*D. N. R.*

"Midnight is past," sings the sailor on the southern ocean: *"Midnight is past; the Cross begins to bend."*

"It is high time to awake out of sleep." Our Lord will come!

"Even so, come, Lord Jesus."

June 24

". . . His own generation . . ." (Acts 13:36.)

WHEN the noted Dr. Stewart of Africa was fifteen years of age he received his first impulse to become a missionary. At the time he was following a plow. Leaning on the handles of the plow, he began to brood over his future. What was it to be? The question flashed across his mind, "Might not I make more of my life than remaining here?" He straightened himself and said, "God helping me I will be a missionary." When this great hero at the age of eighty-six had finished his earthly task the lives of thousands had been changed because of his ministry. With Livingstone he helped heal Africa's open sore. A man who forgot self!

MY GENERATION

"David served his own generation by the will of God." Could you have a nobler motto than that to write on the flyleaf of your Bible? "*I* will serve *my* own generation by the will of God." This is life at its highest and best.

"The great secret of success is to be ready when your opportunity comes."   —*Lord Beaconsfield.*

"Can anything be sadder than work left unfinished? Yes; work never begun."   —*Christina Rossetti.*

June 25

"Being confident of this very thing, that he which hath begun a good work in you will perform it until the day of Jesus Christ." (Phil. 1:6.)

IN ONE of London's galleries there stands an unfinished piece of statuary—crude and imperfect—with barely the outline of a human form emerging. Some one remarked, "The rough block of white marble is here to indicate the crudeness from which these perfect forms have been chiseled." There was the touch of genius in the outline. Why could not the ideal there have been released? Upon closer observation one notices these words inscribed upon the pedestal, "The artist died at this stage of the work." Many a youth has started out as this artist did but died to God and high ideals and went into sin with his life not finished as God had planned it should be.

To each man is given a marble to carve for the wall!
A stone that is needed to heighten the beauty of all:
And only his soul has the magic to give it grace,
And only his hands have the cunning to put it in place.

Yes, the task is given to each man, no other can do:
So the errand is waiting; it has waited ages for you,
And now you appear; the hushed ones are turning their gaze
To see what you do with your chance in the chamber of days.
                                        —*Author Unknown.*

June 26

" *. . . They held their lives cheap.*" (Rev. 12:11, Weymouth.)

HE persecution of the Christians during the reign of Marcus Aurelius was very bitter. The Emperor himself decreed the punishment of forty of the men who had refused to bow down to his image.

"*Strip to the skin!*" he commanded. They did so. "*Now, go and stand on that frozen lake,*" he commanded, "*until you are prepared to abandon your Nazarene-God!*"

Forty naked men marched out into that howling storm on a winter's night. As they took their places on the ice they lifted up their voices and sang:

"*Christ, forty wrestlers have come out to wrestle for Thee; to win for Thee the victory; to win from Thee the crown.*"

. After a while those standing by and watching noticed a disturbance among the men. One man edged away, broke into a run, entered the temple, and prostrated himself before the image of the Emperor.

The captain of the guard, who had witnessed the bravery of the men and whose heart had been touched by their teaching, tore off his helmet, threw down his spear, and disrobing himself, took up the cry as he took the place of the man who had weakened. The compensation was not slow in coming, for as the dawn broke there were forty corpses on the ice.

"*Who shall dream of shrinking,*
By our Captain led?"

. At least a thousand of God's saints served as living torches to illuminate the darkness of Nero's gardens, wrapped in garments steeped in pitch. "*Every finger was a candle.*"

"*A noble army, men and boys,*
The matron and the maid,
Around the Saviour's throne rejoice
In robes of light arrayed;
They climbed the steep ascent of heav'n
Thro' peril, toil and pain,
O God, to us may grace be giv'n
To follow in their train."

June 27

"... Launch out into the deep, and let down your nets for a draught...At thy word I will let down the net."
(Luke 5: 4, 5.)

WHEN Peter made Christ the captain of his boat he was commanded to "launch out into the deep!" When Christ was in control, Peter must no longer stay in the shallows.

Are you hugging the shore of the world? Do you wonder why there is no success in your Christian life? Have you been a Christian for so long, and yet do you still dabble in the world's pleasures? Do you still compromise with the world's standards? Are you still content to come down to the level of the world? Have you never burned your bridges and cut your shorelines and launched out into the deep, with Christ in full control?

If it is a choice between the social evening and the church prayer meeting, which wins?

—Frederick P. Wood.

"Oh, let us launch out on this ocean so broad,
Where the floods of salvation o'erflow;
Oh, let us be lost in the mercy of God,
Till the depths of His fullness we know.

Launch out into the deep! Oh, let the shoreline go;
Launch out, launch out in the ocean divine,
Out where the full tides flow."

A great ship asks deep waters.—*George Herbert.*

June 28

"And I will very gladly spend and be spent for you...."
(2 Cor. 12: 15, R.V.)

I RECALL that once, in the long ago of my student days in this very city, I called on the late Henry Drummond," relates a missionary. "Soon he was telling me of one of his friends who was taking a delicately nurtured young bride to their new home in Central Africa, which was so distant that three months of African travel lay between this missionary home of theirs and the coast."

"What would you say," I asked, "if that young wife were your sister?"

"Say!" he replied; "Say! I'd be proud that I had such a sister!"

What is life for, but to be given away? Only one life have we to give; how can we possibly make more of it! That which is a divine investment of all that is most precious is wholehearted devotion to so magnificent an undertaking!

Serve your own generation. Tomorrow you will be a stranger.

Captains and kings are passing,
Banners of war are furled—
Ours is a vision splendid—
Christ for a broken world.

Glory to all who labored,
Down through the ages gone,
They faced the night of conflict,
We face a glowing dawn.

Ours is a task tremendous,
Ours is the strength of youth,
Let us make all things over
After the ways of truth.

Yet is our strength as nothing,
Never has strength sufficed;
We have a mighty leader,
One is our Master: Christ!

—Selected.

My life shall be a challenge—not a compromise.
—Chas. E. Cowman.

June 29

"He that overcometh shall inherit all things; and I will be his God, and he shall be my son." (Rev. 21: 7.)

OVERCOMERS

WHEN you are forgotten or neglected, or purposely set at naught, and you smile inwardly, glorying in the insult, or the oversight, YOU ARE AN OVERCOMER.

"...To him that overcometh will I give to eat of the tree of life, which is in the midst of the paradise of God." (Rev. 2: 7.)

When you can bear with any discord, any irregularity, and any annoyance, and are content with any food, any raiment, any climate, any society, any solitude, any interruption, YOU ARE AN OVERCOMER.

"He that overcometh, the same shall be clothed in white raiment; and I will not blot out his name out of the book of life, but I will

confess his name before my Father, and before his angels." (Rev. 3: 5.)

When your good is evil spoken of, when your wishes are crossed, your taste offended, your advice disregarded, your opinion ridiculed, and you take it all in patience and loving silence, YOU ARE AN OVERCOMER.

"To him that overcometh will I grant to sit with me in my throne, even as I also overcame, and am set down with my Father in his throne." (Rev. 3: 21.)

When you never care to refer to yourself in conversation or to record your own good works, or itch after commendation; when you can truly "love to be unknown," YOU ARE AN OVERCOMER.

Lord, touch me now with that thrilling touch that makes all the difference between full life and mere existence.

"And they overcame him by the blood of the Lamb, and by the word of their testimony." (Rev. 12: 11.)

> He said not,
>   "Thou shalt not be
>   Tempested;
>   Thou shalt not be
>   Travailed;
>   Thou shalt not be
>   Afflicted:"
> But He said,
>   "Thou shalt not be
>   Overcome!"
>   —Julian of Norwick, A. D. 1373.

June 30

"What man of you, having an hundred sheep, if he lose one of them, doth not leave the ninety and nine in the wilderness, and go after that which is lost, until he find it?" (Luke 15: 4.)

> "O Shepherd with bleeding feet,
> Good Shepherd with pleading voice,
> What seekest Thou from hill to hill?
> Sweet were the valley pastures, sweet,
> The sound of flocks that bleat their joys
> And eat and drink at will.
> Is one worth seeking, when Thou hast of thine
>   Ninety and nine?"

The Master answers:

> *"How should I stay my bleeding feet?*
> *How should I hush my pleading voice?*
> *I who chose death and climbed a hill,*
> *Accounting gall and wormwood sweet?*
> *I seek my own."*

"And when ke hath found it, he layeth it on his shoulders, rejoicing. And when he cometh home, he calleth together his friends and neighbours, saying unto them, Rejoice with me; for I have found my sheep which was lost." (Luke 15: 5, 6.)

"The Lord is my shepherd; I shall not want.
He maketh me to lie down in green pastures: he leadeth me beside the still waters.
He restoreth my soul: he leadeth me in the paths of righteousness for his name's sake.
Yea, though I walk through the valley of the shadow of death, I will fear no evil: for thou art with me; thy rod and thy staff they comfort me.
Thou preparest a table before me in the presence of mine enemies: thou anointest my head with oil; my cup runneth over.
Surely goodness and mercy shall follow me all the days of my life: and I will dwell in the house of the Lord for ever."

— (Psalm 23.)

"The King of Love my Shepherd is!"

July 1

"The thief cometh not, but for to steal, and to kill, and to destroy: I am come that they might have life, and that they might have it more abundantly." (John 10: 10.)

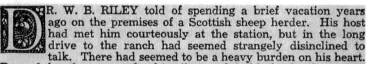

DR. W. B. RILEY told of spending a brief vacation years ago on the premises of a Scottish sheep herder. His host had met him courteously at the station, but in the long drive to the ranch had seemed strangely disinclined to talk. There had seemed to be a heavy burden on his heart. Pressed for the reason for his silence, the old shepherd wept as though his own children had been snatched from him. "I lost sixty-five of my best lambs last night," he said. "Wolves got in." The sympathetic pastor expressed his own grief over this great loss. "And how many sheep did they kill besides?" he asked. The shepherd looked surprised. "Don't you know," he answered, "that a wolf never will take an old sheep so long as he can get a lamb?"

The wolf prefers lambs!

O Lord, make me aware
  of peril in the air
Before the wolf can leap
  upon wee sheep.
Give me the eye that sees
When he is threatening them
Who are so dear to Thee,
  so dear to me.
                                —*Selected.*

July 2

"Now unto him that is able to keep you from falling, and to present you faultless before the presence of his glory with exceeding joy." (Jude 24.)

A WRITER tells of going with a party down into a coal mine. On the side of the gangway grew a plant which was perfectly white. The visitors were astonished that there where the coal dust was continually flying, this little plant should be so pure and white. A miner who was with them took a handful of the black dust and threw it upon the plant, but not a particle adhered. Every atom of the dust rolled off. The visitors themselves repeated the experiment, but the coal dust would not cling. There was a wonderful enamel on the folds of the white plant to which the finest specks could not adhere. As it lived there amid clouds of black dust nothing could stain the snowy whiteness. If He can keep a flower stainless, white as snow, amid clouds of black dust, can He not keep your heart in like purity in this world of sin?

All "inclosed" my lily garden,
  But to One its bloom revealed,
And within its deepest recess
  Springs a living fountain "sealed."

Flows this spring of life from Jesus,
  Back to Him its streams must go,
And the lilies owe their freshness
  To the fountain's constant flow.

Jesus, "Altogether lovely,"
  Spotless Lily of my heart,
Grow within my life forever,
  I am Thine, and mine Thou art.
                —*From Heart Melody.*

As a child of the King, of the true Royal Blood, may I walk today with dignity, never stooping to the allurements of the world. Keep my garments spotless!

July 3

"Wherefore by their fruits ye shall know them." (Matt. 7:20.)

THE TEST

ADELINA PATTI, the great singer, upon her marriage to Baron de Cederstrom, left an order at her home that her letters should all be forwarded to the Cannes post office. When she arrived she went to the post office and asked if there were any letters for the Baroness Adelina de Cederstrom-Patti. "Lots of them," was the reply. "Then, please, will you give them to me?" requested the Baroness. To which the postmaster inquired, "Have you an old letter by which I can identify you?" "No, sir; I have nothing but my visiting card. Here it is." "Oh, that's not enough, madam; anyone can get visiting cards of other people. If you want your letters you will have to give me a better proof of your identity than that." A brilliant idea then struck Mme. Patti. She began to sing. A touching song she chose—the one beginning, "A voice loving and tender"—and never did she put more heart into the melody. Marvelous was the change as the exquisite music broke through the intense silence. In a few minutes the quiet post office was filled with people, and hardly had the singer concluded the first few lines of the ballad when an old clerk came forward and said, trembling with excitement, "It's Patti! Patti! There's none but Adelina Patti who can sing like that!" "Well, are you satisfied now?" the singer asked of the official who had doubted her identity. The only reply which he made was to go to the drawer and hand her the pile of letters.

If we are to convince the world of the divinity of Jesus Christ and His power to transform poor sinful human hearts and lives into His own likeness, then we must prove it by the living testimony of our lives. We must learn to sing the heavenly music.—*Selected.*

> Glad with Thy light, and glowing with Thy love,
> So let me ever speak and think and move
>   As fits a soul new-touched with life from Heaven,
> That seeks but so to order all her course
>   As most to show the glory of that Source
> By Whom her strength, her hope, her life are given.
> —*C. J. P. Spitta.*

July 4

"And let the beauty of the Lord our God be upon us: . . ."
(Psalm 90: 17.)

THE THREADS YOU USE

*Of what are you weaving your life
  today,
  Of fast-fading pleasures or joys
    that stay?
Do you want it completed in lovely
  hues?
  It will all depend on the threads
    you use!*

*Take only the best from the maze
  you find,
  The threads that will strengthen
    your heart and mind;
Just threads you are sure of, beyond
  a doubt,
  Durable threads that will not wear
    out.*

*You will want some colorful, gay
  and bright,
  Beautiful, too, but they must be
    right;
No snags, no knots, no colors that
  run,
  To make you ashamed in the days
    to come.*

*Some of the threads should be sturdy
  and plain
  The better, we know, to withstand
    the strain
Of the noonday sun and the scalding
  tears
  That are sure to come with the
    passing years.*

*To all of your threads you must add
  some gold,
  The wealth of God's Love—it will
    make them hold;*

For, in weaving a life of beautiful
hues,
It always depends on the threads
you use!
—Alice Hansche Mortenson.

July 5

"Ye are our epistles written in our hearts, known and read
of all men: ... written not with ink, but with the Spirit of the
living God; . . ." (2 Cor. 3: 2, 3.)

WHO IS READING YOU?

DR. J. H. FRANKLIN relates a striking experience of a missionary to the islands of the Inland Sea near Japan. One evening a sailor came to him and asked him to call upon a man on another island who was under a deep sense of spiritual need.

The missionary, tired out after a hard day's work, turned to a recent convert and said, "I am dreadfully tired. Won't you go and take him a Bible?" The friend replied, "No, teacher. It is not time to take that man a Bible. That book is yours, and now, thank God, it is mine also, but it is not time to take that man a Bible. Teacher, that man is reading *you* yet awhile."

The missionary could not sleep that night. He kept hearing those words over and over again: "That man is reading you ...." Before daybreak he set out to see the man.

"The Christian is the only Bible the great majority ever look at. Ought we not then so to live as to require no commentary to explain us?"

It was said of a great missionary: "There is no difference between him and the Book."

You are the Bible they will read the most,
They shall see Father, Son, and Holy Ghost
Within its pages. Reading they shall claim
Their great possessions in the fragrant Name.
—Fay Inchfawn.

One example is worth a thousand arguments.

"Dear Master, show me more and more
Thy beauty,
That, gazing on Thy brightness
day by day,
I may reflect a little of Thy lustre;
And thus help others
on their homeward way.

July 6

"Let no man despise thy youth; but be thou an example of the believers, in word, in conversation, in charity, in spirit, in faith, in purity." (1 Tim. 4: 12.)

YOUR IMPRESS

Now what is your niche in the mind of the man who met you yesterday?

He figured you out and labeled you; then carefully filed you away.

Are you on his list as one to respect, or as one to be ignored?

Does he think you the sort that's sure to win, or the kind that's quickly floored?

The things you said—were they those that stick, or the kind that fade and die?

The story you told—did you tell it your best? If not, in all conscience, why?

Your notion of things in the world of trade—did you make that notion clear?

Did you make it sound to the listener as though it were good to hear?

Did you mean, right down in your heart of hearts, the things that you then expressed?

Or was it the talk of a better man in clumsier language dressed?

Did you think while you talked, or but glibly recite what you had heard or read?

Had you made it your own—this saying of yours—or quoted what others said?

Think—what is your niche in the mind of the man who met you yesterday

And figured you out and labeled you; then carefully filed you away?

—*Strickland W. Gillilan.*

Phillips Brooks was the soul of saintliness—saintliness with red blood. To see him walk along a Boston street made the day, if it was dark and gloomy, bright and sunny. The atmosphere of a whole church has been changed by a single beautiful soul within that church; the tone of an entire schoolroom has been made different by the spirit of a noble Christian youth who studied there.

"The influence of a person whose heart God has touched is like a breath of fresh air in a hot room."

July 7

"*. . . Not I, but Christ . . .*" (Gal. 2: 20.)

ONE of the marks of highest worth is deep lowliness. The shallow nature, conscious of its weakness and insufficiency, is always trying to advertise itself and make sure of its being appreciated. The strong nature, conscious of its strength, is willing to wait and let its work be made manifest in due time. Indeed, the truest natures are so free from all self-consciousness and self-consideration that their object is not to be appreciated, understood or recompensed, but to accomplish their true mission and fulfill the real work of life.

> *Climbing the mountain pathway*
> *No lovelier flower I see*
> *Than the shy little violet,*
> *Hiding modestly.*
>
> —*Japanese poet.*

"One day," said Andrew A. Bonar, "a friend of mine, passing down a Glasgow street, saw a crowd at a shop door, and he had the curiosity to look in. There he saw an auctioneer holding up a grand picture so that all could see it. When he got it into position, he remained behind it, and said to the crowd, 'Look at this part of the picture . . . and now at this part,' and so on, describing each detail of it. 'Now,' said my friend, 'the whole time I was there I never saw the speaker, but only the picture he was showing.'"

> *"Not I, but Christ," be honored, loved, exalted;*
> *"Not I, but Christ," be seen, be known, be heard;*
> *"Not I, but Christ," in every look and action;*
> *"Not I, but Christ," in every thought and word.*
>
> *"Not I, but Christ," in lowly, silent labor;*
> *"Not I, but Christ," in humble, earnest toil;*
> *Christ, only Christ! no show, no ostentation;*
> *Christ, none but Christ the gath'rer of the spoil.*
>
> *Christ, only Christ, ere long will fill my vision;*
> *Glory excelling soon, full soon I'll see—*
> *Christ, only Christ, my ev'ry wish fulfilling—*
> *Christ, only Christ, my All in All to be.*
>
> —*Hymnal.*

O Lord, how I long to be centered in Thee, so completely centered in Thee that I do not realize it.

> —*A Little Book of Prayers,*
> *by Oswald Chambers.*

July 8

"Who hath woe? who hath sorrow? who hath contentions? who hath babbling? who hath wounds without cause? who hath redness of eyes? They that tarry long at the wine; they that go to seek mixed wine." (Prov. 23: 29, 30.)

AS I LOOKED around and came to know more of people and things, I found the always unanswerable argument in favor of a young man's abstinence: that is, that the most successful men in America today are those who never lift a wineglass to their lips. Becoming interested in this fact, I had the curiosity to inquire personally into it, and of twenty-eight of the leading business men in the country, whose names I selected at random, twenty-two never touch a drop of wine of any sort. I made up my mind that there was some reason for this. If the liquor brought safe pleasures, why did these men abstain from it? If it is a stimulant to a busy man, why did not these men directing the largest business interests in this country resort to it? And when I saw that these were the men whose opinions in great business matters were accepted by the leading concerns of the world, I concluded that their judgment in the use of liquor would satisfy me.

—*Edward W. Bok, in Christian Herald.*

On the day in 1874 when David Livingstone was buried in Westminster Abbey the streets of London were lined with thousands seeking to pay respect to the memory of the pioneer missionary. In the crowd was noticed an old man, poorly clad, ragged, and weeping bitterly. Some one went to him and asked him why he was weeping when all were seeking to honor the illustrious dead. "I'll tell you why," the old man replied. "Davie (Livingstone) and I were born in the same village, brought up in the same day school and Sunday school, and worked together at the same loom. But Davie went that way, and I went this; now he is honored by the nation, and I am neglected, unknown, and dishonored. I have nothing to look forward to but a drunkard's grave."

"Tread all the powers of darkness down, and win the well-fought day."—*Charles Wesley.*

> *"Yield not to temptation, for yielding is sin;*
> *Each victory will help you some other to win:*
> *Fight manfully onward, dark passions subdue;*
> *Look ever to Jesus; He will carry you through.*
>
> *Ask the Saviour to help you,*
> *Comfort, strengthen, and keep you;*
> *He is willing to aid you,*
> *He will carry you through."*

July 9

"Be still, and know that I am God:..." (Psalm 46: 10.)

THE BLESSING OF QUIETNESS

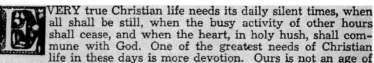VERY true Christian life needs its daily silent times, when all shall be still, when the busy activity of other hours shall cease, and when the heart, in holy hush, shall commune with God. One of the greatest needs of Christian life in these days is more devotion. Ours is not an age of prayer so much as an age of work. The tendency is to action rather than to worship, to busy toil rather than to quiet sitting at the Saviour's feet to commune with Him. The keynote of our present Christian life is consecration, which is understood to mean devotion to active service. On every hand we are incited to work. Our zeal is stirred by every inspiring incentive. The calls to duty come to us from a thousand earnest voices.

Your life needs days of retirement, when it shuts the gates upon the noisy whirl of action and is alone with God.

> *I need wide spaces in my heart*
> *Where faith and I can go apart*
> *And grow serene.*
>
> *Life gets so choked by busy living,*
> *Kindness so lost in fussy giving,*
> *That love slips by unseen.*
>
> *I want to make a quiet place*
> *Where those I love can see God's face,*
> *Can stretch their hearts across the earth,*
> *Can understand what spring is worth,*
> *Can count the stars,*
> *Watch violets grow,*
> *And learn what birds and children know.*
> *—Anonymous.*

Lord, for all who are taxed physically, undertake with Thy sweet strength and sustaining. Prevent the exacting of Satan, and may the joy and strength of God be marvelous today. Cleanse me from flurry, and keep me purely and calmly Thine. Gather me into concentrated peace on Thee. Come in Thy great and quiet almightiness.

—A Little Book of Prayers, by Oswald Chambers.

July 10

"And Jesus, walking by the sea of Galilee, saw two brethren, Simon called Peter, and Andrew his brother, casting a net into the sea: for they were fishers. And he saith unto them, Follow me, and I will make you fishers of men." (Matt. 4: 18, 19.)

THERE is a legend of an artist who long sought for a piece of sandalwood out of which to carve a Madonna. At last he was about to give up in despair, leaving the vision of his life unrealized, when in a dream he was bidden to shape the figure from a block of oak wood which was destined for the fire. Obeying the command, he produced from the log of common firewood a masterpiece. In like manner, many people wait for great and brilliant opportunities for doing the good things, the beautiful things, of which they dream, while through all the plain, common days, the very opportunities they require for such deeds lie close to them in the simplest and most familiar passing events, and in the homeliest circumstances. They wait to find sandalwood out of which to carve Madonnas, while far more lovely Madonnas than they dream of are hidden in the common logs of oak they spurn with their feet in the woodyard."

—*J. R. Miller, D. D.*

Common things are beautiful when they are linked to Christ. It is a great day when we discover God in the common bush.

When we enjoy a closer walk with God, common things will wear the hues of heaven.

Do not wait for the spectacular!

It is very noticeable in all history that the larger part of the great men in every department have sprung from the common people, so far as the absence of wealth or rank, or great ancestry can make them common.

July 11

"O satisfy us early with thy mercy; that we may rejoice and be glad all our days." (Psalm 90: 14.)

HE story is told of a youth who one day found a gold coin on the street. He became a man, but he had acquired the habit of always keeping his eyes on the ground as he walked, expecting to find coins. He never saw the trees, or the flowers which grew in beauty beside the paths; he never saw the purple hills, the lovely valleys, the majestic mountains. To him our Father's lovely world meant only a place in which to look for coins.

Bunyan's man with the muckrake could look no way but down, so he lost his crown.

KIRBY, THE ROSE LOVER

I've been down to Kirby, down to Kirby and his
     roses,
And his peonies and pansies, and his countless
     stock of posies,
And he never mentioned dollars, never talked
     about his neighbors,
Never spoke a word of scandal or the hardship of
     his labors.
But he led me through his gardens, and his eyes
     with kindness glowing,
Like a father to his children, talked of living
     things and growing.

We spent the day with blossoms, stood about and
     talked them over,
Saw the orchards pink with beauty, and the
     meadows white with clover.
And he taught me little secrets of the peonies
     and roses,
As one mother to another all that she has learned
     discloses.
Taught me how and when to plant them, how to know
     wild shoots from true ones,
What to cherish of the old ones, what is worthy of
     the new ones.

Oh, I don't know how to tell it, but I felt my
     soul expanding,
Felt my vision growing wider as with Kirby I was
     standing,
And I thought my little garden could be lovelier
     and brighter,
That my roses might grow redder and my peonies
     grow whiter,
And my life a little finer if I recognized my duty
And thought less of selfish profit and a little
     more of beauty.—Edgar A. Guest.

"One should learn to enjoy the neighbor's garden—the roses straggling over the fence, the scent of lilacs drifting across the road."

July 12

"...They came and saw where he dwelt, and abode with him that day:..." (John 1:39.)

I WONDERED what it was that lured your feet to follow Him upon His homeward way. Was it mere eagerness to see the street and house in which He sojourned and to stay at closer quarters with Him for one day?

...Or, did you feel a strange attractive Power, which lured you from your boat beside the bay; when, heeding not the passing of the hour, and caring not what other folks might say, you made your home with Him for that brief day?

... Perhaps you felt a holy discontent, after the hours spent in that Presence fair? Certain it is, you thenceforth were intent on fishing men; for, from His side you went, and straightway brought your brother to Him there!

... Oh, Andrew! you could never be the same, after the contact of that wondrous day. You ne'er again could play with passion's flame, or harbour pride or hate, or grasp for fame, or give to avarice a place to stay.

... Rather, I think, you might be heard to say, "Something about Him burned my pride away, and cooled my hate and changed it for Love's way .... *After the healing contact of that stay, I must bring Simon to have one such day!"*

... And, ever after, as men passed your way, they would be conscious of some strange, new spell—some unexplained, mysterious miracle. Then, in awe-filled whisper they would say, *"Andrew is greatly altered since that day!"*

... Oh! Wondrous Sojourner on life's dark way. Saviour! Who understands what sinners say, *Grant me to come beneath Thy magic sway, lest, rough-edged, loveless, sin-stained, I should stay, lacking the impress of just such a day!*

—*Eleanor Vellacott Wood.*

July 13

"...Quit you like men, be strong." (1 Cor. 16:13.)

DO NOT pray for easy lives! Pray to be stronger men. Do not pray for tasks equal to your powers. Pray for powers equal to your tasks. Then the doing of your work shall be no miracle, but you shall be a miracle.

—*Phillips Brooks.*

We must remember that it is not in any easy or self-indulgent life that Christ will lead us to greatness. The easy life leads not upward, but downward. Heaven always is above us, and we

must ever be looking up toward it. There are some people who
always avoid things that are costly, that require self-denial, or
self-restraint and sacrifice, but toil and hardship show us the only
way to nobleness. Greatness comes not by having a mossy path
made for you through the meadow, but by being sent to hew out
a roadway by your own hands. Are you going to reach the mountain splendors?—*Selected.*

> *O God, not like a stagnant pool*
> *With tepid depths, let my life be;*
> *But like a stream, undaunted, cool,*
> *That plunges, surges toward the sea.*
>
> *O God, not like a sodden log,*
> *Now dead, though once a stately tree;*
> *But pushing high above the bog*
> *Still upward yearning, let life be!*
> —*J. Gordon Howard.*

SCALE THE HEIGHTS YOU SEE!

July 14

*"For it is God which worketh in you both to will and to do
of his good pleasure."* (Phil. 2: 13.)

GOD'S great works are carried on in silence. All noiselessly
the planets move in their orbits. "There is no speech or
language where their voice is not heard." The dewdrops
form themselves in quiet peacefulness on the summer
grass, and the light of the morning breaks in softness
over the silent earth. There is no crying of "Lo, here!" or "Lo,
there!" before the rising of the sun. Its simple presence is the
only announcement.

So in the spiritual movements we should have more confidence in the undemonstrative influence that is constant than
in the fitful effort that is noisy and sensational. This is a truth
that is too sadly forgotten in these days. We have fallen upon
an age of bustle, trumpet blowing, and advertising. It would
seem as if many believed that they could take the world by storm.
There is more faith in the earthquake than in the Still Small Voice.
We are forgetting that the mightiest power in the world, next only
to the Spirit of God Himself, is the power of Christlike character.
It were well, therefore, that the voices among us were less noisy
and the deeds were more pronounced. Better a star than a meteor;
better a beacon that is steady than a marshfire that is flickering
and changeable. Life is more potent than words. By life, "without a word," things will be accomplished which could not be se-

cured even by the most glowing words "without the life."
—*Wm. M. Taylor, D.D.*

"One great evidence of my abiding in Christ is quietness of spirit. I have my portion elsewhere, and I go on. No matter what it may be, we bring quietness of spirit into all circumstances whilst dwelling with God. The soul is not only happy in God for itself, but it will bring the tone of that place out with it."—*J. N. D.*

"If we are quiet we shall hear.
If we hear we shall be quiet."

"God's noiseless workers own His calm control."

July 15

"For who maketh thee to differ from another? and what hast thou that thou didst not receive? now if thou didst receive it, why dost thou glory, as if thou hadst not received it." (1 Cor. 4:7.)

A GIFT OF PROVIDENCE

FRITZ KREISLER regards his musical ability as a gift from God, and he treats it as a sacred trust.

"I receive messages from men and women located in many parts of the globe telling me that my music gives them happiness," he says. "If that is so, then I am happy — happy that I can bring cheer to at least a few in this sad world of ours. As for the financial end of my art—to be quite truthful, I must admit that, as my dear father did not believe in selling his medical knowledge, so it nauseates me to have to sell my musical ability.

"I was born with music in my system. I knew musical scores instinctively before I knew my ABC's. It was a gift of Providence. I did not acquire it. So I do not even deserve thanks for the music.

"Do you thank birds for flying in the sky, or do the birds charge you fees for singing in the woods? Music is too sacred to be sold.... I never look upon the money I earn as my own. It is public money. It belongs to the public. It is only a trust fund entrusted to my care for proper disbursement.

"So the money I earn I never spend in high living or for my personal pleasure. How can I squander money on myself while there is so much misery, so much hunger in the world? As a matter of fact, to be perfectly healthy the human body does not need much. We create and increase our needs; develop costly habits; then feel miserable when we cannot have things."

In 1860, Franz Liszt, the great musician, wrote ... "Christ crucified, the madness and elevation of the Cross—this is my true vocation." .

"No man can truly say that he has made a success of life unless he has written at the top of his life journal, 'Enter God.'"

—*Robert Louis Stevenson.*

"The world's praise is a puff of wind." —*An Indian saying.*

July 16

"Thou therefore endure hardness, as a good soldier of Jesus Christ." (2 Tim. 2:3.)

"DIE hard, my men, die hard!" shouted Colonel Inglis of the 57th Division to his men on the heights behind the River Albuhera. The regiment was nicknamed "the Die-hards" after that. The tale may have been forgotten, but the name lives on; and in spite of foolish uses, it is a great name. It challenges us. We are called to be the Lord's "Die-hards," to whom can be committed any kind of trial of endurance, and who can be counted upon to stand firm no matter what happens. It is written of Cromwell: "He strove to give his command so strict a unity that in no crisis should it crack." With this aim in view, he made his Ironsides. The result of that discipline was seen not only in victory but in defeat; for his troops, "though they were beaten and routed, presently rallied again and stood in good order until they received new orders." This is the spirit that animates all valiant life; to be strong in will, to strive, to seek, to find, and not to yield is all that matters. Failure or success, as the world understands these words, is of no eternal account. To be able to stand steady in defeat is in itself a victory. There is no tinsel about that kind of triumph.

> *"It's a fight and a hard fight,*
> *And a fight to the end,*
> *For life is no sleep in the clover;*
> *It's a fight for the boy*
> *And a fight for the man,*
> *And a fight until days are all over!"*

The Indians have a saying that when a warrior kills a foe the spirit of the vanquished enters the victor's heart and adds to his strength for every future struggle. In the weird fancy lies a truth. Each defeat leaves us weaker for the next battle, but each conquest makes us stronger.

July 17

"Ponder the path of thy feet, and let all thy ways be established." (Prov. 4:26.)

WALK circumspectly! You have sometimes seen the top of a wall covered with mortar, and in the mortar, pieces of glass, so as to prevent boys from going along. I have seen a cat walk along the top of that wall; and it walks circumspectly—picks its way! With what carefulness it puts down its foot, each time looking for a place *between* those broken bits of glass. You and I have to walk like that if we are going to do anything for God in the world.

—*D. L. Moody.*

Lord Kitchener said this fine thing of General Gordon: "Gordon was a white man without a smudge." That was a soldier's blunt but forceful way of putting it. You know what a smudge is—a smudged copybook—a smudged character—"Gordon was a white man without a smudge."

"Wearing the white flower of a blameless life!"

Let us not cast ourselves needlessly into situations where our most cherished convictions are likely to be assailed by wanton men. Take care of warming yourself by the world's fire.

July 18

". . . A chosen vessel . . ." (Acts 9:15.)

GOD is preparing His leaders, His heroes; and when opportunity comes He can fit them into their places in a moment, and the world will wonder from whence they came and under what mighty leadership had they received their fitness.

ABRAHAM LINCOLN

Child of the boundless prairie, son of
the virgin soil,
Heir to the bearing of burdens,
brother to them that toil;
God and nature together shaped him to
lead in the van,
In the stress of her wildest weather when
the nation needed a man.

Eyes of a smouldering fire, heart of a lion
  at bay,
Patience to plan for tomorrow, valor to
  serve for today;
Mournful and mirthful and tender, quick as
  a flash with a jest,
Hiding with gibe and great laughter the ache
  that was dull in his breast!

Met were the man and the hour—man who
  was strong for the shock!
Fierce were the lightnings unleashed; in the
  midst he stood fast as a rock;
Comrade he was, and commander, he who
  was meant for the time;
Iron in council and action, simple, aloof, and
  sublime.

Swift slip the years from their tether, cen-
  turies pass like a breath;
Only some lives are immortal, challenging
  darkness and death,
Hewn from the stuff of the martyrs, write in
  the star dust his name,
Glowing, untarnished, transcendant, high on
  the records of fame.
                    —Margaret E. Sangster.

Youth! Give to the world a masterpiece!

July 19

"*...Except a corn of wheat fall into the ground and die, it abideth alone: but if it die, it bringeth forth much fruit. . . . if any man serve me, let him follow me . . .*" (John 12: 24, 26.)

THOMAS GAJETAN RAGLAND, a second Henry Martyn in mathematical attainment and in devotion as a missionary, wrote the following three lessons as proved in his experience in India:

1. "Of all qualifications for mission work, and every other work, charity or love is the most excellent." (1 Cor. 13.)

2. "Of all methods of attaining to a position of usefulness and honour, the only safe and sure one is purging our hearts from vainglory, worldliness, and selfishness." (2 Tim. 2:21.)

3. "Of all plans for ensuring success, the most certain is Christ's own—becoming as a corn of wheat, falling into the ground, and dying." (John 12:24.)

That was the law of our Lord nineteen hundred years ago, who lost His life and His fame, who just went around over the world talking to men and women, taking little children up in His arms and ignoring what the world esteemed. Men asked Him to use His masterful gifts of organization to set up a kingdom. They came by force to make Him king, but He went off into the wilderness that He might be alone. At last He actually died and went away without having lifted His finger to perpetuate His movement by any of those devices on which men rely for influence and immortality.

He lost His life. Did He? Why, He has found it again—in tens of millions throughout all the ages over all the world! There are more representatives of Christ today than ever; and they will go on multiplying until the end of time. The corn of wheat fell into the ground and died, and it did not abide alone.

The young Prince of Glory died when He was young. Of His own will and in the conquering strength of a wholehearted decision He went to the Cross for us.

THE SOUL-WINNER'S SECRET

"If it die...much fruit."
(John 12:24.)

There is no field without a seed.
Life raised through death is life indeed.
The smallest, lowliest little flower
A secret is, of mighty power
To live—it dies—buried to rise—
Abundant life through sacrifice.
Would'st thou know sacrifice?
It is through loss;
Thou can'st not save but by the Cross.
A corn of wheat, except it die,
Can never, never multiply.
The glorious fields of waving gold,
Through death are life a hundredfold.
Thou who for souls dost weep and pray,
Let not hell's legions thee dismay.
This is the way of ways for thee,
The way of certain victory.

—*Selected.*

"*Gideon threshed wheat . . . And the angel of the Lord . . . said unto him, The Lord is with thee, . . .*" (Judges 6: 11, 12.)

July 20

"...The place whereon thou standest is holy ground."
(Exod. 3: 5.)

WHEN YOU HAVE FOUND YOUR PLACE

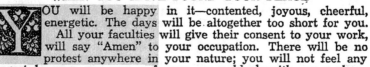

YOU will be happy in it—contented, joyous, cheerful, energetic. The days will be altogether too short for you. All your faculties will give their consent to your work, will say "Amen" to your occupation. There will be no protest anywhere in your nature; you will not feel any regret because you are a farmer, or a blacksmith, or a shoemaker, because whatever your occupation or profession, you will be an artist instead of an artisan. You will not apologize because you are not this or that, for you will have found your place, and will be satisfied.

You will feel yourself growing in your work, and your life broadening and deepening.

Your work will be a perpetual tonic to you. There will be no drudgery in it. You will go to your task with delight and leave it with regret. Life will be a glory, not a grind.

—*Great Thoughts.*

A man I know has made an altar
Of his factory bench.
And one has turned the counter in his store
Into a place of sacrifice and holy ministry.
Another still has changed his office desk
Into a pulpit desk, from which to speak and
*　　write,*
Transforming commonplace affairs
Into the business of the King.
A Martha in our midst has made
Her kitchen table a communion table.
A postman makes his daily round
A walk in the temple of God. . . .

To all of these each daily happening
Has come to be a whisper from the lips of
*　　God,*
Each separate task a listening post,
And every common circumstance
A wayside shrine.
　　　　　—*Edgar Tramp, in Christian Century.*

The surrender of the costliest possession of my life is the key to the treasures of the Kingdom for me.

July 21

"Every man according as he purposeth in his heart, so let him give; not grudgingly, or of necessity: for God loveth a cheerful giver." (2 Cor. 9:7.)

WHEN the English Government sought to reward General Charles George Gordon for his brilliant services in China, General Gordon declined all money or titles, but finally accepted a gold medal inscribed with the record of his thirty-three engagements. It was his most prized possession. But after his death the medal could not be found. Eventually it was learned that he had sent it to Manchester during a severe famine, directing that it should be melted down and used to buy bread for the poor. Under the date of its sending, these words were found written in his diary: "The last and only thing I had in this world that I valued I have given over to the Lord Jesus Christ."

> *It is not what you have that matters,*
> *It is what you do with what you have.*
> —*Sir Wilfred Grenfell.*

Does it seem strange that we should think of making gifts to God? It was not strange in the Jewish religion, nor should it seem so in the Christian religion. Life offers no opportunities fraught with greater meaning than is contained in the idea that we can do something for God. "Sacrificing to God"—whether it be the cattle of the stall, the grain of the field, or the result of the labor of the hand, the essential idea is the same; we are doing something for God, and He is pleased with our gifts.

SACRIFICE

> *"Is sacrifice so hard a thing?*
> *We give a useless seed*
> *To God's kind care, and —lo! —we reap*
> *A harvest for our need."*

When William Borden, Yale University student and multimillionaire, was asked why he should throw his life away in missionary work, his answer was, "You have never *seen* heathenism!" When he was called Home at 25, he left more gifts for missionary work than any man of his age had ever done before. He not only gave away his great fortune but laid down his lovely young life in answering "the call."

"Greater love hath no man than this, that a man lay down his life for his friends." (John 15: 13.)

July 22

" . . . I was not disobedient to the heavenly vision."
(Acts 26: 19.)

WANT to wear out my life for Him!" said David Brainerd when the vision of the compassionate Christ filled his soul. Can there be anything more beautiful, more wonderful, than the victory which crowned the life of that suffering missionary who brought back from his field of service a pitifully broken body but a marvelously triumphant spirit? By a sort of code which he managed with his stubs of legs he communicated this message to his friend, as he lay on his bed in a hospital in England: "You ask me how I am. I have lost my eyesight now, and my voice, no feet and ankles, and no arms, but my heart is far from dead. I have no doubt in these days, and if I had my voice I should sing all the day long. My little room shines with the glory of an invisible Presence, and my heart thrills with the abiding fullness of the joy of God."

Why was he so radiantly happy? Simply this: he had accepted the will of God for his life. He had answered to the call of God, "Here am I, Lord, send me." He had said, "I go," and he went.

> *"It is enough,*
> *I come.*
> *Christ's human face, divinely lit,*
> *And God's love shining out from it*
> *Have conquered.*
> *I come,*
> *It is enough.*
>
> *Is it enough?*
> *I go!*
> *His hand points to the farthest shore*
> *Where human hands outstretched are begging for*
> *The Christ who conquered—lo,*
> *It is enough,*
> *I go!"*

That life is long which answers life's great end. —*Young.*

> *"We go in faith, our own great weakness feeling,*
> *And needing more each day Thy grace to know:*
> *Yet from our hearts a song of triumph pealing;*
> *We rest on Thee, and in Thy name we go."*

July 23

"...Thy Father, which seeth in secret, shall reward thee openly." (Matt. 6:18.)

FAITHFUL UNDER COVER

When to the front you cannot go
Be faithful under cover;
God needs a secret service, too,
The one to help the other.
It may be in the engine-room,
Just firing the old boiler
Where it's dark and lonely, lad;
Be faithful under cover.

First, find the place of secret prayer;
Be faithful under cover;
Fast close the door and linger there—
It is the place of power.
If in the home and kitchen, lass,
Your calling you discover,
In woman's hand is destiny;
Be faithful under cover.

Elijah, in the wilderness,
Was faithful under cover;
God's hidden man was sent to warn
Of dearth, the country over.
Then, if like him to Cherith sent
To wait the coming shower,
He'll keep and feed and cherish you
Be faithful under cover.

Perchance, you've been at battle's front;
Now, faithful under cover;
Your health is gone, you cannot work,
You feel your day is over.
Look up! Cheer up! You're not thro' yet,
God is your gracious Lover;
'Tis in the heart man serves Him best,
Be faithful under cover.

—Mrs. E. W. Grossman.

"To succeed in life," Palmer explains, "live as nearly a selfless life as possible and go beyond what is expected." His motto is "Do all you can and then some." He says it's the "then some" that gets your salary raised. He is firmly convinced that service begins where compensation ends.

July 24

"Set your affection on things above, not on things on the earth." (Col. 3:2.)

A COLLEGE youth was on the verge of making the supreme consecration when the tempter whispered, "There is too much to be sacrificed, for the path of the religious life is hard and stony, and all the pleasures will have to be given up, and you will be miserable to the end of your days."

He slept, and upon awakening in the morning, these words were impressed upon him with overpowering force: "My yoke is easy and my burden is light; only follow me," an all-persuading Voice seemed to say, "and all the years that haunt you shall vanish forever."

Christ's own path led up the hill of Calvary, and there was roughness in the way, but the glory lay beyond the Cross.

God give to you courage to climb up into the mountains where the air is purer and sweeter than in the vales.

THE NAMELESS SEEKER

We are not told his name—this "rich young ruler"
  Who sought the Lord that day;
We only know that he had great possession
  And that—he went away.

He went away—from joy and peace and power;
  From love unguessed, untold;
From that eternal life that he was seeking,
  Back to his paltry gold.

He went away; he kept his earthly treasure,
  But oh, at what a cost!
Afraid to take the Cross and lose his riches—
  And God and Heaven were lost.

So for the tinsel bonds that held and drew him
  What honor he let slip—
Comrade of John and Paul and friend of Jesus—
  What glorious fellowship!

For they who left their all to follow Jesus
  Have found a deathless fame,
On His immortal scroll of saints and martyrs
  God wrote each shining name.

We should have read his there—the rich young ruler—
If he had stayed that day;
Nameless—though Jesus loved him—ever nameless
Because—he went away.
                                        —*Author Unknown.*

"For what shall it profit a man, if he shall gain the whole world, and lose his own soul? (Mark 8: 36.)

Learn to root your soul in timeless things.

July 25

"And herein do I exercise myself, to have always a conscience void of offence toward God, and toward men."
                                        (Acts 24: 16.)

DROP of water on a polished blade may leave very little mark if wiped off instantly. But if it is allowed to remain for days and weeks, how different will be the effect produced! Thus it is with sin. Whether it be in thought or action, the forbidden thing indulged in will gradually intrench itself in your moral being, and if not mortified by the power of the Spirit, it will become a part of yourself in spite of yourself! How all-important, then, to see that no iniquity is having the dominion, and that you are not acquiring any habit that shall yet involve you in eternal loss.

>*"When you have done an evil thing*
>*No matter what its size,*
>*No matter what reward it brings;*
>*Something in you dies."*

"A bad habit is first a caller, then a guest, and at last a master."
                                        —*Talmud.*

"Trifles unnoticed by us may be links in the chain of sin."

There are no *little* sins.

"Sir," said Samuel Johnson, "the chains of habit are generally too small to be felt until they are too strong to be broken. Habits are at first cobwebs—at last cables."

An Indian, asked to define conscience, said, "It is a little three-cornered thing in here. When I do wrong it turns around and hurts very much. If I keep on doing wrong, it will turn until it wears the edges all off, and then it will not hurt any more."

"It is Calvary courage and Calvary calm,
And the character sketched in the fifteenth Psalm,
That I pray for to be such a soul, if I can,
As heaven would hold for a gentleman."

—Selected.

July 26

"... Did not our heart burn within us, while he talked with
us by the way, and while he opened to us the scriptures?"
(Luke 24: 32.)

THE NARROW WAY

'Tis such a narrow pathway,
Yet there's room enough for two,
There's room to walk with Jesus
And for Him to walk with you.
You would lose Him on the broad way,
The crowd would press between,
And only in the narrow path
The heart on Him can lean.

'Tis in the narrow pathway
Your eyes can meet His own,
No need for other counsellors,
Help comes from Him alone;
Oh, blessed, narrow pathway
Where there's but space for two,
Just room to walk with Jesus
And for Him to walk with you.

—Beatrice Cleland.

Ideal companionship is found in Christ.

KINSHIP

Today I walked beside Him
And my littleness of mind
With all its petty meanness
Was left behind.
For something of His presence—
Something lovely and divine—
Something of His largeness
Became as mine.
With Him I felt a oneness
Such as gave me certainty
Of power through a kinship
With the Infinity.

—Edith Dunn Bolar.

July 27

"But Daniel purposed in his heart . . ." (Daniel 1:8.)

BE A decided, *out-and-out* Christian! It is the only way to be happy, safe, and useful.

First, be clear about your standing in Christ, by grace, through faith. There can be no real decision while you doubt this. Accept heartily the Word of God, and for Christ's sake, the salvation promised to those who *believe.* Then risk all for it! Whatever the consequences, make a bold stand for Christ.

This is the *happiest* course. Some believers try to live between Christ and the world. They are never happy, always conscious of inconsistency, always doubting and fearing. In seeking the good opinion of men, they lose the sense of God's favour. Fear *Him,* and you need fear none besides. Be decided and men will soon know what to expect of you.

This is also the *safest* course. Open decision for Christ is a great safeguard against backsliding. Some young believers shrink from it for fear of not "living up to it." This is wrong. Commit yourself openly to Christ's cause and trust Him to keep you.

Moreover, it is the *most useful* course. If you want to do real work for Christ, you *must* be decided. You must live out your profession to have influence with others. Your testimony will have weight as you act out fearlessly what you believe. Reality is one of the great secrets of power. But the salt that has "lost his savour" is good for nothing.

"One foot on sea and one on shore is not the attitude in which steadfastness or progress is possible."—*Alexander Maclaren.*

July 28

"But unto thee have I cried, O Lord; and in the morning shall my prayer come before thee." (Psalm 88:13, Trans.)

IN THE diary of Dr. Chalmers we repeatedly come upon entries which express what may be called *the morning grace of appropriation.* 'Began my first waking minutes with a confident hold of Christ as my Saviour.' 'A day of great quietness.' 'Began the day with a distinct act of confidence in my Saviour; but why not a perennial confidence in my Saviour?'

"The morning makes the day. To think of morning is to think of a bloom and fragrance which, if missed then, cannot be overtaken later in the day. The Lord Jesus stood upon the shore in

the morning and showed Himself to a company of weary, dis-
illusioned men who had toiled all night and taken nothing. He
ever stands upon life's most dreary and time-worn shores, and as
we gaze upon Him the shadows flee away and *it is morning.* 'When
I awake I am still with Thee.' "—*Wings of the Morning.*

Morning by morning waken me, my Father,
   Let Thy voice be the first my soul to greet,
Bidding my spirit rise from earthly slumber,
   And sit a learner at Thy sacred feet.

There, in the stillness, open Thy good treasure,
   The precious things of Christ unfolding still,
And, as Thy Spirit brings them to remembrance,
   Let gratitude and love my spirit fill.

Teach me to do Thy will, Thy pattern show me;
   Reveal Thy purpose for my life each day.
Then for Thy service with fresh oil anoint me,
   And with Thy presence hallow all my way.
               —*Freda Hanbury Allen.*

The hour before the dawn is the hour of inspiration; throughout
the day the stillness of the early morn will remain as a blessing.

Come, O Lord, like morning sunlight!

July 29

*"Ye have not chosen me, but I have chosen you, and or-
dained you, that ye should go and bring forth fruit . . ."*
(John 15: 16.)

HE HAS COMMITTED THE TASK TO US

HE CAME forth to reconcile the world unto God. In this
task He was faithful unto death and wrought a great
redemption. Now He has gone into the Heavens and
committed unto us the ministry of reconciliation. He says,
"Go ye into all the world and preach the gospel to
every creature." Even now, two thousand years later, it appears
as though the task has just begun!

"Oh, let me burn out for God!" cries Henry Martyn. He
plunges, like a blazing torch, into the darkness of India, of Persia,
and of Turkey. The brand plucked from the blaze has soon burned
out. But what does it matter? At its ardent flame a thousand
other torches have been ignited; and the lands that sat so long
in darkness welcome the coming of a wondrous light.
—*F. W. Boreham.*

In simple trust like theirs who heard
  Beside the Syrian sea
The gracious calling of the Lord,
Let us, like them, without a word
  Rise up and follow Thee.

—*Whittier.*

Not of the sunlight,
Not of the moonlight,
Not of the starlight!
O young Mariner,
Down to the haven
Call your companions,
Launch your vessel,
And crowd your canvas,
And, ere it vanishes
Over the margin,
After it, follow it,
Follow the Gleam.

—*Tennyson.*

July 30

"Hide me from the secret counsel of the wicked . . ."
(Psalm 64: 2.)

". . . Lead me to the rock that is higher than I. For thou hast been a shelter for me, and a strong tower from the enemy." (Psalm 61:2, 3.)

". . . Preserve my life from fear of the enemy." (Psalm 64:1.)

THE lion is said to be boldest in the storm. His roar, it is said, never sounds as loud as in the pauses of the thunder; and when the lightning flashes, brightest are the flashes of his cruel eye. Even so, he who "goeth about as a roaring lion seeking whom he may devour" often seizes the hour of human nature's greatest distress to assault us with his fiercest temptations. He tempted Job when he was bowed down with grief. He tempted Jesus when he was faint with hunger. He tempted Peter when he was weary with watching and heart-broken with sorrow.

When the devil's forces are besieging a low soul, he appeals as a rule to the lowest in him. When he is dealing with a high soul he attacks the highest in him; he appears as an angel of light. Even if the ridge line of our soul is but a low one, that crest marks the hottest place of conflict; a few feet farther down spells defeat.

In some of the American lakes it is found that boats are strangely hindered in their progress. They are drawn downwards, because of the magnetic power of deep mud concealed below the surface of the waters. Now, a temptation in the life is like this magnetic mud. It lies in the depths and pulls at everything; it drags down everything; it makes progress difficult.

Save us, O Lord, from the enemy who seeks to take us captive while we are unaware of his devices.

July 31

"Put on the whole armour of God, that ye may be able to stand against the wiles of the devil . . . . And take the helmet of salvation, and the sword of the Spirit, which is the word of God." (Eph. 6: 11, 17.)

GEORGE DOUGLAS tells a story of a young man who was packing his trunk for his first holiday away from home. As a friend stood by, the young man packed one article after the other—his suits, shoes, clothes, books, and his tennis racket and balls. There remained a space just about six inches by four inches; all the rest of the trunk was full. "What are you going to pack there?" asked the friend.

"I have reserved this corner," replied the young man, "to pack a guidebook, a lamp, a looking glass, a volume of poems, a microscope, a telescope, several fine biographies, a package of love letters, a book of songs, some histories, a hammer and a sword. I'm going to put in that little space the *Bible* my mother gave me."

We need to stand on guard against "holiday perils"; that is, the special dangers of boating, bathing, and climbing during the summer vacation. *Then* are we gay, hilarious, venturesome, off our guard! Many a worthy youth has had bitter reason to regret the lapses of gala days.

> *"Gird thy heavenly armour on;*
> *Wear it ever, night and day:*
> *Ambushed lies the evil one;*
> *Watch and pray."*

"My son, be strong," was the admonition of a man one time—a man who loved athletics and who said, "I keep my body under."

Keep this house spiritual and in all ways "exceeding Magnifical."

The soul is not a hovel, but a palace.

August 1

"And without controversy great is the mystery of godliness: God was manifest in the flesh, justified in the Spirit, seen of angels, preached unto the Gentiles, believed on in the world, received up into glory." (1 Tim. 3:16.)

SADHU SUNDAR SINGH was one who had an experience similar to that of St. Paul. When this great Hindu saint was visiting England a modernistic professor asked him to explain what there was in Christianity that he could not find in his Hindu religion that caused him to change his faith. He answered simply, "It was Christ!" The professor wasn't satisfied. "What teaching or doctrine is there in Christianity distinct from that of your former faith," he asked again. The Hindu saint replied, "It wasn't a teaching or a doctrine. It was the living Christ!" Still the professor objected, "Perhaps I haven't made my meaning clear. What is there in the philosophy of Christianity different from the philosophy of Hinduism which caused you to embrace Christianity?" "It was Christ!" was still his answer. Not just a creed, or a doctrine, or a philosophy, but a transforming Christ—crucified, risen, ascended, interceding, and coming again! Christ, divinely revealed to our hearts by the Holy Ghost—Christ in us the hope of glory!

> *Fairest Lord Jesus! Ruler of all nature!*
> *O Thou of God and man the Son! Thee will I cherish,*
> *Thee will I honor, Thou, my soul's glory, joy, and crown!*
>
> *Fair are the meadows, Fairer still the woodlands,*
> *Robed in the blooming garb of spring; Jesus is fairer,*
> *Jesus is purer, Who makes the woeful heart to sing!*
>
> *Fair is the sunshine, Fairer still the moonlight,*
> *And all the twinkling starry host; Jesus is fairer,*
> *Jesus shines purer, Than all the angels heaven can boast!*
> —*Hymn.*

"And Thomas answered and said unto him, My Lord and my God." (John 20:28.)

> *The boundless love of Jesus Christ,*
> *His Deity proclaim;*
> *Jesus is God! The "very God,"*
> *And hallowed be His Name.*
>
> *Jesus is God, and God's Delight,*
> *The Father loves the Son;*
> *The Holy Spirit in His might*
> *Proclaims the Three in One.*

August 2

"... Thou art worthy ... for thou wast slain, and hast redeemed us ... And hast made us unto our God kings and priests: ..." (Rev. 5: 9, 10.)

THE INCOMPARABLE CHRIST

HE CAME from the bosom of the Father to the bosom of a woman. He put on humanity that we might put on divinity. He became Son of Man that we might become sons of God. He came from heaven, where the rivers never freeze, winds never blow, frosts never chill the air, flowers, never fade, and no one is ever sick. No undertakers and no graveyards, for no one ever dies; no one is ever buried.

He was born contrary to the laws of nature, lived in poverty, was reared in obscurity; only once crossed the boundary of the land, in childhood. . . .

In infancy He startled a king; in boyhood He puzzled the doctors, in manhood ruled the course of nature. He walked upon the billows and hushed the sea. He healed the multitudes without medicine and made no charge for His services. . . . He never wrote a song, yet He furnished the theme for more songs than all song writers combined. He never founded a college, yet all the schools together cannot boast of as many students as He has. He never practised medicine, and yet He healed more broken hearts than the doctors healed broken bodies.

He never marshalled an army, drafted a soldier, nor fired a gun, yet no leader ever made more volunteers who have, under His orders, made rebels stack arms or surrender without a shot being fired.

He is the Star of astronomy, the Rock of geology, the Lion and the Lamb of zoology, the Harmonizer of all discords, and the Healer of all diseases. Great men have come and gone, yet He lives on. Herod could not kill Him, Satan could not seduce Him, death could not destroy Him, the grave could not hold Him.

He laid aside His purple robe for a peasant's gown. He was rich, yet for our sakes He became poor. How poor? Ask Mary! Ask the Wise men! He slept in another's manger. He cruised the lake in another's boat. He rode on another's ass. He was buried in another man's tomb. All failed, but He, never! The ever-perfect One—He is the Chief among ten thousand! He is ALTOGETHER LOVELY, and He is my Saviour!

"All I think, all I write, all I am, is based on the Divinity of Jesus Christ, the central Hope of our poor wayward race!" (*Words inscribed on the Gladstone Memorial.*)

—*Selected.*

August 3

"By faith they . . ." (Heb. 11: 29.)

GUARD the citadel of faith, sleep not, but watch and pray. Enemies at every gate are waiting night and day—to storm the walls, or to approach by guile and flattery— using wordy argument and high philosophy.

Guard it well. It's worth the strain, the effort, and the strife. It will be your tower of strength when come the storms of life, a fortress that will stand against the worst that Fate can do, a citadel of faith that none can conquer or subdue.

—*Patience Strong.*

> *FEAR knocked*
> *at the door;*
> *FAITH opened it*
> *And—there was*
> *no one there.*
> —*G. J. G.*

"If there should arise one *utterly believing man,* the history of the world might be changed."—*R. McAdam.*

August 4

". . . Have ye received the Holy Ghost since ye believed? . . ."
(Acts 19: 2.)

THE baptism of the Holy Spirit brings people into harmony with God and godly people, and into active and effective sympathy with the work of God in motive, purpose, and result. It is worth having! But it must be desired and received on God's terms, and in God's measure: by separation from sin and unbelief, and consecration unto God. Solemnly make a contract with God, stamp the contract with the seal of your lips, and God will stamp it with His seal."

—*Reader Harris, K. C.*

Nineteen hundred years ago the Holy Spirit did not reach the end of what He has to tell us!

What is this experience—the baptism with the Holy Spirit? James Brainerd Taylor writes:

"It was on the 23rd day of April, 1822, when I was on a visit to Haddam in Connecticut. Memorable day! The time and place will never be forgotten. For a long time my desire had been that the Lord would visit me and fill me with the Holy Spirit! My cry to Him was, 'Seal my soul forever thine!' I felt that I needed some-

thing I did not possess. At this very juncture I was most delight-
fully conscious of giving up all to God. I was enabled in my heart
to say 'Here, Lord, take me; take my whole soul, and *seal me thine*
—thine now and thine forever!' All was calm and tranquil, and a
heaven of love pervaded my whole soul. The name of *Jesus* was
precious to me! He came as King and took full possession of my
heart."

We may not have an experience precisely similiar to this. The
Spirit has many methods of making His presence known, but there
is born in the consecrated soul a sweet consciousness that it belongs to God. The Dove settles down on its nest. The words we
speak become invested with new power! There is a fellowship
inaugurated with the Lord and with holy souls everywhere,
which is our entrance into "the joy of the Lord."—*F. B. M.*

AN AFRICAN SCHOOLGIRL'S PRAYER: "O Thou, Great
Chief, light a candle within my heart, that I may see what is
therein and sweep the rubbish from Thy rightful dwelling place!"

> "Spirit of the living God, fall ... on me.
> Break me, melt me, mold me, fill me!
> Spirit of the living God, fall ... on me."

August 5

"...*Awake the dawn.*" (Psalm 57:8, R. V.)

PREPARE for the day early, before the world around you
is awake or stirring. The hour before the dawn is the
hour of renewal; throughout the day the stillness of the
early dawn will remain as a blessing. In the stillness,
open your heart; let God reign in your soul. Make your
devotion as simple and as fragrant as the wild rose blooming alone
in the wood, just because it is a wild rose and God made it so!"
—*Some Outdoor Prayers.*

> I am alone. The morning breaks
> And all is quiet here;
> I need but lift my eyes, put forth
> My hand, for God is near.
> Into this blissful, holy calm
> No voice or harsh sound breaks.
> I am content, Enough to be
> With Him, when morn awakes.
> —Kate Browning Pfantz.

"How unspeakably great and wonderful is this early time with
God before each day begins!"

Lord, I love Thy morning
When the sun breaks through:
When the birds are glad with singing,
And the grass is wet with dew:
When all the world is full of living,
And all nature seems to pray,
"Thou hast kept us through the darkness,
Father, guide us through the day!"
For it always will remind me
It was morning in my soul,
On the day I met my Saviour,
When He touched and made me whole.
—Barbara E. Cornet.

With all the birds and flowers and morning stars, we thank
Thee, Lord!

August 6

"Above all, taking the SHIELD OF FAITH, wherewith ye
shall be able to quench all the fiery darts of the wicked."
(Eph. 6:16.)

NO POISONED arrow of doubt can pierce through *that*
shield! "I believe God!" means "I *refuse to believe the*
devil! or my own faithless heart!" And because the mind
is the most vulnerable point of attack, a close-fitting helmet has been provided which, if worn day and night, will
prove ample protection for *the head. Salvation!* That one
word in all its various phases of meaning covers every possible
emergency, and is the unanswerable argument against *all* the
devil's lies. Saved! delivered! redeemed! loosed! and all through
the precious Blood of Christ—the ransom price which has been
paid in full for the emancipation of Satan's slaves! It is when this
blessed truth is believed, that the Holy Spirit is able to use the
sword of the Word of God and the preaching of the Cross for the
dividing asunder of soul and spirit, and the laying bare and criti-
cizing of *the thoughts* and intents of the heart. He will give discernment to recognize when the suggestions in the mind come
from the enemy, and He will strengthen the Christian to say, *No!*
As the child of God becomes aware of the wiles of the devil he
sees the necessity for constant prayer and watchfulness—not for
himself alone, but for the whole Church, for *all* saints.... He
recognizes more fully his responsibility in relation to the whole
Body of Christ.

—The Overcomer.

August 7

*"For as the heavens are higher than the earth, so are my
ways higher than your ways, and my thoughts than your
thoughts."* (Isa. 55: 9.)

*Is there some problem in your life to solve,
    Some passage seeming full of mystery?
God knows, Who brings the hidden things to light.
    He keeps the key.*

*Is there some door closed by the Father's hand
    Which widely opened you had hoped to see?
Trust God and wait—for when He shuts the door,
    He keeps the key.*

*Is there some earnest prayer unanswered yet,
    Or answered NOT as you had thought 'twould be?
God will make clear His purpose by-and-by.
    He keeps the key.*

*Have patience with your God, your patient God,
    All wise, all knowing, no long tarrier He,
And of the door of all thy future life
    He keeps the key.*

*Unfailing comfort, sweet and blessed rest,
    To know of EVERY door He keeps the key.
That He at last when just HE sees 'tis best,
    Will give it THEE.*

                                        —Anonymous.

*"...What I do thou knowest not now; but thou shalt know here-
after."* (John 13:7.)

August 8

*"Let your light so shine before men, that they may see your
good works, and glorify your Father which is in heaven."*
(Matt. 5: 16.)

"ONE of our brilliant young men," writes a leader for a
youth magazine, "has taken a definite position against
everything unchristian in his large high school, and he
does it always with a friendly smile and without self-
righteousness. He became a candidate for the presidency
of the student body. He made it clear that he could not subscribe
to the school dance. With the Testament daily in his pocket, he
was not ashamed to tell his fellow students that he loved Christ

and His Church. Many thought he was extremely foolish. Some laughed at him, but by a large majority he was elected president of over 2,000 high school young people. After serving one term as a junior, they wanted him to become a candidate for re-election. He was given a special certificate by the civic authorities for his great contribution to the program of combating youth delinquency in that community. He dared to be different; yet, he was respected because he had Christianity with real vertebrae.

"Without question, his attitude helped other schoolmates who possessed Christian convictions but who had not his courage to show their colors. He was strong enough to be a leader, and with God's help was able to rally others. Thus, in the end he did not stand alone, after all. Having risked all for Christ, he found that he had been rewarded with friendship, respect, and popularity that was based on *merit*, not merely on the changing whims of the crowd."

> *"Oh, for a life to please my God,*
> *In every little thing—*
> *A holy life, that day by day*
> *To Him will glory bring!*
> *A life lived only 'unto Him,'*
> *No double aim in view,*
> *The outcome of a Christlike heart,*
> *By God made pure and new.*
> *A life that Jesus guides alone,*
> *O'er which He has control!*
> *A life which others seeing, say,*
> *That Jesus owns the whole."*

August 9

"They shall be abundantly satisfied . . ." (Psalm 36: 8.)

SK the eagle that splashes in the glory of the sun if it ever longs for its cage away down among the dim, distant earth scenes. If it ever stops to look at the old cage of former days it is to sing its doxolgy of deliverance and soar away to its home near the sun.

The life of the Spirit-filled heart is the *winged life*. The unsurrendered life is the life of the cage. The best that the cage can give is a momentary thrill that soon gives place to a pitiful beating against the bars.

Our precious Saviour, by His death on the Cross, proclaims "liberty to the captives," and *you* may be set *free;* free, not to take refuge on the branches of a nearby tree, but to "Rise to walk in heaven's own light, above the world and sin, with heart made pure, and garments white, and Christ enthroned within!"

"They shall be abundantly satisfied." The song in your heart will daily be:

> *"Thou, O Christ, art all I want;*
> *More than all in Thee I find."*

Forget the past, throw off your last fear, and leap boldly forward to *complete emancipation!*

August 10

"For it is God which worketh in you both to will and to do of his good pleasure." (Phil. 2:13.)

> *"Walk before God, obey His word,*
> *And yield to His demands;*
> *Beware of calling Jesus, Lord,*
> *And slighting His commands."*

TO KNOW God's leadings, we must have no ends of our own to serve; we shall then be conscious that His eye is resting on us, and when we would turn to the right or to the left, there will be a voice behind us saying, "This is the way; *walk ye in it."* For this, the heart, the eye and the ear need heavenly training, and this we shall never fail to obtain if only we are willing and obedient.

GUIDANCE

We are not mere machines on which God plays as you would on the keys of a piano, but we are so perfectly united to Christ that His thought springs from within as the intuitive thought and feeling of our own mind, and so, it is not so much Christ *and* us, as Christ *in* us. We are not waiting for some extraordinary voice to indicate each step we are to take, but we just run on in simple self-confidence, as you let your pony run on with a loose rein when he is going all right. It is when he is not right, or when the road divides, that you tighten the rein and make him feel your touch. So God leads His people, blending His divine control so naturally and perfectly with the spontaneous action of their own nature that their individuality is not destroyed, and yet they live and move and have their being in His will and presence.

Better not to act at all than to act in doubt.

"For thou wilt light my candle..." (Psalm 18:28) *MY* candle!

Don't drift through life when there's a Pilot waiting to guide you.

August 11

"The cloke that I left at Troas with Carpus, when thou comest, bring with thee, and the books, but especially the parchments." (2 Tim. 4:13.)

CHRISTIAN'S choice of reading is a life-and-death choice when we think of its effect on his devotional life. Many people begin the day by reading this and that until they have no appetite left for the Word of God, and if they read it at all that day they must force themselves to it. Why not read the Bible and then supplement it with choice devotional messages. Great books are the lifeblood of the world's master spirits.

"Good books are the juices squeezed from the cluster of the ages. They represent earth's wisdom and delight and are the footpath across the hills along which the generations have trod. Youth should feel at home in the best thought of all time and every day be eagle-eyed to find the thing to fit their needs in the quest of God!"

Erasmus wrote in his diary: "When I get some money I will get me some Greek books and then some clothes."

"Study your Bible diligently and throw all your novels in the fire," said a university graduate to a group of youth. "The world is sick of reading such books. Spiritual growth is attained by learning to say 'No' to all the thousand influences of the world which 'are not bad' in themselves but which simply take the place meant for Jesus and therefore are deadlier than arsenic or strychnine. Not bad in themselves! God forbid! They compete with Christ. This is their evil. I propose to know nothing but Jesus Christ and Him crucified."

August 12

"Know ye not that ye are the temple of God, . . ." (1 Cor. 3: 16.)

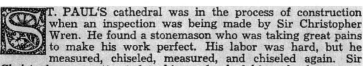

T. PAUL'S cathedral was in the process of construction when an inspection was being made by Sir Christopher Wren. He found a stonemason who was taking great pains to make his work perfect. His labor was hard, but he measured, chiseled, measured, and chiseled again. Sir Christopher was attracted to him and asked him why he was so painstaking and precise. His reply was, "I am building a cathedral."

"We are building day by day
A temple the world cannot see;
Building, building, for eternity."

If you are to have a good tomorrow you must lay the right foundation today. A foundation of wood, hay, or stubble will never support a character-making building.

An aged low-caste woman in India was once asked the price of a temple in the process of building. She turned to the missionary in surprise and said: "Why, we do not know! It is for our god; we don't count the cost."

We are building every day
In a good, or evil way,
And the structure as it grows,
Will our inmost self disclose.
Build it well, whate'er you do,
Build it straight, and strong and true;
Build it clean, and high and broad,
Build it for the eye of God.
                    —*I. E. Dickenza.*

He who builds with God, builds not alone.

August 13

"Through thy precepts I get understanding; therefore I hate every false way." (Psalm 119:104.)

N THE heart of every youth, down below all other wants and aspirations there is a profound longing to know the way of the spiritual life. The world is crying, "What shall I do to be saved?" Of all books the Bible is *the only one* that answers that universal cry.

There are other books which set forth morality with more or less correctness; but there are none that suggest a blotting out of the record of the misspent past or an escape from the penalty of the broken law.

There are other books which have poetry; but there are none which sing the songs of salvation or give a troubled soul the peace that floweth like a river.

There are other books which have eloquence; but there are none which enable us to behold God Himself with outstretched hands pleading with men to turn and live.

There are other books which have science; but there are none that can give the soul a definite assurance of life, so that it can say, "I know Whom I have believed."

"I believe the Bible because 'it finds me.' " Those are the words
of Coleridge; and I make them mine. It found me perplexed with
a youth's fear of the unknown; it calmed my fears and gave me
the hope that "maketh not ashamed." It has found me once and
again in the Vale of Baca and wiped away my tears. It has found
me and helped me in seasons of weakness and discouragement.
It has found and never failed me!

And when I come to the border line between time and eternity
it shall find me there and give me a rod and staff to lean upon.

Yes, the Bible is a book to live and die by.

> "Break Thou the bread of life, Dear Lord, to me,
> As Thou didst break the loaves Beside the sea;
> Beyond the sacred page I seek Thee, Lord;
> My spirit pants for Thee, O living Word.
>
> Bless Thou the Truth dear Lord, To me— to me—
> As Thou didst bless the bread By Galilee;
> Then shall all bondage cease, All fetters fall;
> And I shall find my peace, My All in all."

August 14

"For ever, O Lord, thy word is settled in heaven."
(Psalm 119: 89.)

EW of the followers of Darwin's theory of evolution realized how he later felt about the results of his own specu-
ulations. Lady Hope tells of calling upon Darwin and
finding him reading the book of Hebrews, which he de-
scribed as "a royal book." Lady Hope spoke of creation
and of the treatment the Genesis account of it had received at the
hands of some. Darwin fairly wrung his hands as a look of agony
came over his face. "I was a young man," he said, "with unformed
ideas. I threw out queries, suggestions, wondering all the time
about everything. The ideas took like wildfire. People made a
religion of them. Oh, if I could only undo it!" A few weeks
later he went to his reward.

> "Of all sad words of tongue or pen,
> The saddest are these, 'It might have been!' "

THE BOOK

The books men write are but a fragance blown
From transient blossoms crushed by human
hands;
But, high above them all, splendid and alone,
Staunch as a tree, there is a Book that stands

Unmoved by storms, unchallenged by decay;
The winds of criticism would profane
Its sacred pages, but the Truth, the Way,
The Life are in it—and they beat in vain.

O traveler from this to yonder world,
Pause in the shade of God's magnificent,
Eternal Word—that tree whose roots are curled
About our human need. When strength is spent,
Stretch out beneath some great, far-reaching limb
Of promise, and find rest and peace in Him.
                                        —Helen Frazee-Bower.

August 15

"Ye are the light of the world. . . ." (Matt. 5: 14.)

GOD is caring about our testimony on earth *for Him*; and if I am only little enough in my own eyes, He will say, "I can bring out a ray in you, and place you exactly where it can shine." You may have very little light, but think of the glimmer of the glowworm as it shines out so very brightly on a dark night!

To be able to say, "I am the Saviour's prize; I have fallen to His lot," makes everything bright, "for the Lord is my light and my salvation."

A little star shone singly in the night,
And thought "How very feeble is my light!
There's not a traveler who will see his way,
Who will be guided by my tiny ray.
But I will not go out—the more will I
Attempt to shine in this vast, darkened sky."

Down in the world there was a weary soul
Striving alone to see the clouded goal.
Full of despair, she wrestled all the night,
But saw no shining of a guiding light.
She said, "There is no moon, I am so sad,"
And lost the very little hope she had.

But through her narrow window did she see
A point of brightness gleaming fervently.
It was the single star. She cried aloud,
And hoped anew for passing of the cloud.
When morning came, with all its golden light,
She said, "I found the Saviour in the night.

"I found Him through a star—it must have been
The Star of Bethlehem that I have seen,
For to the Lord it led—and so I came
And saw the hills of Heaven all aflame,
All shining with the glory of that star,
Whose small but steady light had called afar."

O little star! be not afraid thy light
Will be too feeble to be seen at night.
However small, if steady, it will be
Lighting the roadway to Eternity.
They know in Heaven, where the angels are,
A soul was lighted by a little star.
                                        —*Vivien Jameson.*

August 16

"...*The house that is to be builded for the Lord must be exceeding magnifical,...*" (1 Chron. 22:5.)
"*Know ye not that your body is the temple of the Holy Ghost? ...*" (1 Cor. 6:19.)

SLAVERY to habits that destroy body and mind has been the Waterloo of many a promising athlete. What a pathetic sight is that of a young person, capable of doing really big things, but handicapped by intemperate living and lacking in self-control! It is only a question of time until he becomes a castaway upon the scrapheap of human wreckage. No fight is so severe as the fight with self. No victory is so great as the conquering of self.

To be able to say "Yes" or "No" at the right time is an indication of a God-controlled life. Such a life is obtainable through the Lord Jesus Christ. "*I can do all things through Christ which strengtheneth me.*"

There is a deep experience for every soul, where sin is seen in all its horrid ugliness, where the Blood of Calvary's Lamb is appropriated with all its cleansing and transforming power, and where the living Christ is admitted to the holiest of all in the being, and is allowed to take full charge, where the "old man" with all his evil propensities is relegated to the place where he belongs—the cross of crucifixion—and "a new creation" in which all the old things are passed away and all things become new, is manifested.

Make it yours today!

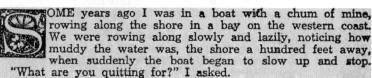

August 17

*"Be sober, be vigilant; because your adversary the devil,
as a roaring lion, walketh about, seeking whom he may
devour."* (1 Peter 5:8.)

SOME years ago I was in a boat with a chum of mine, rowing along the shore in a bay on the western coast. We were rowing along slowly and lazily, noticing how muddy the water was, the shore a hundred feet away, when suddenly the boat began to slow up and stop. "What are you quitting for?" I asked.

"Why," he said, "I am not quitting, but the old boat is caught on something. We must have run into the mud."

I said, "Why there's plenty of water here. Put your oar down."

He took his oar out of the oarlock, and reached down. The water was five or six feet deep. Then slowly over the edge of the boat there came the slimy arm of a devilfish. He jumped back from it, and I jumped back, snatched the oar, and began to hack at the arm that had fastened to the boat. Then on the other side another arm began to come up. We realized our danger and took the two oars, and began to pole for the shore until we got near enough so that we could jump clear off the boat and get out of the danger.

In days since then I have looked back at that moment, and it has seemed to me a picture of a youth passing through life's experiences without any serious sense of danger, when all of a sudden out of the muddy depths of a perilous place some vicious arm reaches up, and before he knows it, the trend toward the right begins to slow up, and he is in the arms of danger. Young people! do not let anybody ever laugh you into the idea of thinking there is no peril in the sins all around us! These sins can seize you, and they can seize me; people as good as we are going down every day. No! I need the Saviour's help and I need it greatly! You need Him, and you need Him now.

—*A. W. Beaven.*

"I need Thee, loving Shepherd,
I need Thy constant care,
To guide me on life's journey,
And all the way prepare.
I need Thine arms around me,
To hold me lest I fall:
O more and more I need Thee—
My only Hope, my All."

August 18

"... When I have a convenient season, ..." (Acts 24:25.)

"CONVENIENT" is a word that has no place in serious life. When seriously ill we do not defer sending for the doctor until it is convenient. How much rather, then, shall we promptly deal with the crisis of the soul! *"Choose ye this day whom ye will serve."* Listen to the wise words of Dr. Temple: "If you want to live a Christian life, do not dally with your purpose; do not fancy that you will find it easier to win your way by degrees, and that by a gradual change you can attain the same end, with less pain than you fear will be given by a sudden wrench. Nothing can be a greater mistake!

Press into the enemy's citadel *at once!* Do not wait outside until he has had time to shoot you down. In with your heart and soul! Priceless opportunities pass!

—Dr. Watkinson.

"Child, follow me," the Master said,
 As he knocked full loud at my chamber door;
  But the morn was fair, and my heart was gay,
  "I'll dally a while on the primrose way,
 And I'll come" said I, "when the morning's o'er."

"Child, follow me," the Master said,
 As he lingered patiently at the gate;
  Gray shadows were falling, the night was near;
  "Life's joys are so sweet, and my friends so dear,
 "I will come," said I, "when the night is late."

"Child, follow me," the Master cried,
 As he walked away through the darkness deep;
  And the night had fallen, and the birds were still;
  "Linger," said I, "at the foot of the hill,
 And I'll come when the world is hushed in sleep."

"Master, I come," I cried at length,
 "Heart weary to serve at thine own dear side,
  Thou hast called me long, but I come at last."
  (But his eyes were dim and his strength was past,
 And not long could he follow the Crucified).

—Author Unknown.

He marches past our door—the Shepherd with the Cross!

 "Into my heart. Into my heart.
 Come into my heart, Lord Jesus;
 Come in today, come in to stay;
 Come into my heart, Lord Jesus."

August 19

"...How much owest thou unto my Lord?" (Luke 16:5.)

WHERE IS THY TALENT?

MANY talents are being hid "in the earth" today. And it is not just the one-talent men and women who are doing it! Afraid of being considered peculiar and unwilling to be reproached for Christ's sake, countless numbers are letting the "earth" have their ability. Living for the things of this world, which must end with time, is as surely hiding talents in the earth as literally burying them far beneath the surface of the ground would be.

Every note in the organ is needed for the full expression of noble harmony. Every instrument in the orchestra is required unless the music is to be lame and broken. Sir Michael Costa was once conducting an orchestra in London. One of the instrumentalists, playing a piccolo, was suddenly impressed with his own unimportance as a minor contributor to the mighty volume of harmonious sound. So he stayed his fingers and the piccolo was silent. Immediately Sir Michael raised his hand and cried, "Stop! Where's the piccolo?" Every other instrument in the orchestra was incomplete without the co-operation of the piccolo!

God has endowed no two souls alike, and every soul is needed to make the music of "the realm of the blest."

> Bring to God your gift, my brother,
> He'll not need to call another,
>   You will do;
> He will add His blessing to it,
> And the two of you will do it,
>   God and you.
>   —R. E. Neighbour.

What is that in thine hand? Is it a musical instrument, or the gift of song? Is it a ledger, or a school book? A typewriter or a telegraph instrument? Is it an anvil or a printer's rule? Whatever it is, give it to God, in loving service!

"But the manifestation of the Spirit is given to every man to profit withal. For to one is given by the Spirit the word of wisdom; to another the word of knowledge by the same Spirit; to another faith by the same Spirit ... to another the working of miracles; to another prophesy; ... but all these worketh that one and the selfsame Spirit, dividing to every man severally as he will." (1 Cor. 12: 7-11.)

August 20

". . . Ethiopia shall soon stretch out her hands unto God."
(Psalm 68: 31.)

EMPEROR HAILE SELASSIE'S TESTIMONY

T A recent Bible-Testimony-Fellowship meeting in London, Haile Selassie, ruler of Ethiopia, was invited to give a personal testimony. He said in part: "From early childhood I was taught to appreciate the Bible, and my love for it increases with the passage of time. All through my troubles I have found it a source of infinite comfort. *'Come unto me all ye that labour and are heavy laden, and I will give you rest'*—who can resist an invitation so full of compassion! Because of this personal experience in the goodness of the Bible, I resolved that all my countrymen should find the truth for themselves. Therefore, in spite of great opposition, I caused a new translation to be made from our ancient language into the language which the old and the young understood and spoke. . . . Today man sees all his hopes and aspirations crumbling before him. He is perplexed, and knows not whither he is drifting. But he must realize that the Bible is his refuge and the rallying point of humanity. In it man will find the solution of his present difficulties and guidance for his future action, and unless he accepts with clear conception the Bible and its great message, he cannot hope for salvation. For my part, I glory in the Bible."

Look, ye saints, the sight is glorious;
See the Man of sorrows now;
From the fight returned victorious,
Every knee to Him shall bow:
Crown Him, crown Him, crown Him, crown Him!
Crowns become the Victor's brow.

Hark, those bursts of acclamation!
Hark, those loud triumphant chords;
Jesus takes the highest station:
O what joy the sight affords!
Crown Him, crown Him, crown Him, crown Him!
King of Kings, and Lord of lords.
                                                    —Hymnal.

"Wherefore God also hath highly exalted him, and given him a name which is above every name: that at the name of Jesus every knee should bow, of things in heaven, and things in earth, and things under the earth; and that every tongue should confess that Jesus Christ is Lord, to the glory of God the Father."
(Phil. 2:9-11.)

August 21

"For ye are laborers together with God: . . ." (1 Cor. 3: 9.)

N A little shop on a back street a man makes a mariner's compass. It is taken on board a great ship, and by means of its trembling needle the vessel is guided over the sea unerringly to its destination. A *man* made the compass. Yes, a man *and* God. A man did the mechanical work, put the wonderful instrument together; but it was God who put into the magnet its mysterious power. God and man are co-workers; and without God man can do nothing; nevertheless God's perfect work needs man's best.

It is a supreme privilege that we can be associated with God in the carrying on of His work. We count it an honor to be associated with distinguished human beings. An essayist writes: "I should have felt it to be a great honor to carry Shakespeare's bag, or to polish Milton's shoes, or to have picked up Raphael's brush." What an infinitely greater privilege it is to become, as Paul says, "labourers together with God."

> *So near is grandeur to our dust,*
> *So near to God is man—*
> *When duty whispers low "Thou must"*
> *The youth replies, "I can!"*
> —*Ralph Waldo Emerson.*

"I can . . . through Christ."

August 22

". . . Filled with all the fulness of God." (Eph. 3:19.)

T A recent youth conference a young man related an epoch-making crisis in his life which lifted him into a new realm of Christian experience. The greatest of the promises became daily facts, proving to him that they were literally true.

"For a long time," he said, "I made no progress, until one day I went alone into a quiet place and falling upon my knees I cried, 'O Christ of Galilee! O Christ of Gethsemane! O Christ of Calvary! —I give all of *myself* to Thee; give *Thou* all of *Thyself* to me!' This prayer was answered with an overflowing fullness."

He prayed a definite prayer and received a definite answer!

> *"Breathe on me, Breath of God,*
> *Until my heart is pure.*

Breathe on me, Breath of God,
Till I am wholly Thine,
Till all the earthly part of me
Glows with Thy fire divine."

August 23

"Thou therefore endure hardness, as a good soldier of
Jesus Christ." (2 Tim. 2:3.)

LUXURIOUSNESS is rarely the cradle of giants. It is not unsuggestive that the soft and beautiful tropics are not the home of the strong, indomitable, and progressive peoples. The pioneering and progressive races have dwelt in sterner and hardier climes. The lap of luxury does not afford the elementary iron for the upbringing of strong and enduring life. Hardness hardens; antagonism solidifies; trials innure and confirm. How commonly it has happened that men who, in soft circumstances, have been weak and irresolute, were hardened into fruitful decision by the ministry of antagonism and pain.

Thou, Great God, who girdest the soul as Thou dost gird the world by zones of stars and glories of star-sown night, gird us with God so that we shall feel, as we go into the battle with tightened girdle at our loins, that God is our strength and makes war through us. Amen.

—*Bishop Quayle.*

"Give me hard tasks, with strength that shall not fail;
Conflict, with courage that shall never die!
Better the hill-path, climbing toward the sky,
Than languid air and smooth sward of the vale!

Better to dare the wild wrath of the gale
Than with furled sails in port forever lie!
Give me hard tasks, with strength that shall not fail;
Conflict with courage that shall never die!

Not for a light load fitting shoulders frail,
Not for an unearned victory I sigh;
Strong is the struggle that wins triumph high,
Not without loss the hero shall prevail;
Give me hard tasks, with strength that shall not fail!"

Nothing earthly will make me give up my work in despair. I encourage myself in the Lord my God and go forward.

—*David Livingstone.*

August 24

"I am not eloquent . . ." (Exod. 4: 10.)

NOTHING is more dishonoring to God, or more dangerous for us, than a mock humility. When we refuse to occupy a position which the grace of God assigns us, because of our not possessing certain virtues and qualifications, this is not humility, for if we could but satisfy our own consciences in reference to such virtues and qualifications, we should then deem ourselves entitled to assume the position. If, for instance, Moses had possessed such a measure of eloquence as he deemed needful, we may suppose he would have been ready to go. Now, the question is, how much eloquence would he have needed to furnish him for his mission? The answer is, without God no amount of human eloquence would have availed; but with God the merest stammerer would have proved an efficient minister. This is a great practical truth.

Unbelief is not humility, but thorough pride. It refuses to believe God because it does not find in self a reason for believing. This is the very height of presumption.—*C. H. M.*

> *"Move to the fore,*
> *Say not another is fitter than thou*
> *Shame to thy shrinking! Up! Face thy task now.*
> *Own thyself equal to all a soul may,*
> *Cease thy evading—God needs thee today.*
> *Move to the fore!*
>
> *"God Himself waits, and must wait till thou come;*
> *Men are God's prophets though ages lie dumb.*
> *Halts the Christ Kingdom with conquest so near?*
> *Thou art the cause, thou soul in the rear.*
> *Move to the fore!"*

Find your purpose and fling your life out into it; and the loftier your purpose is, the more sure you will be to make the world richer with every enrichment of yourself.
—*Phillips Brooks.*

"Our sufficiency is of God." In Him are the mighty overcoming energies which accomplish the possible and the impossible with equal readiness. "There is One with us," says Dr. Speer, "to Whom the impossible is His chief delight."

August 25

"Looking unto Jesus the author and finisher of our faith; . . ."
(Heb. 12: 2.)

Faith is looking away from your own faith—unto Jesus.

SOME people try to have faith in their own faith, instead of faith in Jesus. Christ. They keep looking for a subjective condition, They ought to be looking to an objective Christ. True faith pays no attention whatever to itself. It centers all its gaze upon Christ. For *faith* is not our Saviour. Faith is simply an *attitude* of the soul, through which *Jesus saves*. When Satan cannot beguile us in any other way he gets us to scrutinizing our faith, instead of looking unto Christ. That man has the strongest heart who is the least conscious of its existence. And that faith is the strongest which pays no attention to itself. You may weaken the heart by centering your anxious attention upon it. So, nothing will quicker weaken faith than the constant endeavor to discover it. It is like the child's digging up of the seed to see if it is growing. It is a curiosity which brings disaster to the seed. It is not a man's faith, but his *faith in Christ* which saves him. To be looking unto Christ is faith. To be looking unto anything else, even unto faith, is trouble to the soul.

Therefore do not worry about your faith. Do not always be scanning it. Look away from it altogether—unto Jesus. For faith alone is naught. It is only faith *in Jesus* that counts. Take care that you are depending upon Jesus to save, and faith will take care of itself.

August 26

"Moreover it is required in stewards, that a man be found faithful." (1 Cor. 4:2.)

I SUPPOSE that there has been no man in the world more distinguished for sound wisdom in the field of medicine than Sir William Osler. At the time of his death he was Regius Professor of Medicine in Oxford University. He had received honorary degrees from almost every high-class university and college in the world. He was an authority on good literature. He was a prince of good fellows, a great lover of children, and those who knew him best said his clearest title was "the friend of young men." He had been a greatly honored citizen in Philadelphia and in Montreal, as well as in Baltimore, where he had a large part in the making of Johns Hopkins Medical School; and he had done graduate work in his early life in Berlin, Vienna, and Edinburgh. *Where did he start?* Under what auspices did he make his beginning? In a little frontier settlement on the edge of the forest in eastern Canada, twelve miles from the nearest doctor. His father was a missionary, a university man from England, who with his bride came out to that wild primitive country. His circuit riding took him away from home four days out of every week. If he ever had a bridge over which to cross those abundant Canadian rivers it was made of floating logs fastened together in primitive fashion, which sometimes sank when he stepped upon it.

—*Selected.*

"It is not your entrance but your exit that really counts."

August 27

"And for their sakes I sanctify myself, ..." (John 17:19.)

ON THE walls of memory I have hung an exceptionally stirring picture. Here stands *a boy* in a little room of his young personal interests and affairs—a room full of algebra and grammar and music and baseball and budding friendships and slowly-settling purposes, pursuits and plans. He is thinking of a great man-making experience in another life most precious, most significant to us all—his future.

There is *a man*, Washington, the richest of all the land, sure of ease, secure in position, furnished with comfort, fond of quiet, with a beautiful home in a setting of rare loveliness, enough but not too many affairs to occupy and exercise his talents. In the full vigor of his early prime, he kneels at the feet of his mother to receive her blessing ere he sets out on his journey to assume command of the armies of his country in the struggle for independence.

What is really happening as he kneels at his mother's knee? It is something like this:

"Here on this day and in this act of dedication and purpose, I lift myself out of my little, personal, quiet, easy role of a gentleman-farmer on Mt. Vernon estates, up out of the affairs of ploughs and horses and crops and profits, into the service of my country, cost what it may!"

He needs the voice of God, the strength of God, the touch of God, the impulse of God, and he seeks it in prayer.

He is leaving all behind, setting his feet in a path where trouble, privation, anxiety, burden, misunderstanding, danger and sacrifice unknown surely await him.

All that is great in any life you may recall—any life worthy to be enshrined in the memory of men—will find its keynote in this phrase:

"For their sakes I sanctify myself." (Jesus.)

Remember Valley Forge, you young American princes!

"Undertake something which asks that you devote yourself, dedicate yourself, and only God's record books shall be roomy enough to sum it up."

August 28

"And Samuel said, Hath the Lord as great delight in burnt offerings and sacrifices, as in obeying the voice of the Lord? Behold, to obey is better than sacrifice, . . ." (1 Samuel 15: 22.)

IF TWO angels were to receive at the same moment a commission from God, one to go down and rule earth's grandest empire, the other to go and sweep the streets of its meanest village, it would be a matter of entire indifference to each which service fell to his lot, the post of ruler or the post of scavenger; for the joy of the angels lies only in obedience to God's will, and with equal joy they would lift a Lazarus in his rags to Abraham's bosom, or be a chariot of fire to carry an Elijah home.

—*John Newton.*

"The heavenly places and the kitchen are at the same elevation. We can discharge the humblest duty while still breathing the air of the mountaintops."

LIFE VICTORIOUS

I have heard my Master calling, and His voice is music sweet;
And He bids me march right forward, not dream of a retreat.
He says His land of Beulah lies before me out of sight,
Where reigns the deathless daylight never shadowed by the night.
He bids me do my duty, though humble it may be,
And do what thing lies nearest in glad humility;
For Christ is one that serveth, and thinks no service mean
That helps the world's endeavor to help its heart be clean.

So I walk highways and byways; and my hands are rough with
*   toil,*
As I try to make a garden out of hard, infertile soil;
But I see God's flowers a-growing where there grew no flowers
*   before,*
And my life is full of gladness, and I work God's work the more.
Bless God! My life is holy like a temple with its calm;
And I envy not an angel with his harp-string and his palm;
For I am God's own helper; and He calls me by my name,
And says my work is holy as a sacrificial flame.

—*From The Blessed Life, by Bishop Quayle.*

August 29

"But God forbid that I should glory, save in the cross of our Lord Jesus Christ, by whom the world is crucified unto me, and I unto the world." (Gal. 6: 14.)

BEETHOVEN was in the habit of playing his symphonies on an old harpsichord, as a test. They would thus be made to stand out in their true character, with nothing to hide their faults, or exaggerate their beauties.

Thus wisely may we test our character, endeavoring to ascertain how it manifests itself—not on great and rare occasions, or before the public eye, where there is a chance for display and applause—but in private, in the little, homely everyday duties, which attract no particular attention and reward us with no praise.

If in the retired nook of your own breast, in the regulation of your thoughts and feelings; if in the bosom of your family, in the monotonous round of home life each day, you preserve a sweet, serene temper, and go forward cheerfully, taking a real pleasure in duty as duty, and in all these little matters honestly strive to serve and please the heavenly Master; if, in a word, your piety sounds well on such an unpretending harp, it is good, genuine, tested; it will one day win acclamation from a vaster and nobler throng than ever was thrilled by the genius of Beethoven.

—Selected.

Every character has an inward spring; let Christ be in it. Every action has a keynote; let Christ set it!

—Drummond, in The Changed Life.

August 30

"...Be filled with the Spirit." (Eph. 5:18.)

WE MUST empty by filling," said a divinely enlightened woman, Ellice Hopkins; and a wise man has said, "Nothing is ever displaced until it is replaced." In these two utterances lies the secret (if it be a secret) of all reform.

Here we learn that nature abhors a vacuum. We cannot pump the darkness out of a room; we must empty it by filling it with light. One tallow dip will do more to exclude darkness than a thousand steam pumps. The only way to shut out disease is to fill the veins with health. In morals we must banish the degrading by the elevating; not by prohibition, but by substitution.

The popular superstition which credits every deserted house

with being haunted and peoples it with bad spirits has a germ of truth. If the demon be excluded and the soul be swept and garnished, yet, if it be empty, the demon will return with seven other spirits more wicked than himself. The Holy Spirit, by entering the soul, empties it of evil spirits, and by dwelling in the soul, filling it to the utmost, He maintains the exclusion of the bad.—*H. L. Wayland, D.D.*

> *"Come, O Lord, like ocean flood-tides*
> *Flowing inland from the sea;*
> *As the waters fill the shallows,*
> *May our souls be filled with Thee!"*

As comes the breath of spring so the Holy Spirit comes to our souls. He comes like dawning day; He comes like songs of morn; and His presence is like summer to the soul. His joy shines forth, and then *life* blossoms to its goal.

> *"Thou hast bought me to possess me;*
> *In Thy fullness Lord, come in!"*

"Have ye received the Holy Ghost since ye believed?"

August 31

"And as thy servant was busy here and there, he was gone. . ." (1 Kings 20:40.)

> *He came to you, for in His gentle voice*
> *He'd much that He would say.*
> *Your ears were turned to earth's discordant sounds,*
> *And so—He went away.*
>
> *He came; and in His hand He had a task*
> *That He would have you do,*
> *But you were occupied with other things,*
> *And so you missed that too.*
>
> *He would have touched you; and His touch could thrill,*
> *And give you quickening power;*
> *But earthly things enveloped, and you could*
> *Not feel Him in that hour.*
>
> *—Selected.*

The most powerful thing in your life is your opportunity. It is also the most irretrievable. We must have clearness of vision if we are to see it and lay hands upon it as it hurries past us on very quiet feet. It disappears as utterly as the day has gone.

God, give us vision, courage, and a quiet mind!

Duties are pressing upon me,
  And the time for work is brief,
What if, with purblind vision,
  I neglect the very chief?
What if I do with ardor
  What a thousand could, maybe,
And leave undone forever
  What was meant for only me?
                    —*Charlotte Fiske Bates.*

September 1

". . . He that cometh to God MUST BELIEVE THAT HE IS, and that he is a REWARDER of them that diligently seek him." (Heb. 11:6.)

THERE is a story lodged in a little bedroom of one of these dormitories which I pray God His recording angel may note, allowing it never to be lost," said Dr. Horace Bushnell at a chapel service in Yale University, the school which he had left as an earnest but somewhat doubting young man, but to which he returned some years later as a mighty winner of souls. As a student, God to him was not a reality. One day in his room in the dormitory this thought possessed him: "If there is a God, as I rather hope there is, and very dimly believe to be, He must be a right God. Will He not help me, or, perchance, even be discovered by me?" He dropped on his knees and began to pray: "Take the dimness of my soul away! Reveal Thyself to me!"

Now the decisive moment had come! He prayed to the dim God, dimly felt, confessing the dimness for honesty's sake, and asking for help that he might begin a right life.

It would seem a very dark prayer but was, nevertheless, the truest and best he could make; however, his prayer and his vow were so profoundly meant that his soul was borne up unto God's help, as it were, by some unseen chariot, and permitted to see the opening of heaven even before he opened his eyes: He rose, and it was as if he had received wings! The whole sky was luminous about him. It was the morning, as it were, of a new eternity. After this, all troublesome doubt of God's reality was gone—for he had found Him! A Being so profoundly felt must inevitably be!

"If I ask Him to receive me,
  Will He say me, Nay!
Not till earth and not till heaven
  Pass away!"

September 2

"After this manner therefore pray ye: . . ." (Matt. 6:9.)

THE LAW OF PRAYER ACTION

FIRST, there must be an understanding—a working agreement, a fixed invariable Law of Prayer Action. Secondly, there must be a time and place spent in communication in accord with the working agreement. Thirdly, sooner or later the known results will come.

But what is the Law of Prayer Action?

1. The prayer must be in Jesus' name.

2. The prayer must be by a man in full touch with Jesus in heart, habit, and life.

3. The prayer must be in harmony with the teaching of the Bible.

4. The prayer must be actual, simple, definite and confident— "in faith believing." —Dr. S. D. Gordon.

GOD HEARS OUR PRAYERS

If radio's slim fingers
Can reach out in the air
And pluck the sweet
Melodies found lingering there

And send them at once to both you and me
Direct to our homes or wherever we be;

If the old refrain on the violin
Can reach us so clearly above earth's din,
If the voice that is singing sweet and low
Is not torn asunder by storm clouds of woe;

If whispering hope from the strings of the harp
Can travel for miles, speak to our heart;
If the strains of the organ we can hear through the night,
And pleads in the darkness, "Lead kindly light";

If all of these things we can hear in the air,
Then why should we doubt that God hears our prayers?

Faith should not show surprise at the perfect answer to prayer.
—Cobb.

"In the life of Lord Lawrence we are told that when someone deprecated prayer for rain as useless to change the order of nature, the great Indian statesman and Christian said: 'We are told to pray and that our prayers will be answered; that is sufficient for me!'"

September 3

"But Daniel purposed in his heart that he would not defile himself . . ." (Dan. 1:8.)

NOBLE heart-purpose is the strongest watchman over external conduct. It is the purposeless life that has no defenses. An ocean liner, with engine power, and helm, and compass, and destination, can cut her way through the most tumultuous seas. A liner, destitute of helm, and compass, and errand, is at the mercy of every fierce and unfriendly sea. Daniel had the mighty safeguard of "a purpose true," and every time an unfriendly circumstance beset him he held firmly to his course.

We turn from Daniel to the apostle Paul. He, too, had a purpose which dominated everything: "For me to live is Christ." That sovereign ambition was always on the throne. In every moment Christ must be honored! In every issue Christ must be glorified! The body must do nothing which will impair its fine fitness as a servant of Christ. The mind must entertain no suggestion which will make it a less holy temple for Christ. The heart must allow no sentiment or desire to sit at its table which would be an affront to Christ. The apostle led everything up to this pure and lofty purpose, and by it everything was accepted or condemned.

My soul! Cultivate the companionship of a glorious purpose! Never be caught in spiritual indolence. Let thy flag be always unfurled, and let this be emblazoned upon it: "For me to live is Christ!"

Have we the conviction that life is a commission for a great task?

"Help me to live a great life, so that I can assist in Thy great plans."

"Standing by a purpose true,
Heeding God's command,
Honor them, the faithful few!
All hail to Daniel's Band!

"Dare to be a Daniel,
Dare to stand alone,
Dare to have a purpose firm!
Dare to make it known."

September 4

". . . If thou canst believe, all things are possible to him that believeth." (Mark 9:23.)

SELDOM have we heard a better definition of faith than was given once in one of our meetings by a dear old colored woman as she answered the question of a young man, *how to take the Lord for needed help.*

In her characteristic way, pointing her finger toward him, she said with great emphasis: "You've just got to believe that He's done it, and it's done." The great danger with most of us is that, after we ask Him to do it, we do not believe that it is done, but we keep on "helping Him," and getting others to help Him; and waiting to see how He is going to do it.

Faith adds its "Amen" to God's "Yea," and then takes its hands off, and leaves God to finish His work. Its language is, "Commit thy way unto the Lord; trust also in him; and he worketh" (R.V.)
    —*Days of Heaven upon Earth.*

"I simply take Him at His word,
I praise Him that my prayer is heard,
And claim my answer from the Lord;
I take, He undertakes."

September 5

"How shall we sing the Lord's song in a strange land?"
(Psalm 137: 4.)

THE NOTE of the nightingale is never heard outside the borders of a certain area," says an English writer. "You never hear it north of York. You never hear it west of the river Exe. You may take the eggs and have them hatched in Scotland and carry the fledglings to our Scottish woods, but never will the birds come north again to give us that wonderful music of the night. Outside a certain limit they are silent."

There are frontiers for the voice of heaven as there are for the voice of every singing bird. But the frontiers are not geographical; they are moral and have to do with character. They are determined by what a man desires and by the deepest craving of his soul.

A great man once said that no theological statement had ever satisfied him like the voice of Jenny Lind singing, "I *Know* That My Redeemer Liveth!"

Jenny Lind said, "I sing for God." She did. That is why she lives and sings today, though dead.

> If I had a voice, oh, a strong, strong voice,
> I would tell to the ends of the earth,
> To the sorrowing ones who have no relief,
> Of the depths of a holy mirth.
>
> If I had a voice, a persuading voice
> That could tell of His heart of love,
> It would turn everyone from all self and from sin
> To the Lord of the heaven above.
>
> If I had a voice, just a tender voice
> With a wooing and winning power,
> I might say the sweet word that my Lord would give
> That would change a life—in an hour.
>
> —Anon.

September 6

". . . He that believeth shall not make haste." (Isa. 28:16.)

ONE OF THE greatest mistakes in life is *hasty* praying. We rush into God's presence and try in a few hurried sentences to solicit His help, but not at the expense of spending the necessary time in communion and fellowship with Him! Quick-firing guns must have time to cool, but how little space do *we* devote to the cooling processes of our souls! If we only realized the true nature of prayer we should understand that it is better to entreat God to make speed to save us than that we should hasten forth to our duties, to the neglect of prayer.

One who knew Luther well wrote thus to Melancthon: "I cannot admire enough the extraordinary cheerfulness, constancy, faith, and hope of that man in these trying and vexatious times. He constantly feeds these gracious affections by a very diligent study of the Word of God. Then not a day passes in which he does not employ in prayer at least three of his very best hours. Once I happened to hear him in prayer. *Gracious* God! What spirit and what faith there is in his expressions! He petitions God with as much reverence as if he were in the Divine presence, and yet with as firm a confidence as he would address a father or friend."

The great Wilberforce wrote to his son: "Let me conjure you not to be seduced into neglecting, curtailing, or hurrying over your morning prayer. Of all things, guard against neglecting God in the closet. There is nothing more fatal in the life and power of religion. How much better I might serve God if I cultivated a closer communion with Him." Haste in prayer means fever and failure. Time spent in prayer is time saved.

"Steal away to Jesus." He is not far from thee at this moment.

September 7

"And the Lord said unto the servant, Go out into the high-ways and hedges, and compel them to come in, that my house may be filled." (Luke 14:23.)

A BRAZILIAN girl, aged twenty-one, who is a graduate of an American college, wrote:

"It was in my girlhood that I first heard about the work among the savages in our jungle lands. My heart flamed with pure passion for souls, and I was then only nine years old. Now I am all on fire for Christ, and the supreme ambition of my life is to go to the place where no one else will go, to surrender my best youthful days to His service. I have counted the cost, but to me it appears as no cost at all, when I think of my loving Saviour and Friend who has satisfied the deepest longings of my heart."

> I dare not idle stand,
> While upon every hand
> The whitening fields proclaim the harvest near;
> A gleaner I would be,
> Gathering, dear Lord, for Thee,
> Lest I with empty hand at last appear.
>
> I dare not idle stand,
> While on the shifting sand,
> The ocean casts bright treasures at my feet;
> Beneath some shell's rough side
> The tinted pearl may hide,
> And I with precious gift my Lord may meet.
>
> I dare not idle stand,
> While over all the land
> Poor, wandering souls need humble help like mine;
> Brighter than the brightest gem
> In monarch's diadem,
> Each soul a star in Jesus' crown may shine.
>
> —Selected.

September 8

"And all things, whatsoever ye shall ask in prayer, believ-
ing, ye shall receive." (Matt. 21:22.)

Let this poem be dedicated to the lads whose homes are on the
range amid the great, wide spaces—out where the deer and
antelope roam. Here they may build an altar under the sky and
find God's presence.

A COWBOY'S PRAYER

Oh, Lord, I've never lived where churches grow,
 I love creation better as it stood
That day You finished it so long ago,
 And looked upon Your work and called it
  good.

I know that others find You in the light
 That filters down through tinted window
  panes,
And yet I seem to feel You near tonight
 In this dim, quiet starlight on the plains.

I thank You, Lord, that I am placed so well;
 That You have made my freedom so complete,
That I'm no slave of whistle, clock or bell,
 Or weak-eyed prisoner of wall or street.

Just let me live my life as I've begun,
 And give me work that's open to the sky;
Make me a partner of the wind and sun,
 And I won't ask a life that's soft or high.

Let me be easy on the man that's down;
 And make me square and generous with all;
I'm careless sometimes, Lord, when I'm in town,
 But never let them say I'm mean or small.

Make me as big and open as the plains,
 As honest as the horse between my knees,
Clean as the wind that blows behind the rains,
 Free as the hawk that circles down the breeze.

Forgive me, Lord, when I ·sometimes forget,
 You understand the reasons that are hid,
You know the little things that gall and fret,
 You know me better than my mother did.

Just keep an eye on all that's done and said,
Just right me sometimes when I turn aside,
And guide me on the long, dim trail ahead
That stretches upward toward the Great
Divide.

—*Author Unknown.*

September 9

"*For all the promises of God in him are yea, and in him Amen, ...*" (2 Cor. 1: 20.)

YOU have lost the key to a chest, and after trying all the keys you possess, you are obliged to send for a locksmith. The tradesman comes with a huge bunch of keys of all sorts and sizes. To you they appear to be a singular collection of rusty instruments. He looks at the lock and tries first one key and then another. He has not touched it yet; and your treasures are still out of your reach. Look! he has found the suitable key; it almost touches the bolt, but not quite. He is evidently on the right track now. At last the chest is opened, for the right key has been found.

This is a correct representation of many a perplexity. You cannot get at the difficulty so as to deal with it aright and find your way to a happy result. You pray but have not the liberty in prayer which you desire. A definite promise is what you want. You try one and another of the inspired words, but they do not fit. You try again, and in due season a promise presents itself which seems to have been made for the occasion; it fits as exactly as a well-made key fits the wards of the lock for which it was originally prepared. Having found the identical word of the living God, you hasten to plead it at the throne of grace, saying, "O my Lord, Thou hast promised this good thing unto Thy servant; be pleased to grant it!" The matter is ended; sorrow is turned to joy; prayer is heard.—*C. H. Spurgeon.*

"I have a key in my bosom, called *Promise,* that will, I am persuaded, open any lock." Then said Hopeful, "That's good news, good brother; pluck it out of thy bosom and try."—*Pilgrim's Progress.*

"*But oh, what light and glory,*
Would shine o'er all our ways,
If we always would remember
That He means just what He says."

September 10

"... I believe God, that it shall be even as it was told me."
(Acts 27: 25.)

BELIEF IS CONFIDENCE IN GOD'S WORD

BELIEVING does not come by trying. If a person were to make a statement of something that happened this day, I should not tell him that I would try to believe him. If I believed in the truthfulness of the man who told the incident to me and who said he saw it, I should accept the statement at once. If I did not think him a true man, I should, of course, disbelieve him; but there would be no trying in the matter. Now, when God declares there is salvation in Christ Jesus I must either believe Him at once or make Him a liar.   —*Charles H. Spurgeon.*

> *"O listen not to those who would steal*
> *our rights away,*
> *And make us doubt God's promise, which*
> *stands secure today;*
> *Begone such worldly wisdom, but rather let us*
> *say,*
> *It shall be as it was told me by the Lord."*

"All faith roots in the faithfulness of God."

September 11

"Give attendance to reading, . . ." (1 Tim. 4: 13.)

TELL me what you read, and I will tell you whether you are becoming like the strong oak that stands deep-rooted, ready for the sudden storm, or like the flimsy tumbleweed that is rolled across the fields by every caprice of the wind. I will tell you whether you will grow as the straight, tall fir tree grows, or be like the little garden shrub that never grows at all, or never casts any cool shade. I will always know if your leaves are green and your fruit faithful like the tree planted by the rivers of water, or dry as the sagebrush on the desert; whether you are tender and fragrant like the rose, or prickly and bitter like the thistle.

When the importance of good literature is urged upon them, people often say, "I just haven't time!" Some excuse themselves in what they read by saying, "But this is perfectly innocent and. harmless." No doubt it apparently may be, but is it positively helpful? In reality much of the so-called *harmless* reading matter in many of our homes is harmful in the very fact that it is not helpful. It is idle. It consumes quantities of time and interest and brain room without giving much eternal quality in return.

The next time you find yourself reading, ask yourself these questions: Is this strengthening my character, or slowly, subtly undermining it? Does this raise my ideals and sensibilities, or does it accustom me to worldliness and sin, until I gradually lose my protest and feel that some things are not so bad after all? Does it make me a better Christian? In reading this am I exhibiting high standards or low standards in my mental food and entertainment? Does my choice indicate refined or cheap tastes? Is this reading leading my mind along the way of least resistance; does it put my mental powers to sleep as a sedative, making me mentally lazy, and unfitting me for real thinking, or does it stimulate and sharpen my mental faculties? Does it leave me with a little feeling of pollution, or a sense of wholesomeness and well-being? Do I feel as though I have had a mental bath or as though I needed one? Does it increase my relish for the Bible and good, solid reading, or does it dull that relish and make such reading appear tame and uninteresting? Is it the best kind of reading I could be doing at this moment?
—*Excerpts from a Sermon.*

What we read mirrors our character!

September 12

"A wonderful and horrible thing is committed in the land."
(Jer. 5: 30.)

THIS sounds somewhat repulsive to start with, perhaps; yet it is the first lesson to learn in the school of God. There are many designations and descriptions of sin in God's Word. Here it is exposed in its real light. It is "wonderfully horrible." All sin, even the tiniest—as men regard it—is utterly revolting in the eyes of a holy God. It necessitated the agony of Calvary. It nailed precious hands and feet to a Roman Cross. Sin is never beautiful, though it may be attractive. A native Congo pastor once used this illustration: "Sin is not always sordid and low. Often it comes in most beautiful garb. But does that lessen or help us bear the misery of its results? A carrier goes to bring a load for the missionary. As he walks along the road, there is a flash from the bushes, and he feels the treacherous sting of a deadly serpent. When he turns to look at it, does he care whether it is gorgeous or beautiful? Does it matter to him whether it is the most beautiful snake in existence, or whether it is drab and ugly? Its sting is in his body. Its poison is already in his blood. Ugly or beautiful, the creature means but one thing—*death!* Even so with sin. It can be in the most attractive surroundings, or in the most beautiful attire; it can also be ugly and repulsive. But the wages is the same—*death!*

Many a temptation comes to us in fine, gay colors that are but skin deep.   —*Matthew Henry.*

> O God of peace, strong is the enemy,
>   But Thou art nigh,
> And he must fall beneath our feet, because
>   Of Calvary.
>
> Give us calm confidence of victory,
>   Lord of the fight;
> And when the enemy comes like a flood
>   Put him to flight.
>
> Mighty the weapons of our warfare are
>   Through Thee alone;
> Oh, lead us to the battle, captain us,
>   Most Mighty One.
>   —*A. W. C.*

September 13

"I beseech you therefore, brethren, by the mercies of God, that ye present your bodies a living sacrifice, holy, acceptable unto God, which is your reasonable service." (Rom. 12: 1.)

ONCE an Indian lived alone, hunting and trapping in the Selkirk Mountains. His family had all been killed by a band of white hunters, and he grew up a wild man. At length another trapper, a white man, came to the mountains to live. He was kind and patient, and gradually the wild boy came to trust him and to love him. Slowly he entered into the love of Jesus Christ, as the white man taught him. After many months of thought, one moonlit night on top of a noble peak, the young Indian dressed himself in all his heathen finery, took his friend's hand, knelt and prayed silently. Then he rose and made his confession of his new purpose, suiting the action to the word:

> "Indian lay down blanket,
> Indian lay down pipe.
> Indian lay down tomahawk.
> *Indian lay down Indian."*

Well may all of us learn a lesson from that child of the forest. What Christ requires of us is not some modifications, more or less complete, of our old life of sin and selfishness and doubt, but that we walk with Him in entire newness of life. "Indian must lay down Indian!"

September 14

"...That in all things he might have the pre-eminence."
(Col. 1: 18.)

AFTER President Garfield was assassinated he was taken to a quiet, isolated house where he could have absolute quiet and rest in his fight for life, and a special railway was constructed to facilitate the bringing of doctors, nurses and loved ones to his bedside. The engineers laid out the line to cross a farmer's front yard, but the determined old farmer refused to grant the right of way, until they explained to him that it was for the President; then he exclaimed:

"That is different! If that railroad is for the President, you can run it right through my house."

Are you willing to give Jesus right of way across your front yard? It may run right through some of your plans or social engagements or business appointments, but will you give Him the right of way?

Recognize God's right through your life!

Anything which makes Christianity its second object makes Christianity no object. God will put up with a great many things in the human heart, but there is one thing He will not put up with in it—a second place. He who offers God a second place offers Him no place. —*John Ruskin.*

September 15

"Then the spirit ... said unto me, Go, shut thyself within ..."
(Ezek. 3: 24.)

> *"'Tis good to be with Jesus*
> *From all the world apart.*
> *Enjoying sweet communion,*
> *That blessed 'better part.'"*

GET a place, some familiar place, for being alone with God—and a time. What time, it is not for me to say. I would not have anybody to be bound by rules concerning times or anything else; but have a time—times if you will—but a time at least. We shall all agree that, for the young, strong, and healthy, there is no time like the morning. Remember that God can do a wonderful amount of work in five minutes, if you can spare no more, but He can do nothing in five minutes, if you ought to give Him sixty. All this is between yourself and Him. Have a time, the time when the door is shut, the best beloved on earth excluded, the soul brought face to face with God.

A Christian lad, giving a testimony for Jesus, told his secret when he said that from the time of his conversion he trusted the Lord with his morning hour; and the way he spoke of it indicated the radiancy of the light that shone from him then. Loving youth, do you want a glad and rejoicing life? Do you want to live by the wells that never dry up or freeze? There is no hour like that of morning prime for fellowship with God. The filling of that hour will overflow into all the hours that follow.

"Do not have your concert first, then tune your instruments afterwards. Begin the day with the Word of God and prayer, and get first of all in harmony with Him."—*J. Hudson Taylor.*

"Happy is the youth whose morning is spent with Jesus. Early seekers make certain finders."

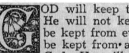

"When morning gilds the skies
My heart awaking cries,
Let Jesus Christ be praised!"

September 16

"He will keep the feet of his saints ..." (1 Samuel 2: 9.)

GOD will keep the feet of those who walk in His paths. He will not keep the feet of those who simply seek to be kept from eternal perdition; but of those who wish to be kept from all steps that accord not with the glory of God. He will keep the feet of those who commit all their steps into His keeping. He will keep them from frequenting the society of the wicked, from approaching the precipice of temptation, from that prosperity which bringeth a snare, from circumstances which are likely to be adverse to their piety and usefulness, from the burden of care, from the excessive pressure of responsibility, from erroneous doctrines, from vain speculations, from supineness and a bland confidence, from the fear of death, and from a serious misinterpretation of His providences.

He will not keep them from trials, privations, bereavements, worldly losses, perplexing combinations, inward conflicts, the tongue of slander and the misjudgment of friends. But He will keep them *above* these, and bring them off more than conquerors. He will keep them by the promises, by the commandments, by the example of Christ, by that of other saints, by the preaching of the Gospel, by the Sabbaths and by prayer meetings, by giving them the love of private prayer, and by leading them to self-examination. Sometimes, when a broad sea stretches before them, they are ready to say, "We are safer where we are." But they are pressed forward. Then a path is opened for them through the depths of the sea, and their feet are kept.

—*Rev. George Bowen.*

September 17

"...Perfect and complete in all the will of God." (Col. 4:12.)

WHEN Shackleton wanted two volunteers to join his party for the South Pole, fifty thousand young men applied. Youth is fascinated by the challenge of some rugged task. The Calvary spirit is our primary need in all our service for Christ.

> Your goal was not some island of the
> blessed,
> A zone of gardens, sweet with pink
> and chrome;
> You had not thought to find at last a
> home
> Where you might pause, by labors un-
> oppressed.
>
> Fearless and strong, you set upon your
> quest;
> Ice-fanged the ways that lured your
> dauntless ship,
> Endless the night that held you in its
> grip
> But stout the heart that beat within
> your breast.
>
> You are of the Norman breed, brave
> Viking soul;
> You rode the icebergs as a summer sea;
> Their crystal peaks, their cold, strange
> mystery
> Lured on and on, till God revealed
> your goal.
> —*The Spirit of Amundsen.*

> "My goal is God Himself, not joy, nor peace,
> Not even blessing, but Himself, my God;
> 'Tis His to lead me there, not mine, but His—
> At any cost, dear Lord, by any road."

All great men and women travel the way of the Cross. Be not afraid of the rugged mountain-climb. With Him scale the heights today!

September 18

*"And be not conformed to this world: but be ye transformed
by the renewing of your mind, that ye may prove what is
that good, and acceptable, and perfect, will of God."*
(Rom. 12:2.)

AT BAALBEC in a quarry lies a magnificent column—the
largest worked stone in the world—almost detached and
ready for transportation. In the ruined Temple of the
Sun nearby is a niche still waiting for it after forgotten
centuries. So large, so good, yet a failure, because it
never filled the place for which it was quarried and hewn.

The unused column may represent the possibilities in a human
life—the empty niche, the opportunities! How many lives that
never fulfill the bright possibilities before them!

"If you are in the *wrong* place, the *right* place is vacant."

God has *just one person to come at the right moment*; a place
which no one can fill *but that person and at that time!*

> *Whate'er your place, it is
> Not yours alone, but His
> Who sent you there.*
> —*John Oxenham.*

Ask God if you are in His chosen place.

> *"Our life is but a little holding lent
> To do a mighty labor. We are one
> With heaven and the stars when it is spent
> To do God's will."*

It is possible for us to miss God's plan for our lives.

September 19

*"Now in the place where he was crucified there was a
garden; ..."*
(John 19:41.)

THE *Cross* was the crowning service of Christ's life! It
was love going to the uttermost. To John it was no
mere coincidence that in the place of that supreme
surrender there should be the fragrance and the blos-
soming of flowers. One might have thought to find
a desert there. One might have counted on a bleak and dreary
scene. What struck the mystical eye of the apostle was that
everything was the opposite of that! Christ died! He gave Him-

self for man! He poured out His life in full surrender! And in the place where all this happened was a garden!

John hints that there is always a garden when we share in the self-surrender of our Lord. Let any person willingly lay down his life for others; let him surrender what is dearest to him in self-abandonment of love, and the strange thing is that everything grows beautiful, and the flowers begin to blossom at his feet in a way they never did before. It seems to be a hard, bleak life; the life of a continuous self-denial. It *seems* to rob one of many a sweet thing which is the gift of God. Surrender up thy life with its freedoms and its sweet and secret pleasures; turn thy days into an arid desert where no passionate flowers can ever grow! But John saw it was entirely otherwise. Live for self, and you move into a wilderness. Sooner or later the scenery grows desolate; the fragrance disappears; the world grows cold and meaningless and ugly. Lose your life for the sake of others who need you, and in the place where you are crucified there is a *garden!*

Self-surrender is the road to service. Self-denial is the way to song. To be made captive by the Lord Jesus Christ is to have the freedom of the universe. Then one goes back to this quiet word of John and begins to understand the depth of it: *"In the place where He was crucified there was a garden!"*

—*George H. Morrison, D. D.*

September 20

"And call upon me in the day of trouble: . . ." (Psalm 50: 15.)

IN A factory where delicate fabrics are woven the operators are required, when the threads at any time become tangled, to press a button which calls the foreman to come and put matters right. On one occasion, however, a woman who was an old hand at the work thought she could disentangle the threads without the foreman's help, but she made things much worse. When the foreman did come she said, "I did my best, sir."

His answer was, "Remember that doing your best is to send for me."

When things get in a tangle, doing our best is sending for the Master, asking Him to straighten them out for us.

> Once in an eastern palace wide
> A little child sat weaving;
> So patiently her task she plied,
> The men and women at her side
> Flocked round her, almost grieving.

"How is it, little one," they said,
"You always work so cheerily?
You never seem to break your thread,
Or snarl or tangle it, instead
Of working smooth and clearly."

"I only go and tell the King,"
She said, abashed and meekly;
"You know He said 'In everything.'"
"Why, so do we!" they cried, "we bring
Him all our troubles weekly."

She turned her little head aside;
A moment let them wrangle;
"Ah, but," she softly then replied,
"I go and get the knot untied
At the first little tangle!"
                    —*Selected.*

HE IS ABLE

"The fingers that wove the rainbow into a scarf,
And wrapped it around the shoulders of the dying storm;
The fingers that painted the lily bell
And threw out the planets;
The fingers that were dipped in the mighty sea of eternity
And shaken out over this old planet,
Making the ocean to drop and the rivers to stream—
The same fingers can take hold of these tangled lives
And make them whole again.
For He can make the crooked straight."

September 21

"Look not thou upon the wine when it is red, when it
giveth his colour in the cup, when it moveth itself aright.
At the last it biteth like a serpent, and stingeth like an adder."
                    (Prov. 23:31, 32.)

TRIFLING WITH A SERPENT

THERE is a fable that a serpent found himself surrounded with a ring of fire and said to a man standing near, "Lift me out." The answer was, "If I do, you will bite me.' Over and over the serpent pledged himself that he would not do it, and finally, the fable goes, the young man reached over and lifted the serpent from his perilous position. But he was no sooner safe than his fangs protruded, and he made ready to strike with the sting of death.

"But you promised that you would not," said his rescuer. "I

know I did," said the serpent, "but it is my nature to sting, and I can't help it."

And this is true of strong drink. Men trifle with it, and they imagine that when they choose to do so, they can break themselves free from its power; but it is its nature to sting and kill and destroy, and no one is so strong that he can overcome it in his own strength, if it once gets a hold upon his life.

—*Selected.*

A MESSAGE TO YOUTH.

"You may think that you have self-control enough to take care of yourself. But the chances are that your self-control will be no more than pasteboard against a Gatling gun if you tamper with temptation and once begin the indulgence. If you want a clear head; if you want a sound heart; if you want a clear conscience; if you want a healthy body; if you want money in your pocket and credit to your name, put your foot right down and say that you are going to abstain from the use of intoxicating liquors, and keep the faith."

—*Exchange.*

The journey of a thousand miles begins with the first step. Watch your step!

September 22

"Thou therefore endure hardness, as a good soldier of Jesus Christ." (2 Tim. 2:3.)

IN THE noble struggle for freedom and a united Italy against seemingly unconquerable foes and insuperable difficulties, Garibaldi flung forth to his dispirited forces this challenge: "Soldiers! What I have to offer you is fatigue, danger, struggle and death; the chill of the cold night in the open air, and heat under the burning sun; no lodgings, no munitions, no provisions, but forced marches, dangerous watchposts, and the continual struggle with the bayonet against batteries. *Those who love freedom and their country, follow me!*" They answered the call.

"A brave man inspires others to heroism, but his own courage is not diminished when it enters into other souls; it is stimulated and invigorated."   —*Washington Gladden.*

I shall go across battlefields and into twisting storms that I may have an experience of the Father's care, protection, and glorious deliverances! I am to share in the tremendous experiences of the great!

I am builded not as a skiff but as an ocean liner to sail the high seas of the universe.

September 23

"Brethren, let every man, wherein he is called, therein abide with God." (1 Cor. 7:24.)

NDER the elms on College Hill a freshman sat looking off toward the sunset. He was looking through the glory of departing day into his own grey future. He was fighting for a quiet and trustful submission to the inevitable.

The boy was country born and bred. All his life he had dreamed of college and the theological seminary, and then the ministry. From the little red schoolhouse at the crossroads below his father's farm he had entered the Free Academy in the near-by city and was graduated at the head of his class. Then he suffered a severe illness. The doctors told the ambitious student that his only hope of recovery was a complete change of occupation. For two years he ploughed and sowed and harvested and hardly looked inside the covers of a book. Finally he seemd so far recovered that he thought he might enter the college of his choice.

But the first week of study brought back the old pain and dizziness. Gradually he came to realize that he must surrender his ambition, give up the ministry, and go back home to the farm. He wrestled long before peace came. The next day he packed his books and his trunk, said good-bye to his teachers and to the friends he had made, and went quietly home.

Steadily and successfully he applied himself to the work of a farmer. His manner of life was a kind of visible conscience for his neighbors. He toiled long hours from Monday morning until Saturday night, but he was always in his place at the morning and evening services of the little country church, and he was constant in attending the midweek prayer meeting. He taught in the Sunday school and was a source of strength to the Young People's Society. The church made him an elder, and as the older men were carried one by one to their last resting place, he became the recognized intellectual, moral, and religious leader of the community.

He never stood in the pulpit, but as a Christian farmer he exerted a spiritual influence that any man might covet.

—*The Youth's Companion.*

> *To some Christ calls: "Leave boat and bay,*
> *And white-haired Zebedee";*
> *To some the call is harder: "Stay*
> *And mend the nets for Me."*
>
> —*Selected.*

"... So shall his part be that tarrieth by the stuff: they shall part alike." (1 Samuel 30:24.)

September 24

"Thou wilt keep him in perfect peace, whose mind is stayed on thee; because he trusteth in thee." (Isa. 26:3.)

ISS AMY CARMICHAEL gives a beautiful illustration from nature of this kind of trust. The sunbird—one of the tiniest of birds, a native of India—builds a pendant nest, hanging it by four frail threads, generally from a spray of valaris. It is a delicate work of art, with its roof and tiny porch, which a splash of water or a child's touch might destroy. Miss Carmichael tells how she saw a little sunbird building such a nest just before the monsoon season, and felt that for once bird wisdom had failed; for how could such a delicate structure, in such an exposed situation, weather the winds and the torrential rains? The monsoon broke, and from her window she watched the nest swaying with the branches in the wind. Then she perceived that the nest had been so placed that the leaves immediately above it formed little gutters which carried the water away from the nest. There sat the sunbird, with its tiny head resting on her little porch, and whenever a drop of water fell on her long, curved beak, she sucked it in as if it were nectar. The storms raged furiously, but the sunbird sat, quiet and unafraid, hatching her tiny eggs.

We have a more substantial rest for head and heart than the sunbird's porch! We have the promises of God! Are they not enough, however terrifying the storm?

> *"Like a bird that found its nest,*
> *So my soul has found its rest*
> *In the center of the will of God."*

September 25

"My son, give me thine heart, and let thine eyes observe my ways." (Prov. 23:26.)

HE rich young ruler consecrated a part but was unwilling to consecrate the whole. He hallowed the inch but not the mile. He would go part of the way but not to the end. And the peril is upon us all. We give ourselves to the Lord, but we reserve some liberties. We offer Him our house, but we mark some rooms "private." And that word "private," denying the Lord admission, crucifies Him afresh. He has no joy in the house so long as any rooms are withheld.

Dr. F. B. Meyer has told us how his early Christian life was marred and his ministry paralyzed, just because he had kept back one key from the bunch of keys he had given to the Lord. Every key save one! The key of one room kept for personal use, and the Lord shut out. And the effects of the incomplete consecration were found in lack of power, lack of assurance, lack of joy and peace.

The "joy of the Lord" begins when we hand over the last key. We sit with Christ on His throne as soon as we have surrendered all our crowns, and made Him the sole and only ruler of our life and its possessions. The last touch of consecration lands us in the very heart of God's eternal peace.

Give God the key to all the inner rooms of your heart, and follow! The issue is transcendently glorious.

"He had great possessions." Did he? or did great possessions have him?

Possession comes through giving, not giving through possession.

September 26

"And God spake..." (Genesis 46: 2.)

ANY man may hear the voice of God. When man will listen, God speaks. When God speaks, men are changed. When men are changed, nations are changed.

In the ancient days *God spake*, and the wonderful things which He told Moses on the mountaintop have inspired mankind for centuries.

Down through the years men of God have heard His voice. *God spake* to George Muller, and he became the modern apostle of faith. Hudson Taylor heard Him speak as he walked by the seashore on a memorable Sabbath morning, and in obedience to that Voice he launched forth into inland China, establishing mission stations in every province of that vast country.

God spake to Dr. A. B. Simpson, and he stepped aside from a well-beaten path and like Abraham of old, "went forth, not knowing whither he went." Today, *The Christian and Missionary Alliance*, operating in more than twenty mission fields of the world, is the result of his obedience, and untold numbers have been blessed through his ministry.

Charles Cowman heard the "soft and gentle Voice," when *God spake* saying, "Get thee out of thy country, and from they kindred, and from thy father's house, unto a land that I will shew thee." The result—*The Oriental Missionary Society*, with hundreds of mission stations dotted all over the Orient! And now its activities have extended into The Land of the Southern Cross and embrace the wide world.

When Isaiah heard the voice of the Lord saying, "Who will go for us?" he quickly answered, "Here am I; send me."

"I heard Him call, 'Come, follow,' that was all,
My gold grew dim, my heart went after Him,
I rose and followed, that was all;
Who would not follow if he heard Him call?"

September 27

"...That it may bring forth more fruit."   (John 15:2.)

TWO years ago I set out a rosebush in the corner of my garden. It was to bear yellow roses, and it was to bear them profusely. Yet, during those two years, it did not produce a blossom!

I asked the florist from whom I bought the bush why it was so barren of flowers. I had cultivated it carefully, had watered it often, had made the soil around it as rich as possible; and it had grown well.

"That's just the reason," said the florist. "That kind of rose needs the poorest soil in the garden. Sandy soil would be best and never a bit of fertilizer. Take away the rich soil and put gravelly earth in its place. Cut the bush back severely. Then it will bloom."

I did—and the bush blossomed forth in the most gorgeous yellow known to nature. Then I moralized: that yellow rose is just like many lives. Hardships develop beauty in the soul; they thrive on troubles; trials bring out all the best in them; ease and comfort and applause only leave them barren.—*Pastor Joyce.*

The finest of flowers bloom in the sandiest of deserts as well as in the hothouses. God is the same Gardener.

September 28

"I have prayed that your own faith may not fail: . . ."
(Luke 22: 32, Trans.)

CHRISTIAN, take good care of thy faith, for recollect, that *faith is the only means whereby thou canst obtain blessings.* Prayer cannot draw down answers from God's throne except it be the earnest prayer of the man who believes.

Faith is the telegraphic wire which links earth to Heaven, on which God's messages of love fly so fast that before we call, He answers, and while we are yet speaking, He hears us. But if that telegraphic wire of faith be snapped, how can we obtain the promise?

Am I in trouble? I can obtain help for trouble by faith. Am I beaten about by the enemy? My soul on her dear Refuge leans by faith.

But take faith away, then in vain I call to God. There is no other road betwixt my soul and Heaven. Blockade the road, and how can I communicate with the Great King?

Faith links me with Divinity. Faith clothes me with the power of Jehovah. Faith insures every attribute of God in my defense. It helps me to defy the hosts of hell. It makes me march triumphant over the necks of my enemies. But without faith how can I receive anything from the Lord?

Oh, then, Christian, watch well thy faith. "If thou canst believe, all things are possible to him that believeth."
—C. H. Spurgeon.

"Faith, mighty faith, the promise sees,
    And looks to that alone,
Laughs at impossibilities,
    And cries, 'It shall be done!'"

Queen Victoria said, "We are not interested in the possibilities of defeat. They do not exist!"

September 29

"This is the day which the Lord hath made; we will rejoice and be glad in it." (Psalm 118:24.)
"I was glad when they said unto me, Let us go into the house of the Lord." (Psalm 122:1.)

A FREQUENT visitor at Mount Vernon wrote: "No company ever prevented George Washington from attending church. I have often been at Mount Vernon on Sabbath morning when his breakfast table was filled with guests, but to him they furnished no pretext whatever for neglecting his God and losing the satisfaction of setting a good example. For instead of staying at home out of false complaisance to them, he always invited them to accompany him.

THE SHEPHERD'S HEART

I pondered quite a while at home
Before I came to church today,
I longed the wooded hills to roam,
To worship God in my own way;
"I'm only one, I do not count,"

And this excuse served very well
Till, coming from its steeple mount,
I heard the sound of my church bell.
Then coming through the church door
  wide,
I found my Lord expecting me,
His nail-pierced hands drew me in-
  side,
He said, "My child, I've watched for
  thee,"
Now seated here within my place,
The ninety and nine come back to me,
And oh, the pain on my Lord's face,
When one stray lamb he cannot see!
  —Myrtle R. Stacy.

"...*As his custom was, he went into the synagogue on the sabbath day,* ..." (Luke 4: 16.)

September 30

"If I take the wings of the morning, . . ." (Psalm 139:9.)

THE *morning* is the time of wonderful light, dewy freshness, music, joy and promise! And youth is the morning hour of life. It is the time of lovely light, glad music, the delicacy of dew, the wonderful joy and promise of that which is to be. It is the time of vision, of high, happy and wide-ranging ambitions and eagerness. It is the time for wings, for he who would rise aloft must have wings, and the morning is the winged time. Those two wings of the morning are FAITH and FIDELITY. There is no lofty life, there are no high clear spaces of the upper air possible except by the use of the two wings of the morning.

But these two wings may be crippled by two weights which may hold us down in the dim, dusty, dreary, lower levels of life—FEAR and FOLLY. Nothing cripples the wings of faith like being afraid to seek and hear the truth, afraid to listen to one's own deeper voices, afraid to honor the best and obey the highest. It is folly not to follow the great, gifted, far-seeing Christian leaders of the centuries.

Drop those weights of FEAR and FOLLY! Take the wings of the morning and fly. Stretch those wings of FAITH and FIDELITY. Challenge them to your great adventure. Test them! Try them! Mount to the heights! Then the high places and the far horizons and the clear, infinite sky shall be yours with its radiance and its peace. Wings are yours! "Take the wings of the morning"—sure, serene, courageous, and unafraid!

October 1

"So he fed them according to the integrity of his heart; and guided them by the skilfulness of his hands. (Psalm 78: 72.)

THE most interesting thing in the world is to live a great life. God has a plan for every life, a really great plan. God never made anything cheap or uninteresting. He has equipped every life for a great career, and a great destiny. He challenges you to a wonderful friendship with Him. Out of this friendship shall come your development, your empowering, your guidance—your success. God is interested in you. He has great things for you to accomplish during your lifetime. You alone can wreck your own life. Mistakes there may have been a plenty, but sin and life's blunders He corrects and cures. The Holy Spirit has been given to us to lead us into all truth. He is our Teacher, our Protector, our Inspirer, our Guide. He was commissioned to make sure of the greatness of every life. His mode of procedure is to build the life of Jesus into the life of each Christian in a wonderfully precious friendship. The Holy Spirit fuses the will of man into the will of God. So the great thing in all life is to live to please God. What we are, what we say, what we do is saturated with the life of Jesus. The very atmosphere is full of quietness, peace, and love. Such a life will go through the world comforting, cheering, healing, and inspiring other lives. Fortunate, indeed, the community that has a few individuals who thus go through life. One such nature can influence an entire community, just as one flower will fill a whole room with sweet odors."   —*Dean Dutton, D. D.*

"The one greatest act of a lifetime is to accept the Creator's full lifetime program and enter into rich fellowship with Him, here and now."

October 2

"...Neither will I offer...unto the Lord my God of that which doth cost me nothing. .... (2 Samuel 24: 24.)

THE following story is told of a young African convert who was saved out of the vilest savagery. She came on Christmas Day—the Lord's birthday—with her gift to Him. "These African Christians were very poor—a few vegetables or a bunch of flowers was all they could bring— a coin worth a penny or two would have been a valuable gift. But here came this girl of sixteen, and from under her dress she drew a coin worth eighty-five cents and handed it to the missionary as *her* gift to the Saviour she loved. He was so amazed that he could hardly accept it but said little until after the service, when. he enquired how she had obtained a fortune like that. And then she explained that in order to give Christ an offering that satisfied her own heart she had gone to a neighboring planter and had bound herself out to him as a slave for the *rest of her life* for this sum of eighty-five cents. Thus her gift was the equivalent of the whole strength and service of the rest of her life, and she had brought it and laid it down at the feet of her Lord."

> *"Only the best, only the best,*
> *Is good enough for Jesus!"*

October 3

"And thine ears shall hear a word behind thee, saying, This is the way, walk ye in it, when ye turn to the right hand, and when ye turn to the left." (Isa. 30:21.)

THIS is the season when migratory birds are winging their way toward warmer climes. What is it that prompts them to fly for hundreds of miles each year to the balmy southland and to return again in the springtime to the exact spot which they left in the autumn? For want of a better term, we call it *instinct.* One authority states that the word means "inward impulse"; "a natural propensity that incites animals to the actions that are essential to their existence and development"; or, "a propensity prior to experience and independent of instructions."

The authorities in charge of one of the oldest missions on the Pacific Coast state that the swallows, which make their homes in the walls of this historic institution, migrate with the utmost regularity. During a record of sixty-eight years, it is said that they have never been a day late or early in their arrival at this mission. One press reporter affirms that "For the first time in the known mission history, the swallows were several hours late in arriving last March." This was supposed to have been due to a storm at sea.

How can men doubt that there is an all-wise God who has placed within these tiny creatures such mysterious powers? It is only because of the taint of sin and the deception of Satan that men do not obey a higher instinct and seek protection and rest under the shelter of the Almighty.

> *No chart or compass have the birds*
> *That migrate ev'ry year;*
> *They know they will be shown the way—*
> *They feel no doubt or fear.*

Can we not be as filled with faith—
Our minds as free from doubt?
Can we not trust in God above
To point our pathway out?
                    —Anonymous.

"I like to watch the swallow turn its face to the ocean and set fearlessly over the waters. If I had no other proof of lands beyond the sea, the instinct of the swallow would satisfy me."
                    —F. W. Boreham.

"I see my way as birds their
        trackless way;
    I shall arrive—what time, what
        circuit first,
    I ask not — —
    He guides me and the bird, in
        His good time."

October 4

"Be not deceived; ..." (Gal. 6: 7.)

SIN as a caterpillar is bad enough, but sin as a butterfly is a thousand times worse.

"If sin in its grossest form be thus dangerous, what must be the unmeasured power of sin when it puts on the robes of beauty? For the purpose of impressing upon my mind the beauty of the butterfly, I read a volume lately written by a popular entomologist with this as my sole objective. It is said that the finest Mosaic picture contains as many as 870 tesserae, or separate pieces to the square inch of surface, but upon the same small space of a butterfly's wing the entomologist has counted no less than 150,000 separate glittering scales, each scale carrying in it a gorgeous color, beautiful and distinct.

"On every wing there is a picture as varied as the rainbow. Every wing is iridescent with different lights that shift and change. Here are patches of blue, and spots of purple, and lines of green, and aurelian, and red. Every wing is speckled and mottled, flecked and tinted. Here are fringes of snow-white, and waves of crimson, and whole chains of little crescents. The poets call the butterfly 'a flying and flashing gem,' 'a flower of paradise, gifted with the magic power of flight.' They tell us that its wings are as rich as the evening sky.

"I want to magnify the transmutation of the caterpillar into the butterfly. I want to set into great prominence the great contrast between the crawler and the flyer. And why? That I may remind you that *the butterfly is only a caterpillar beautified with wings.* It is only a painted worm decked in a velvet suit, and adorned with sparkling gems. Egg and caterpillar and butterfly, the three forms of this creature's existence, are one and of the same nature. It speaks, too, of the power of Satan to transform himself into an angel of light, and of the power of sin to make itself attractive, and of the power of error to deck itself in robes that resemble the robes of truth, so that even the very elect of God are in danger of being deceived. For example, 'Sin beautifies itself by assuming and wearing the wings of wit,' as do immorality and lust in some of our popular literature, the wings of fashion, the wings of art, and wings of attractive and pleasing names."   —*David Gregg, D. D.*

"Be not deceived!"

October 5

"*I can do all things through Christ which strengtheneth me.*" (Phil. 4:13.)

WHEN the kite sails with a loose string, it drops, because there is not enough opposition to keep it afloat; and when men have no odds against them in life, nothing to draw out their vital force of opposition, they also soon trail along the ground. This is the meaning of temptation; it is discipline. We do not enter the world ready-made; we are engaged in the making of ourselves, and in the process, temptation must needs play a tremendous part.
—*W. J. Dawson,* in *The Divine Challenge.*

YOU CAN CONQUER TEMPTATION

One time in my boyhood I was fighting a terrific temptation, about which my mother knew nothing except that boys of that age had fights that were real. I had led in prayer at morning devotions and must have dropped some word in my prayer that was a window through which my mother looked into my soul and saw that a fight was going on. After prayers were over, and I had stepped into the hall to get my cap as I was going to school, I remember mother's coming out, putting her hand on my shoulder and saying:

"Go on, my boy! You will win!"

And I did, too.

This is a vital value of Christianity. When you put your life in touch with Jesus Christ it puts behind you the lift of a great companionship. You do not fight alone. He stands behind you and says, "Go on! Do what is right! You can win. Play the game!"

—*A. W. Beaven.*

"While praying to be delivered from a temptation, do not peep at it through your fingers."

> "*Every time that we yield to temptation*
> *It is easier for us to do wrong;*
> *Every time we resist temptation,*
> *It is easier for us to be strong.*"

"A good traffic rule on the road of life: 'When you meet temptation, turn to the right.' "

October 6

"*...If a man love me, he will keep my words: and my Father will love him, and we will come unto him, and make our abode with him.*" (John 14:23.)

THE great need of the age is a new *God-consciousness*. If we are His children the Lord proposes to keep us company in every hour of life. "Lo, I am with you always and all the day."

God is a person, a Person to whom we can say, "Thou"; a Person who can speak to us as a man speaketh to his friend and who can become to us a heavenly Father. Thus we may come to be at peace with Him, and to be His child forevermore.

When you meet a friend on the street, and he recognizes you, you always return the bow, unless you wish rudely and intentionally to repulse him. This is the secret of enjoying the Lord's presence. Recognize His presence, and He will respond. Recognize Him in your heart. Many persons are waiting for the Lord to reveal Himself, but they themselves never recognize His presence in them. "Know ye not," says the Apostle Paul, "that ye are the temple of the Holy Ghost, which is within you?" Recognize this fact. Speak to Him in your heart, and He will speak to you. Call His dear name; wait in silence for Him to speak from within and sweet and quick as the echo, will come the answering whisper of love, "Here am I."

—*Dr. A. B. Simpson.*

The Master needed companionship — "Let *us* go hence."

> "*Warm, sweet, tender, even yet*
> *A present help is He,*
> *And faith has still its Olivet,*
> *And love its Galilee.*"

October 7

"Buying up your opportunity, . . ." (Eph. 5:16, R. V.)

SCOTCH botanist sallied forth to the hills one bright day to study his favorite flowers. Presently he plucked a heather bell and put it upon the glass of his microscope. He stretched himself at length upon the ground and began to scrutinize it through the microscope. Moment after moment passed, and still he lay there gazing, entranced by the beauty of the little flower. Suddenly a shadow fell upon the ground where he lay. Looking up, he saw a tall, weather-beaten shepherd gazing down with a smile of half-concealed amusement at a man spending his time looking through a glass at so common a thing as a heather bell. Without a word the botanist reached up and handed the shepherd the microscope. He placed it to his eye and began to gaze. For him, too, moment after moment sped by while he gazed in enraptured silence. When he handed back the glass the botanist noticed that the tears were streaming down his bronzed cheeks and falling on the ground at his feet. "What's the matter," said the botanist. "Isn't it beautiful?" "Beautiful?" said the shepherd. "It is beautiful beyond all words. But I am thinking of *how many thousands* of them I have trodden under foot!"

Priceless opportunities pass. We can lose them! We trample upon them, and they are lost forever!

October 8

"God has kindled a flame in my heart to make me a world's beacon. . . ." (2 Cor. 4:6, Weymouth.)

LAMPS do not talk; but they do shine. A lighthouse sounds no drum; it beats no gong; and yet, far over the waters its friendly spark is seen by the mariner.
—*Spurgeon.*

Every Christian ought to be in his human measure a new incarnation of the Christ, so that people shall say, "He interprets Christ to me."—*Rev. J. R. Miller, D. D.*

HIS LAMPS

His lamps we are,
To shine where He shall say:
And lamps are not for sunny rooms
Nor for the light of day;
But for dark places of the earth,
Where shame and wrong and crime have
birth,

Or for the murky twilight grey,
Where wandering sheep have gone astray,
Or where the Lamp of Faith grows dim,
And souls are groping after Him.
And as sometimes a flame we find
Clear-shining through the night,
So dark we cannot see the lamp,
But only see the Light,
So may we shine, His love the flame,
That men may glorify His Name.
—A. J. F.

In his beautiful and gripping story, *"Black Rock,"* Ralph Connor informs us that Graeme once said to him, "Now Connor, don't rage. Craig will walk where his light falls; and I should hate to see him fail; for if he weakens like the rest of us, my North Star will have dropped from my sky."

Each of us is a sort of North Star for someone else. Each must live his own life in the sense that no one can live it for him. However, if we fall far short of our ideals and of the hopes that our loved ones have for us, we have not only injured ourselves, but have caused somebody's North Star to drop from the sky.

October 9

"...What think ye of Christ?..." (Matt. 22:42.)

JESUS challenges the attention of the world by His great versatility. He meets all the needs of all classes and conditions of men.

Call the roll of the world's workers and ask, "What think ye of Christ?" Their answers amaze us by their revelation of these qualifying attributes of the Saviour. He is:

To the Artist—the One Altogether Lovely.
To the Architect—the Cornerstone.
To the Astronomer—Sun of Righteousness.
To the Baker—the Living Bread.
To the Doctor—the Great Physician.
To the Educator—the Great Teacher.
To the Farmer—the Sower and Lord of the Harvest.
To the Newspaper man—the Good Tidings of Great Joy.
To the Servant—the Good Master.
To the Student— the Incarnate Truth.
To the Theologian—the Author and Finisher of our Faith.
To the Builder— the Sure Foundation.
To the Carpenter—the Door.
To the Preacher—the Word of God.

To the Banker—the Hidden Treasure.
To the Biologist—the Life.
To the Toiler—the Giver of Rest.
To the Sinner—the Lamb of God who taketh away Sin.

There is a Russian legend—(you will remember that it is only a legend)—that when our Lord was on earth an artist wanted to paint His picture. He could successfully paint other folk, but every time he tried to paint Christ he failed. At length he went to our Lord and asked the reason, and Christ smiled at him and said: "No one can paint a picture of Me for anyone else, for if he did, it would be said that the Christ was thus and thus; every one must paint his own picture."

October 10

"...Ye were not redeemed with corruptible things, as silver and gold...But with the precious blood of Christ,..."
(1 Peter 1:18, 19.)

NE of the richest spots on earth is Johannesburg. It is rich because of its apparently limitless supplies of gold. But think of that wealth plus all the pearls of the South Seas and all the diamonds of the East! Think of the jewels of the world and the treasures of State, and then you would not have reached the value of a single soul!

"Say, knowest thou what it is or what thou art?
    Knowest thou the importance of a soul immortal?
Behold this midnight glory of the stars,
    Amazing pomp, worlds upon worlds,
Ten thousand add and twice ten thousand more;
    Then weigh the whole—one soul out-weighs them all."

Oh, that we had a passion to save others! It was a pledge between that holy India missionary, known as "Praying Hyde," and God—that each day he should win at least four souls.
And Brainerd tells us that one Sunday night he offered himself to be used by God and for Him. "It was raining, and the roads were muddy; but this desire grew so strong that I kneeled down by the side of the road and told God all about it. While I was praying, I told Him that my hands should work for Him, my tongue speak for Him, if He would only use me as His instrument—when suddenly the darkness of the night lit up, and I knew that God had heard and answered my prayer; and I felt that I was accepted into the inner circle of God's loved ones."

One youth on fire with the love of Jesus may set the whole universe ablaze.

October 11

"But if we walk in the light, as he is in the light, we have
fellowship one with another, and the blood of Jesus Christ
his Son cleanseth us from all sin." (1 John 1:7.)

OME time ago the front door bell in our home went
out of order. For some reason only a faint sound came
from it, so we sent for a repairman. What was wrong?
Spider webs were discovered inside of it and were hindering the vibration of sound.

"Oh, those cobwebs! Those hindering things which dull our
witness. What are they? Some habit, self-indulgence, friendship, or pastime? Or is it sloth, pride, indulgence, worldliness,
self-seeking, love of praise, selfish motives, undisciplined life,
or self-will?

"Let God cleanse them away! Your life will never ring true
as long as they remain." —*Selected.*

"Nothing between my soul and the Saviour
So that His blessed face may be seen;
Nothing preventing the least of His favor,
Keep the way clear! Let nothing between."

October 12

"And Moses said unto the Lord, O my Lord, I am not elo-
quent...but I am slow of speech, and of a slow tongue."
(Exod. 4:10.)

ONE OF GOD'S FARMERS

(The conversion of Bishop William A. Quayle as told by
himself.)

THINK of the funny men I have had preach to me, and
I remember how some of them did tear the beautiful
garment of dramatic expression into small ribbons and
did not care about the ribbons at all; and I remember
when I heard them fall on the 'whom's' and the 'who's'
and all the ridiculosities of speech. Yet I remember some of
those men who could not get it arranged whether they should
say 'who' or 'whom,' who brought you up until you fell on the
outstretched Hand, and caught the foot of the Cross. I would
not say I like people to be ungrammatical; but I would rather
hear some people who are ungrammatical and divine, than hear
other people who are grammatical and utterly human.

"The preacher came over to me and said, 'Billy, you belong
with Jesus!' He was a kindly man, and he wore threadbare, out-

of-date clothes, and spoke with much tenderness. He said that there was a Sower who went out to sow, and that there was a great harvest. And everybody paid heed. Then he came and put his hand on my shoulder and said, 'Billy, God wants you to be one of his farmers.' And I came up the aisle of the old log schoolhouse; not to the chancel—there wasn't anything but a dictionary in the schoolhouse, so I came up and bowed at the dictionary. And oh, the wind was wild that night! It was as stormy as on the wild sea, the storm that beat upon that prairie schoolhouse. The wind had its chance and blew as it did on the Sea of Galilee; and it seemed to me that Christ came over and said, 'Boy, what do you want down here?'—and I said, 'I want Thee, O Christ!' And he said, 'I have come!' "

"Great lives spring from great awakenings."

October 13

"...Count it all joy when ye fall into divers temptations; Knowing this, that the trying of your faith worketh patience."
(James 1:2, 3.)

G OD can make a stepping-stone of Satan himself for advancing His own work!" And all this teaches me how I must think about my temptations. I must look upon temptation as opportunity. I must regard it, not as something to be feared, but as something to be used. And so it is that the apostle counsels us to *count it all joy* when we fall among temptations! They are often full of menace, but splendid wealth lies behind the guns! Refuse to yield, and the wealth is yours! Our manifold temptations are just the threatening side of manifold treasures. If we overcome the tempter, we shall return in power. In great temptations we are being favored with a shining opportunity, and we are to count it all joy. Let us fight the good fight of faith, assured that every victory will make us nobler soldiers. And let us fight in the holy fellowship of the Captain of our salvation, who, Himself being tempted, turned His wilderness into a place of springs, and who will so strengthen His disciples that their wilderness and solitary place shall be glad, and their desert shall rejoice and blossom as the rose.

—*Dr. J. H. Jowett.*

Temptation sharp? Thank God a second time!
Why comes temptation but for man to meet
And master and make crouch beneath his foot,
And so be pedestalled in triumph? Pray:
"Lead us into no such temptations, Lord!"

Yea, but, O Thou whose servants are the bold,
Lead such temptations by the head and hair,
Reluctant dragons, up to who dares fight,
That so he may do battle and have praise!
                    —Robert Browning.

Roar he or purr, he is a conquered foe!

October 14

"He was oppressed, and he was afflicted, yet he opened not his mouth: he is brought as a lamb to the slaughter, and as a sheep before her shearers is dumb, so he openeth not his mouth." (Isa. 53:7.)

NEVER allow yourself to answer again when you are blamed," says Alexander Whyte. "Never defend yourself. Let them reprehend you, in private or in public, as much as they please. Let the righteous smite you; it shall be a kindness; and let them reprove you, it shall be an excellent oil, which shall not break your head. Never so much as explain your meaning, under any invitation or demand whatsoever. 'It is the mark of the deepest and truest humility,' says a great saint, 'to see ourselves condemned without cause, and to be silent under it. To be silent under insult and wrong is a noble imitation of our Lord.' O my Lord, when I remember in how many ways Thou didst suffer, Who in no way deserved it, I know not where my senses are when I am in such a haste to defend and excuse myself. Is it possible I should desire anyone to speak good of me, or to think it, when so many ill things were thought and spoken of Thee! What is this, Lord; what do we imagine to get by pleasing words? What about being blamed by all men, if only we stand at last blameless before Thee!"

The day when Jesus stood alone
And felt the hearts of men like stone,
And knew He came but to atone—
That day "He held His peace."

They witnessed falsely to His word,
They bound Him with a cruel cord,
And mockingly proclaimed Him Lord;
"But Jesus held His peace."

They spat upon Him in the face,
They dragged Him on from place to place,
They heaped upon Him all disgrace;
"But Jesus held His peace."

My friend, have you for far much less,
With rage, which you called righteousness,
Resented slights with great distress?
—Your Saviour "held His peace."
                                        —L. S. P.

October 15

"O Lord, I know that the way of man is not in himself:
it is not in man...to direct his steps." (Jer. 10:23.)

WE WERE at the foot of Mount Blanc in the village of Chamouni. A sad thing had happened the day before. A young physician had determined to reach the heights of Mt. Blanc. He accomplished the feat, and the little village was illuminated in his honor; on the mountainside a flag was floating that told of his victory.

"After he had ascended and descended as far as the hut, he wanted to be released from his guide; he wanted to be free from the rope and insisted on going on alone. The guide remonstrated with him, telling him it was not safe; *but he was tired of the rope* and declared that he would be free. The guide was compelled to yield. The young man had gone only a short distance when his foot slipped on the ice, and he could not stop himself from sliding down the icy steeps. The rope was gone, so the guide could not hold him nor pull him back. Out on the shelving ice lay the body of the young physician.

"The bells had been rung, the village had been illumined in honor of his success; but alas, in a fatal moment he refused to be guided; *he was tired of the rope.*

"Do you get tired of the rope? God's providences hold us, restrain us, and we get tired sometimes. *We need a guide,* and shall *until* the dangerous paths are over. *Never get disengaged from your Guide.* Let your prayer be 'Lead Thou me on,' and sometime the bells of heaven will ring that you are safe at Home!"
                                        —C. H. Spurgeon.

HIS WAY

God bade me go when I would stay
('Twas cool within the wood);
I did not know the reason why.
I heard a boulder crashing by
Across the pathway where I stood.

He bade me stay when I would go;
"Thy will be done," I said.
They found one day at early dawn,
Across the way I would have gone,
A serpent with a mangled head.

No more I ask the reason why,
Although I may not see
The path ahead, His way I go;
For though I know not, He doth know,
And He will choose safe paths for me.
                    —*The Sunday School Times.*

October 16

"Let no man despise thy youth; but be thou an example of the believers, in word, in conversation, in charity, in spirit, in faith, in purity. (1 Tim. 4:12.)

JOSEPH, while still in his teens, was carried into Egypt and there began to do the work which God had planned for him.

Abraham Lincoln as a boy stood in the slave market of New Orleans, and there in his youth he made a resolution which shaped his life and the destiny of his nation.

Napoleon Bonaparte at sixteen was a lieutenant, and in his thirties was master of France and Europe.

Thomas Edison began the study of chemistry in the basement of his home when he was only eleven. As a boy he studied telegraphy and was ready to go to work as an operator when his opportunity came.

Florence Nightingale when just a girl decided to give her life to nursing.

Madame Curie, with her husband, discovered radium at thirty.

Raphael painted his wonderful works as a young man and died at the age of thirty-seven.

Daniel was a youth when he withstood the idolatry of Babylon.

David was called from the tending of his father's sheep to the throne when only twenty.

We are told in Joshua 6:23 that the spies who went to spy in the Promised Land were young men.

Edward Gibbon, the great historian, began his studies at seventeen and at twenty-four was publishing his historical works.

Josephus, the Jewish historian, was an authority on Jewish law at fourteen.

Every youth has a quest to make,
For life is the King's highway,
And a joyous heart is the script we take,
On the road of everyday.

Every youth has his gifts to guard,
  As he fares to a far-off goal;
A body pure, and a mind unmarred,
  And the light of a lovely soul.

Every youth has a task of his own,
  For the Father has willed it so.
Youth seeks the way, and He alone,
  Can show him the path to go.

Every youth has a lovely Guide,
  From the vale to the mountain crest;
For the unseen Friend who walks beside,
  Is the Way and the End of the quest.
                                  —*Mary S. Edgar.*

October 17

"...But in every thing by prayer and supplication with thanksgiving let your requests be made known unto God."
                                              (Phil. 4:6.)

IT IS said of the late Billy Sunday that when he was converted and joined the church, a Christian man put his arm on the boy's shoulder and said, "William, there are three simple rules I can give you, and if you will hold to them, you will never write 'backslider' after your name: Take fifteen minutes a day to listen to God talking to you (meaning the study of His Word); take fifteen minutes a day to talk to God; take fifteen minutes each day to talk to others about God."

Billy Sunday was deeply impressed and determined to make these the rules of his life. From that day he made it a rule to spend the first moments of each day alone with God and His Word. Before he read a letter, looked at a paper, or even read a telegram, he went to the Bible so that the first impress of the day might be that which he received from God.

Among students years ago this motto was used:
  WATCH THE MORNING WATCH!

At the gray dawn, while yet the world is sleeping,
  And the sweet matins of the birds begin,
One who hath held me in His holy keeping
  Stands at the threshold, waiting to come in.

Oft has He knocked to give me gentle warning;
  My heart seemed willing, but my flesh, how weak!
Until one morning, O that blessed morning
  When my own name I heard Him speak!

Yes, 'twas my name; no other voice could speak it
  To stir my heart and melt my very soul;
And I arose so quickly to obey it,
  Flung wide the door, and gave Him full control.

O, then I feasted on divinest beauty,
  The altogether lovely, loving One,
While blessing me, threw radiance round each duty
  That in His name should on that day be done.

Peace fell upon me while to Him I listened;
  And in that sacred hour I talked with Christ
As ne'er before, and we together christened
  With tears of joy, new joy, our sacred tryst.

Can I afford to miss such rare communion?
  To let the health of my own soul decline?
May Christ forbid; His grace secures the union
  While I am truly His, as He is mine.
                        — Selected.

October 18

"I delight to do thy will, O my God:..." (Psalm 40:8.)

 WELL-KNOWN doctor, when dying, said, "I have found happiness since I lost my own will." True happiness is found in doing God's will. Every true blessing depends on obedience to that will. The One whose delight it was on earth to do God's will enjoined His disciples to pray on this wise, "Thy will be done on earth as it is in heaven." Thus the doctor was right; when the will is surrendered to God and His Word obeyed, blessing results.
                                              —*L. O. L.*

Machines work best under restraint. Unbridled power is destructive. Character is controlled by the same law. We are most free and most useful when we work within the will of Another—the will of God.
"We are limited until we lose ourselves in His limitless power."

> *"Make me a captive, Lord,*
>   *And then I shall be free;*
> *Force me to render up my sword,*
>   *And I shall conqueror be.*

I sink in life's alarms
When by myself I stand,
Imprison me within Thy arms
And strong shall be my hand.

"My heart is weak and poor,
Until it master find:
It has no spring of action sure—
It varies with the wind:
It cannot freely move
Till Thou hast wrought its chain;
Enslave it with Thy matchless love,
And deathless it shall reign."

October 19

"Hearken, O daughter, and consider, and incline thine ear;
...So shall the king greatly desire thy beauty: for he is thy
Lord; and worship thou him." (Psalm 45:10, 11.)

A LADY of rank is not dependent upon her dress or her equipage for her position. It is the lack of real greatness that makes the society butterfly eager to attract attention by her gaudy display. 'There is no creature so diminutive in its real proportions, when really reduced to its actual dimensions, as the dude and the daughter of fashion.' "

TERTULLIAN ON DRESS

Let women paint their eyes with tints of chastity, insert into their ears the Word of God, tie the yoke of Christ around their necks and adorn their whole person with the silk of sanctity and the damask of devotion; let them adopt that chaste and simple, that most elegant style of dress, which so advantageously displays the charms of real beauty, instead of those preposterous fashions and fantastical draperies of dress which, while they conceal some few defects of person, expose many defects of mind and sacrifice to ostentatious finery all those mild, amiable, and modest virtues by which the female character is so pleasingly adorned. Clothe yourself with the silk of piety, the satin of sanctity, with the purple of modesty; so shall you have God Himself to be your suitor.

Modesty is the charm of true womanhood. What is loud and bold and risky is degrading and will be prayerfully and studiously avoided by those who have the fear of God before their eyes.

Our outward adorning should be, and is, a reflection of the Spirit—"the hidden man of the heart." Where the mind is light and vain, the dress will reveal it by being showy and foolish. A Christian's dress will never attract attention to the wearer. It will be suitable and becoming to the station in life and will indicate that within there is "a meek and quiet spirit, which is in the sight of God, of great price."

—*George Goodman.*

October 20

"If we live in the Spirit, let us also walk in the Spirit."
(Gal. 5: 25.)

WO friends were cycling through Worchestershire and Warwickshire to Birmingham. When they arrived in Birmingham I asked them, among other things, if they had seen Warwick Prison along the road. "No," they said, "we hadn't a glimpse of it!" "But it is only a field's length from the road!" "Well, we never saw it!" Ah, but these two friends were lovers! They were so absorbed in each other that they had no spare attention for Warwick Prison!

"Walk in the Spirit, and ye shall not fulfill the lusts of the flesh." That great companionship will make us negligent of carnal allurements. The world, the flesh, and the devil may stand by the wayside and hold their glittering wares before us, but we shall scarcely be aware of their presence.

This is the only real and effective way to meet temptation. We must meet it with an occupied heart. We must have no loose and trailing affections. We must have no vagrant, wayward thoughts. Temptation must find us engaged with our Lover. We must "offer no occasion to the flesh." Walking with the Holy One our souls are clean above the meanesses and the vulgarities which are pregnant with destruction. Our safety is in our elevation. "Because he hath set his love upon me, therefore will I deliver him: I will set him on high because he hath known my name."

—*Dr. J. H. Jowett.*

There's a secret God has whispered
To His hidden ones alone;
'Tis a secret, sweeter, stranger,
Than thy heart has thought or known.

Holy secret, how it cleanses
All the heart from self and sin;
Crowding out the power of evil,
By the life of Christ within.
—*Dr. A. B. Simpson.*

October 21

"Blessed is that servant, whom his lord when he cometh shall find so doing." (Matt. 24: 46.)

STORY is related, which has to do with the Second Coming of our blessed Lord and the general dissemination of this precious truth. At last it reached the colored people in the south as they worked in the cotton fields. Said one of the old colored brethren, *"What's de use of us pickin' cotton if de Lawd is comin' back?"* And scores of others agreed. The cotton pickers stopped their work and the cotton wasted in the fields. Everybody was busy attending conferences and camp-meetings, singing the praises of God, and looking for His return.

The following winter was one of great need and privation, because their crops had been so woefully neglected.

Then one of their number, an evangelist, began preaching on this text: *"Blessed is that servant, whom his lord when he cometh shall find so doing."* Before long the colored people were once again tilling their ground and picking cotton in the rows.

"Work, for the night is coming, Work thro' the morning hours;
Work, while the dew is sparkling, Work 'mid springing flow'rs
Work when the day grows brighter, Work in the glowing sun;
Work, for the night is coming, When man's work is done.

"Work, for the night is coming, Work thro' the sunny noon;
Fill brightest hours with labor, Rest comes sure and soon.
Give ev'ry flying minute Something to keep in store;
Work, for the night is coming, When man works no more."

"OCCUPY TILL I COME!"

"When He calls me, I will answer;
I'll be somewhere working when He comes!"

October 22

"Let the words of my mouth, and the meditation of my heart, be acceptable in thy sight, O Lord, my strength, and my redeemer." (Psalm 19:14.)

HERE is no one thing that *love* so much needs as a sweet voice to tell what it means and feels; and it is hard to get and keep it in the right tone. One must start in youth and be on the watch night and day, at work and play, to get and keep a voice that shall speak at all times the thoughts of a kind heart. A kind voice is like a lark's song to a hearth and home. It is to the heart what light

is to the eye. It is a light that sings as well as shines. Train
it to sweet tones now, and it will keep in tune through life.

THE LANGUAGE JESUS SPOKE

I want to know the language Jesus spoke,
  Pure words, uncritical and ever kind;
At Jesus' voice the sleeping dead awoke,
  The sick were healed, and sight came to
    the blind.

I'd rather know the language of my King,
  Than perfectly to speak my native tongue,
I'd rather, by my words, glad tidings bring,
  Than win applause and fame on fields
    far-flung.

Oh, Master, let me daily with Thee walk,
  The secret of Thy words to me confide;
Then let the world be conscious when I talk
  That I received instruction at
    Thy side.
                                        —*Author Unknown.*

"*And all bare him witness, and wondered at the gracious
words which proceeded out of his mouth....*" (Luke 4:22.)

October 23

"*Love covereth . . .*" (Prov. 10: 12.)

IF WE have not been able to discover the good thing in
our brother fellow servant; if our eye has detected only
the crooked thing; if we have not succeeded in finding
the vital spark amid the ashes, the precious gem among
the surrounding rubbish; if we have seen only what
was of one's nature, then let us with a loving and delicate hand
draw the curtain of silence around our brother or speak of him
only at the throne of grace.—*C. H. M.*

"Let us all resolve: first, to attain the grace of silence; second,
to deem all fault-finding that does no good; third, to practice the
grace and virtue of praise."—*Harriet Beecher Stowe.*

You said your say:
Mine answer was my deed.
                    —*Tennyson.*

TO KNOW ALL IS TO FORGIVE ALL

If I knew you and you knew me—
If both of us could clearly see,
And with an inner sight divine
The meaning of your heart and mine,
I'm sure that we would differ less
And clasp our hands in friendliness;
Our thoughts would pleasantly agree
If I knew you and you knew me.

If I knew you and you knew me,
As each one knows his own self, we
Could look each other in the face
And see therein a truer grace.
Life has so many hidden woes,
So many thorns for every rose;
The "why" of things our hearts would see,
If I knew you, and you knew me.
—Nixon Waterman.

October 24

"And to love him...is much more than all...sacrifices."
(Mark 12:33, R.V.)

LIVINGSTONE, ON SACRIFICE

PEOPLE talk of the sacrifice I have made in spending so much of my life in Africa. Can that which is simply paid back as a small part of a great debt we owe to our God be called a sacrifice? Is that a sacrifice which brings its own best reward in healthful activity, the consciousness of doing good, peace of mind, and a bright hope of a glorious destiny hereafter?

"Away with the word in such a view and with such a thought! It is emphatically no sacrifice. Say, rather, it is a *privilege*. Anxiety, sickness, suffering, or danger, now and then, with a foregoing of the common conveniences and charities of this life, may make us pause, and cause the spirit to waver and the soul to sink, but let this be only for a moment.

"All these are nothing when compared with the glory which shall hereafter be revealed in and for us. I never made a sacrifice. Of this we ought not to talk when we remember the great sacrifice which was made by Him who left His Father's throne on high to give Himself to us."

"MY JESUS, MY LORD, MY LIFE, MY ALL,
I AGAIN DEDICATE MY WHOLE SELF TO THEE."

The above words were found in Dr. Livingstone's diary under date of the day Stanley left him after failing to persuade him to take the only possible opportunity of returning home.

David Livingstone when but twenty-three years of age was exploring the Dark Continent.

October 25

"...Called to belong to Jesus Christ." (Rom. 1:6, Weymouth.)

HERE must be a full and complete surrender of ourselves to God before there can be full blessedness. On Advent Sunday, December, 1873, I utterly yielded myself and my all to Him and utterly trusted Him to accept and keep me.—*Frances Ridley Havergal.*

God registers dates. The recording angel watches from on high.

> I'm yielded, Lord—
>   Take Thou my heart, and reign therein
>   To keep it pure
>   And free from sin.
>
> I'm yielded, Lord—
>   Oh, take my life and live through me,
>   That those who look,
>   Thy life may see.
>
> I'm yielded, Lord—
>   Take Thou my will—blend it with Thine,
>   Thy perfect will
>   Henceforth is mine.
>
> I'm yielded, Lord—
>   Then take my lips, my hands, my feet,
>   And make them for
>   Thy service meet.
>
> I'm yielded, Lord—
>   That I am not my own I clearly see;
>   And when Thou called'st
>   I did yield to Thee.

Now take my all—my Lord, I all resign;
What claim have I on that which is not
    mine?
On that which Thou has bought? 'Tis
    Thine alone.
Called to BELONG to Thee, I'd be Thine
    own.
                    —Mary E. Thomson.

Dr. Jowett prayed: "Lord, may there be no gaps in my consecration. May my life be all of one piece.... May sin make no rent!"

October 26

"Give therefore thy servant an understanding heart...that I may discern between good and bad:..." (1 Kings 3:9.)

HEAR the testimony of John Wesley's mother: "Would you judge of the lawfulness or unlawfulness of pleasure? Take this rule: Whatever weakens your reason, impairs the tenderness of your conscience, obscures your sense of God, or takes off the relish of spiritual things; in short, whatever increases the strength and authority of your body over your mind, that thing is sin to you, however innocent it may be in itself."

The North American Indians have a saying among themselves which they use concerning a person who is keen of discernment and quick to detect secret dangers — "He hears a cataract."

Guard your intuition or discernment as a gift from God.

"And shall make him of quick understanding [keen of scent or smell, (Hebrew)] in the fear of the Lord:..." (Isa. 11:3.)

October 27

"...Gentleness,..." (Gal. 5:22.)

NE day at an auction a man bought a cheap earthenware vase for a few pennies. He put into the vase a rich perfume—the attar of roses. For a long time the vase held this perfume, and when it was empty it had been so permeated with the sweet perfume that the fragrance lingered. One day the vase fell and was broken to pieces, but every fragment still smelled of the attar of roses.

We are all common clay—plain earthenware—but if the love of

Christ is kept in our hearts it will sweeten all our lives, and we shall become as loving as He. That is the way the beloved disciple learned the lesson and became so devoted. He leaned on Christ's breast, and Christ's gentleness filled all His life.

> As John upon his dear Lord's breast,
> So would I lean, so would I rest;
> As empty shell in depths of sea,
> So would I sink, be filled with Thee.
>
> Like singing bird in high blue air,
> So would I soar, and sing Thee there.
> Nor rain, nor stormy wind can be,
> When all the air is full of Thee.
>
> And so, though daily duties crowd,
> And dust of earth be like a cloud,
> Through noise of words, O Lord, my Rest,
> Thy John would lean upon Thy breast.
> —Rose from Brier.

October 28

"But seek ye first the kingdom of God, and his righteousness; and all these things shall be added unto you."
(Matt. 6:33.)

THE worst calamity which could befall any human being would be this—to have his own way from his cradle to his grave; to have everything he liked for the asking, or even for the buying; never to be forced to say: "I should like that, but I can't afford it; I should like this, but I must not do it," never to deny himself, never to work, and never to want. That man's soul would be in as great danger as if he were committing great crimes.   —*Charles Kingsley.*

Resolve to spurn the self-centered life!

Life is all a Pilgrim's way—the way that Christian trod—through pain, despair, and hardship to the kingdom of his God.... So many things lie hidden to ensnare you as you go—Self-pity, Fear and Vanity, these things will overthrow your happy hopes, and all the splendid things you meant to do—and blot out of your sight the shining goal you had in view.... So plod along, good pilgrim, plod along the stony road—don't waste your time in grumbling—every man must bear his load; for every misspent moment there will be a price to pay—for opportunities we've missed along the Pilgrim's way.

It matters not if we be clad in rags or finery—Beneath the

tatters and the gems the eye of God can see—Man looks upon the outward form, deceived by every art—But God, discerning motives, can look down into the heart.

—*Patience Strong.*

"While saints in heaven Thy glory sing,
Let me on earth Thy likeness wear."

October 29

"By a new and living way,..." (Heb. 10:20.)

 HERE is a beautiful story of the boyhood of Agassiz. The family lived in Switzerland. One day Louis and a younger brother were crossing a lake near their home and came to a crack in the ice which the smaller boy could not leap over. The older one then laid himself down across the crack, making a bridge of his body, and his brother climbed over him. There is always a need for human bridges over gaps and yawning crevices, and let no one say that this is asking too much, even of love. We remember that the Master said He was the *Way*, a bridge; that He laid His precious life across the great impassable chasm between sin and Heaven, that men might walk over on Him from death to life. If it was fit that the Master should make of Himself such a bridge, can any service we may be called to do in helping others be too costly, too humble?

In the Mohawk valley there is a sign which reads:
"JESUS SAITH,...I AM THE WAY, THE TRUTH, AND THE LIFE." (John 14:6.)

> *"Without the Way there is no going,*
> *Without the Truth there is no knowing,*
> *Without the Life there is no living."*

God made one only way. No other road
Leads up to the heights to that divine abode.

God made one only way! One living way!
Wouldst thou find Him? O wander not astray.
Strange paths wind on, as far as eye can see.
Christ is the only way of life for thee.

God made one only way! Set thy feet here,
Where His dear footprints even yet are clear.
The Way! Yea! The beginning and the end,
Is Christ Himself, thy Master and thy Friend.
                    —*Edith Hickman Dival.*

October 30

"For we are labourers together with God:..." (1 Cor. 3:9.)

OD never gave a man a thing to do concerning which it were irreverent to ponder how the Son of God would have done it." You are only as the carpenter's tools, and you will do no good unless the carpenter's Son shall use you.

Antonio Stradivari, born in 1644, was the most famous of all violin makers:

> "...God be praised.
> *Antonio Stradivari has an eye*
> *That winces at false work and loves the true—*
>   *When my Master holds*
> *Twixt chin and hand a violin of mine,*
> *He will be glad that Stradivari lived,*
> *Made violins, and made them of the best,*
> *The masters only know whose work is good;*
> *They will choose mine, and while God gives men skill,*
> *I give them instruments to play upon,*
>   *God choosing me to help Him."*
>   —George Eliot.

May my work today be well done! May nothing be turned out half done.

"I was deeply impressed by what a gardener once said to me concerning his work. 'I feel sir,' he said, 'when I am growing the flowers or raising the vegetables, that I am having a share in creation.'

"I thought it a very noble way of regarding his work."

Dr. Charles and Dr. William Mayo kept this motto in their office: "If you make even a mousetrap well, the world will wear a path to your doorstep."

October 31

"...Christ shall be magnified in my body, whether it be by life, or by death." (Phil. 1:20.)

OME years ago at the opening of a Disarmament Conference, in the midst of a speech King George was making, some one tripped over the wires of the Columbia Broadcasting Company, tearing them loose and interrupting the service. The chief operator quickly grasped the loose wires in his bare hands, holding them in contact, and for twenty minutes the current passed through while repairs were being made. His hands were slightly burned, but through them the words of the King passed on to the millions of listeners and were heard distinctly. Without his courage and endurance the King's message would have failed to reach its destination.

The King of Heaven has chosen to send His message to a lost world through human wires. Every faithful missionary and every Christian who gives his or her support is a human wire through which the King's voice is reaching the lost with a message of peace, vastly more important than the message from London.

For the missionary, it is often a costly business. Some men and women must suffer the loss of every earthly thing, stoop with weariness, waste away with fevers in far-off places, even die— but it pays to HOLD ON. Only thus can men hear the voice of the King. The Church of God needs more men who are willing to TAKE HOLD and HOLD ON.

Love through me, love of God!

The thrill that went through the civilized world when Livingstone's death and all its touching circumstances became known did more for Africa than he could have done had he completed his task and spent years in this country following it up. From the worn-out figure kneeling at the bedside in the hut in Ilala an electric spark seemed to fly, quickening hearts on every side.

November 1

"My voice shalt thou hear in the morning, O Lord; in the morning will I direct my prayer unto thee, and will look up." (Psalm 5:3.)

THE PEEP O' DAY

MORNING! The air is fresh; the birds sing at their best. It is a new birth of time. Sameness is relieved, abolished; this is another day. "My voice shalt thou hear in the morning, O Lord; in the morning will I direct my prayer unto thee, and will look up." (Psalm 5:3.) Surely this is the voice in melody. Mere statement would not suffice; it must be in music. It is the voice in song and also in prayer with the upward look. What a morning glory!

But how early? Rather, how soon after awaking should praise and prayer begin? If there can be nothing in sleep to disturb God's care of us and love for us, shall we, who are the recipients of His marvelous grace, allow Satan to steal the first waking moments and fill them with fears and murmurs and groans and sighs, allowing praise and prayer to be deferred until after this robbery? What subtlety!

For what is sleep? If our Lord "giveth unto his beloved in

sleep" (Psalm 127:2 R. V. marg.), then sleep is a time of special receiving from Him. It is the opposite to worry and struggle and murmur. It is the time when He carries us, as it were, in His safekeeping over to the very verge of eternity, and after refreshing us there, lo, when we awake He has brought us back to a new world, a new day—a fresh-born, a God-made day! Who then watched and cared? Why, when we were all unconscious, He brought us safely to this symbolized resurrection. Who? Who did it? Who but our Lord! And shall we allow Satan to steal these first waking moments at "the peep o' day," whether we awaken early or late?

Lord, claim my every day, my every hour—and this one at "the peep o' day."

—Dr. Henry Ostrom.

> *"Alone with Thee, amid the mystic shadows,*
> *The solemn hush of nature newly born;*
> *Alone with Thee in breathless adoration,*
> *In the calm dew and freshness of the morn."*

November 2

"...Because thou hast been faithful in a very little,..."
(Luke 19:17.)

GOD prepares us for the greater crusades by more commonplace fidelities. Through the practice of common kindnesses God leads us to chivalrous tasks. Little courtesies feed nobler reverences. No man can despise smaller duties and do the larger duties well. Our strength is sapped by small disobediences. Our discourtesies to one another impair our worship of God.

And thus the only way to live is by filling every moment with fidelity. We are ready for anything when we have been faithful in everything. "Because thou hast been faithful in that which is least!"—that is the order in moral and spiritual progress, and that is the road by which we climb to the seats of the mighty. We cannot prepare to be good missionaries by scamping our present work. When every stone in life is "well and truly laid" we are sure of a solid, holy temple in which the Lord will delight to dwell. The quality of our greatness depends upon what we do with "that which is least."

THE BUSINESS OF THE DAY

It's just the way we carry through
The business of the day
That makes and molds the character—
The things we do and say;

The way we act when we are vexed;
The attitude we take;
The sort of pleasures we enjoy;
The kind of friends we make.
It's not the big events alone
That make us what we are;
And not the dizzy moments when
We're swinging on a star.
It's just the things that happen as
Along the road we plod.
The little things determine what
We're really worth to God.
—Patience Strong.

Can the Master count on me today?

November 3

"Greater love hath no man than this, that a man lay down his life for his friends." (John 15:13.)

SADHU SUNDAR SINGH passed a crowd of people putting out a jungle fire at the foot of the Himalayas. Several men, however, were standing gazing at a tree the branches of which were already alight.

"What are you looking at?" he asked. They pointed to a nest of young birds in the tree. Above it a bird was flying wildly to and fro in great distress. The men said, "We wish we could save that tree, but the fire prevents us from getting near to it."

A few minutes later the nest caught fire. The Sadhu thought the mother bird would fly away. But no! she flew down, spread her wings over the young ones, and in a few minutes was burned to ashes with them.

Let us have love heated to the point of sacrifice!

We mean a lot to Some One;
And 'tis everything to me
That to God His wayward children
Were worth a Calvary.
It's the meaning of my Sunday,
And to Saturday from Monday
It is my hope that one day
My Saviour I shall see.
Though the day be dark and dreary,
Here's comfort for the weary—
We mean a lot to Some One
Who died for you and me.
—Value and Other Poems.

November 4

"...That in all things he might have the pre-eminence."
(Col. 1:18.)

THERE was a strange bonfire in the city of Ephesus many years ago. Many of the new believers who had used curious arts brought their books together and burned them before the eyes of all. They counted the value of them and found it to be fifty thousand pieces of silver—so mightily had the Word of God grown and prevailed!

It is particularly helpful to consider the cost of this Ephesian bonfire! Books were burned in order that their owners might be purged of the stain of possessing and perusing them. It is impossible to pass by this event without suggesting that many books and periodicals of the present day ought to meet the same fate that overtook the wicked books of these homes in Ephesus. But the point to be considered here is that those who accepted the faith of the Saviour whom Paul preached were willing to sacrifice down to the minutest detail and on to the greatest cost, anything that would hinder them from receiving His favor and being used to carry on His mission.

Have we surrendered from our souls and banished from our lives everything that would hinder the cause of Christ? Do we hate compromises? Do we detest the thought that there may be still impurities and inconsistencies in our character? Are we willing to make, if necessary, a huge bonfire of all things big and little that may offend the Saviour and spoil our work?

The great surrender is different for every life. Some cherish one thing and some another. But if we would truly cherish Christ and live in His favor there must be no hidden idols, no unacknowledged or half-acknowledged motives which are not pure.

November 5

"And we know that all things work together for good to them that love God, to them who are the called according to his purpose." (Rom. 8:28.)

HE WAS weaving.

"That is a strange looking carpet you are making!" said the visitor.

"Just stoop down and look underneath," was the reply.

The man stooped. *The plan was on the other side,* and in that moment a light broke upon his mind.

The Great Weaver is busy with His plan. Do not be impatient; suffice to know that you are part of the plan and that He *never errs.* Wait for the light of the later years and the peep at the other side. *Hope on!*

> *White and black, and hodden-gray,*
> *Weavers of webs are we;*
> *To every weaver one golden strand*
> *Is given in trust by the Master hand;*
> *Weavers of webs are we.*
>
> *And that we weave, we know not,*
> *Weavers of webs are we.*
> *The thread we see, but the pattern is known*
> *To the Master weaver alone, alone;*
> *Weavers of webs are we.*
> *—John Oxenham.*

Of many of the beautiful carpets made in India it may be said that the weaving is done to music. The designs are handed down from one generation to another, and the instructions for their making are in script that looks not unlike a sheet of music. Indeed, it is more than an accidental resemblance, for each carpet has a sort of tune of its own. The thousands of threads are stretched on a great wooden frame, and behind it on a long bench sit the workers. The master in charge reads the instructions for each stitch in a strange chanting tone, each color having its own particular note.

The story makes us think of our own life web. We are all weavers, and day by day we work in the threads—now dark, now bright—that are to go into the finished pattern. But blessed are they who feel sure that there is a pattern; who hear and trust the directing Voice, and so weave the changing threads to music.

—W. J. Hart.

November 6

"I hate vain thoughts: but thy law do I love."
(Psalm 119:113.)

HUGH T. KERR, in referring to the story that Napoleon once stabled his cavalry in Cologne Cathedral, comments: "But that is of little or no account in comparison to giving hospitality to evil imaginations, profanity, vulgarity, and all the demons of the house of shame within the sacred inclosure of the temple in which the Spirit of God dwells."

A young man once said to the writer with anguish in his voice,

"My chief trouble is with my mind; if only I could control my thoughts!" The counsel he received was this: "Remember that it is impossible to think two thoughts at the same time. Run a good thought in, and the bad one is bound to leave. Keep practicing this habit, and, by God's help, you will slowly but surely be 'transformed by the renewing of your mind.' "

Open the door, let in the air;
The winds are sweet, and the flowers
    are fair;
Joy is abroad in the world today;
If our door is wide, it may come in this
    way.
      Open the door!

Open the door, let in the sun;
It hath a smile for every one;
It hath made of the raindrops gold
    and gems;
It may change our tears to diadems.
      Open the door!

Open the door of the soul; let in
Strong, pure thoughts which shall
    banish sin.
They will grow and bloom with a grace
    divine,
And their fruit shall be sweeter than
    that of the vine.
      Open the door!

Open the door to the heart; let in
Sympathy sweet for stranger and kin;
It will make the halls of the heart so
    fair
That angels may enter unaware.
      Open the door!
          —Author Unknown.

"Let vain thoughts no more thy thoughts
    abuse,
But down in darkness let them lie."

Think truly, and thy thoughts
Shall this world's famine feed.
      —Bonar.

November 7

"And forgive us our debts, as we forgive our debtors."
(Matt. 6:12.)

OULD you have strength to suffer wrong in the spirit in which Christ did? Accustom yourself in everything that comes to you to recognize the hand and will of God. This lesson is of more consequence than you think. Whether it be some great wrong that is done you, or some little offence that you meet in daily life, before you fix your thoughts on the person who did it, first be still and remember God allowed this trouble to come to you to see if you would glorify Him in it. This trial, be it the greatest or the least, was sanctioned by God and was His will concerning you. Therefore recognize and submit to God's will in it. Then in the rest of soul which this gives, you will receive wisdom to know how to behave in it. With your eye turned from man to God, suffering wrong will not be so hard as it seems.

We are the young sons and daughters of the King and should exhibit that graceful tact and Christian courtesy which can bear and forbear. Don't reprove and find fault, but encourage, bless, help! Be thou the rainbow in the storm of life.

> *Have you an ancient wound? Forget the wrong—*
> *Out in my West a forest loud with song*
> *Towers high and green over a field of snow*
> *Over a glacier buried far below.*
> —*Edwin Markham.*

The strength of your conquest ever becomes your sword.
—*Emerson.*

Life is too short to nurse one's misery. Hurry across the lowlands, that you may spend more time on the mountaintops.
—*Phillips Brooks.*

November 8

"He that spared not his own Son, but delivered him up for us all, how shall he not with him also freely give us all things?" (Rom. 8:32.)

HE highest life represents more, not less life than the lower life. We speak of giving up habits and indulgences, but this is a misleading form of speech. The pauper gives up his rags, when he is clad. The lame man gives up his crutches when he is healed. But these are not sacrifices. The Christian man throws away all that hampers his freedom as the slave surrenders his chains when he steps forth into liberty. Christ's call is to the free, the abundant, the unencumbered life. —*Robert Speer.*

Hast thou heard Him, seen Him, known Him,
    Is not thine a captured heart?
Chief among ten thousands own Him,
    Joyful choose the better part.

What has stripped the seeming beauty
    From the idols of the earth?
Not a sense of right or duty,
    But the sight of peerless worth.

Not the crushing of those idols,
    With its bitter void and smart;
But the beaming of His beauty,
    The unveiling of His heart!

'Tis that look that melted Peter,
    'Tis that Face that Stephen saw,
'Tis that Heart that wept with Mary
    Can alone from idols draw.

Draw and win and fill completely,
    Till the cup o'erflow the brim;
What have we to do with idols
    Who have companied with Him?
              —*Author Unknown.*

There is no true separation *from* the things which Jesus calls us to leave, without a corresponding separation *unto* things which are incomparably better. One hardly likes to speak of it as compensation, because the "unto" is so infinitely more than the "from"; it is like talking of a royal friendship compensating for dropping a beggar's acquaintance, or the whole of England for a brass farthing, or palace life for "giving up" workhouse life!

November 9

"Therefore my heart is glad, and my glory rejoiceth: my flesh also shall rest in hope." (Psalm 16:9.)

IT IS now more than one hundred years since the emancipation of the slaves of the British West Indian colonies. Historians tell a beautiful story of this momentous event. The day set for their emancipation was the first day of August. The night before, many of them, it is said, never slept at all. Their hearts were so eager with expectation they could not close their eyes. Thousands of them gathered in their places of worship for prayer and praise to God for bringing to them this freedom. Some of their brethren were sent to the nearby hilltops to view the first gleams of the coming dawn. These reported by signal to the waiting ones below when the dawn of the great and jubilant day was breaking. Day of all days was it to them, when they should pass from the thralldom of human ownership to the liberty and independence of the new life. Who can picture the hope that thrilled their innermost hearts as they watched for the dawn of that day!

Likewise, a great emancipation day is coming for the children of God! The enthrallment of sin is to be forever broken; infirmities are to give place to infinities; corruption is to be changed to incorruption; mortality is to clothe itself with immortality; feeble and changeable fellowship is to be transmuted into endless and unbroken communion with our Lord; limitation and imperfection of service is to give way to boundlessness and perfectness of ministry throughout all eternity. And all this is to come with the coming of the Lord Jesus Christ!

He is coming! He is on the road and traveling quickly. The sound of His approach should be as music to our hearts! Ring out, ye bells of hope!

> *"Faith looks back and says,*
> *'Christ died for me';*
> *Above, and cries,*
> *'He lives for me';*
> *Forward, and whispers,*
> *'He comes for me.'"*

November 10

". . . Handle me, and see; for a spirit hath not flesh and bones, as ye see me have." (Luke 24:.39.)

IS YOUR soul a chaos waiting for Christ's order—an agony waiting for His peace—a mine waiting for Him to open it and discover the gold that is hidden in it? Let Christ stop being an idea, and become a *Person* to you this day. —*Samuel M. Shoemaker.*

WHERE ART THOU?

Where are You, God?
I looked abroad
And saw but desert land and drear;
O surely YOU could not be here!
Upon the broad expanse of sea,
I sensed Your all-immensity.

No voice I heard,
No holy word.
O surely in the ripened grains,
Or on deserted woodland lanes,
O surely in approaching storm
I would behold His mystic form.

But, blinded, I
Had passed Him by,
Nor knew I that the Master wept,
Until His formless love had crept
Within my heart, and broken, sore,
I met Him at my very door.
                    —*Luella Valentine Dahlstrom.*

"In the cool of the day He walks with me,
In the rose-bordered way He talks with me;
In love's holy union, and sacred communion,
In the garden of my heart."

There is no god but God!—to prayer—lo: God is great!—*Byron.*

November 11

"For with God nothing shall be impossible." (Luke, 1:37.)

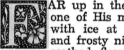FAR up in the Alpine hollows, year by year God works one of His marvels. The snow patches lie there, frozen with ice at their edge from the strife of sunny days and frosty nights, and through that ice crust come, unscathed, flowers that bloom.

Back in the days of the bygone summer the little soldanel plant spread its leaves wide and flat on the ground to drink in the sun's rays, and it kept them stored in the root through the winter. Then spring came and stirred the pulses even below the snow shroud, and as it sprouted, warmth was given out in such strange measure that it thawed a little dome in the snow above its head.

Higher and higher it grew, and always above it rose the bell of air till the flower bud formed safely within it; and at last the icy covering of the air-bell gave way and let the blossom through into the sunshine, the crystalline texture of its mauve petals sparkling like snow itself as if it bore the traces of the flight through which it had come.

The fragile thing rings an echo in our hearts that none of the jewel-like flowers nestled in the warm turf on the slopes below could waken. We love to see the impossible done; and so does God!

Face it out to the end, cast away every shadow of hope on the human side as an absolute hindrance to the Divine, heap up all the difficulties together recklessly and pile as many more on as you can find; you cannot get beyond the blessed climax of impossibility. Let faith swing out to Him. He is the God of the impossible.—*Selected.*

November 12

"He that dwelleth in the secret place of the most High shall abide under the shadow of the Almighty." (Psalm 91:1.)

*In the secret of his presence how my soul delights
   to hide!
Oh, how precious are the lessons·which I learn at
   Jesus' side!
Earthly cares can never vex me, neither trials lay
   me low;
For when Satan comes to tempt me, to the secret
   place I go.*

*When my soul is faint and thirsty, 'neath the shadow
   of his wing
There is cool and pleasant shelter and a fresh and
   crystal spring;
And my Saviour rests beside me, as we hold communion sweet:
If I tried I could not utter what he says when thus
   we meet.
Only this I know: I tell him all my doubts, my griefs,
   and fears.
Oh, how patiently he listens! and my drooping soul
   he cheers.
Do you think he ne'er reproves me? What a false
   friend he would be
If he never, never told me of the sins which he must
   see!
Would you like to know the sweetness of the secret
   of the Lord?
Go and hide beneath his shadow; this shall then be
   your reward.
And whene'er you leave the silence of that happy
   meeting place,
You must mind and bear the image of the Master
   in your face.*
      —Ellen Lakshmi Goreh, (An Indian Christian.)

November 13

"...For I do always those things that please him."
(John 8: 29.)

THE pilot of a United States revenue cutter was asked if he knew all the rocks along the coast. He replied, "No, it is necessary to know only where there are no rocks." Could there be a more excellent answer to a soul troubled by trying to decide from day to day *what is* and *what is not* conformity to the world? The settled purpose to please Him in all things will bring us into deep water where there are no rocks. *Halfheartedness*, which Thomas Fuller says "consists in serving God in such a manner as not to offend the devil," takes the soul into a very shallow water indeed, with rocks on every hand.

Get out into the channel and stay there! Keep off the rocks and reefs!

"Satan holds out a lying promise of new regions, and while it perpetually deceives the seafarer with the faint hope of discoveries, it continually entangles him in adventures from which he can never get loose."

"Jesus, Saviour, pilot me, Over life's tempestuous sea;
Unknown waves before me roll, Hiding rocks and treach'rous shoal;
Chart and compass came from Thee; Jesus, Saviour, pilot me."

—*Hymnal.*

November 14

"...There they dwelt with the king for his work."
(1 Chron. 4: 23.)

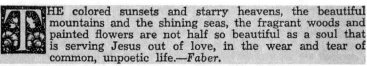

THE colored sunsets and starry heavens, the beautiful mountains and the shining seas, the fragrant woods and painted flowers are not half so beautiful as a soul that is serving Jesus out of love, in the wear and tear of common, unpoetic life.—*Faber.*

"Does the wildflower bloom less carefully, and are the tints less perfect because it rises beside the fallen tree in the thick woods where mankind never enters? Let us not bemoan the fact that we are not great, and that the eyes of the world are not upon us."

When I am tempted to repine
That such a lowly lot is mine,
There comes to me a voice which saith
"Mine were the streets of Nazareth."

So mean, so common, and confined,
And He the Monarch of mankind!
Yet patiently He traveleth
Those narrow streets of Nazareth.

But if through honor's arch I tread
And there forget to bend my head,
Ah! let me hear the voice which saith,
"Mine were the streets of Nazareth."
—Nettie Rooker.

The most saintly spirits are often existing in those who have never distinguished themselves as authors or left any memorial of themselves to be the theme of the world's talk; but who have led an interior angelic life, having borne their sweet blossoms unseen like the young lily in a sequestered vale on the bank of a limpid stream.—Kenelm Digby.

November 15

"By the grace of God I am what I am:..." (1 Cor. 15:10.)

NOTHING gives such upright dignity of mien as the consciousness, "I am what I pretend to be. About me there is no make believe."

"Individuality is the only thing the individual possesses which he could patent. There is just one of a kind; but one is enough. To be an echo is not to be a contribution. Elisha was not eliminated by Elijah. Be just yourself."

A mastering yet unassuming personality is a rare posession.

BE WHAT YO' AM

De sunflower ain't no daisy, and de melon
    ain't no rose;
Why is dey all so crazy, to be sumfin else
    dat grows?
Jes' stick to de place you's planted, and
    do de bes' yo' knows;
Be de sunflower or de daisy, de melon or
    de rose.

Don't, yo' be what yo' ain't, jes' yo' be
   what yo' is;
If yo' am not what yo' are, den yo' is not
   what yo' is;
If yo' is jes' a little tadpole, don't yo' try
   to be a frog;
If you's only de tail, don't try to wag de
   dawg.

Pass roun' de off'ring plate, if you can't
   exhawt and preach.
If you's a little pebble, don' try to be
   de beach;
When a man is what he isn't, den he isn't
   what he is;
And as sure as I is talkin', he is gwine
   to get his.

—*Anon.*

God makes no duplicates. Each life is purposeful, original, precious.

November 16

"And every man that hath this hope in him purifieth him-self, even as he is pure." (1 John 3:3.)

BACK in the vast hinterland in South America lived a young man who had found the Lord Jesus Christ as his Saviour—a living, risen Christ! As he walked and talked with the Master a strong conviction came to him that in order to keep the close companionship of the pure and sinless One, he too must have a pure heart and live a cleansed life. But—he was clinging to an idol! One morning he went out for a stroll into the woods, determining to settle the matter once and forever. A woodman's axe had felled a huge tree, and he found the log and sat upon it there in the wilds—alone with his thoughts, the Word of God, and a decision to be made. He took from his pocket the Bible he had never been allowed to read in his old days, and these words brought conviction to his heart: *"From all your filthiness and from all your idols I will cleanse you."* Reaching into his pocket he pulled out a packet of the cherished evil weed, and threw it into a deep gulley. He then lifted his heart to God in prayer for deliverance from the habit. He prayed, "Oh, wash me, Lord, without, within! Make me clean! Come and dwell in the best room of my life! Possess me wholly!" And then in the forest stillness the answer came and assurance that God had heard, that every fetter was broken, that no longer he was to be a slave, but one free in Christ Jesus! The Holy Spirit entered the cleansed temple, and for many weeks and months he has been a faithful witness—*one* youth among a thousand university students! "And Jesus, looking upon him, loved him."—*Selected.*

Be ye clean, O youth who bear the name of the sinless Christ!

November 17

"And they that be wise shall shine as the brightness of the firmament; and they that turn many to righteousness as the stars for ever and ever." (Daniel 12:3.)

WHO does not thrill to read the testimony of saintly James Chalmers, missionary to New Guinea, who proclaimed with triumph his unalterable choice: "Recall the twenty-one years, give me back all its experiences, give me its shipwrecks, give me its standings in the face of death, give me back my surroundment of savages with spears and clubs, give me back again the spears flying about me with the club knocking me to the ground—give it all back to me, and I will still be your missionary!"

Someone has said, "Live heroically and die triumphantly." This was literally true of Chalmers, whose consecration ever urged him to deeds of valor for Christ, and who is honored throughout eternity to wear a martyr's crown.

> *"Christ, alone, can save the world;*
> *But Christ cannot save the world alone."*

A Chinese Christian, Lough Fook, was so touched by the condition of the coolies in Demarara that he sold himself into slavery in order to win them for Christ. He was the means of two hundred being led to Christ before he died five years afterward.

MY RESOLVE: "I will always do a little more than just enough."

> *"March we forth in the strength of God,*
> *With the banner of Christ unfurled,*
> *That the light of the glorious Gospel of Truth*
> *May shine throughout the world.*
> *Fight we the fight with sorrow and sin,*
> *To set the captives free*
> *That the earth may be filled with the glory of God*
> *As the waters cover the sea."*

November 18

"Is not this the carpenter?" (Mark 6:3.)

"This is my beloved Son, in whom I am well pleased."
(Matt. 3:17.)

IT SUITS our best sense that the One who spoke of putting our hand to the plow, and taking the yoke upon us, should have made plows and yokes Himself, and people do not think His words less heavenly for not smelling of books and lamps. Let us not make the mistake of those Nazarenes: *that Jesus had been a carpenter* was to them poor credentials of divinity, but it has been *divine credentials to the poor* ever since. Let us not be deceived by social ratings and badges of the schools.

Carey was a cobbler, but he had a map of the world on his shop wall, and outdid Alexander the Great in dreaming and doing.

What thoughts were in the mind of Jesus at His workbench? One of them was that the kingdoms of this world should become the kingdoms of God—*at any cost!*

—*Selected.*

Yes, yes, a carpenter, same trade as mine!
How it warms my heart as I read that line.
I can stand the hard work, I can stand the poor pay,
For I'll see that Carpenter at no distant day.
—*Rev. Maltbie D. Babcock.*

"The Carpenter of Nazareth made common things for God."

A man was making a flower box; the corners were true, for he was particular. Another said, "It's just to hold dirt and does not need to be perfect." The answer came, "But my spirit does." "The Carpenter of Nazareth never made anything less than His best."

November 19

"Brethren, if a man be overtaken in a fault, ye which are spiritual, restore such an one in the spirit of meekness; considering thyself, lest thou also be tempted." (Gal. 6:1.)

I REFUSE the cheapening, mildewing, spoiling power of faultfinding. I refuse to dwell upon the faults of others. I refuse to think of them, much less to speak of them.

I will constantly say when tempted to look at or speak of human faults, frailties, or weaknesses—"what would my life be like should I have been born as they, environed as they, abused as they have been?"

. I will seek a picture. As by a flash of divinely illuminated imagination, I will think of what all such would be should they be what the Father planned them to be.

It shall be my high resolve NEVER to criticize! If I must speak of faults it shall be only after much prayer and with the motive of seeking to find a way for them out into larger things.

·"He knoweth our frame; he remembereth that we are dust." So should we.

—Selected.

> "Judge not the heart, thou cans't not see.
> What looks to thy dim eyes a stain;
> In God's pure light may be a scar,
> Brought from some well-won battlefield,
> Where thou would'st only faint and yield."

November 20

"...Men ought always to pray, and not to faint."
(Luke 18:1.)

IS IT hypocritical to pray when we don't feel like it? Perhaps there is no more subtle hindrance to prayer than that of our *moods*. Nearly everybody has to meet that difficulty at times. Even God's prophets were not wholly free from it. Habakkuk felt as if he were facing a blank wall for a long time. What shall we do when moods like this come to us? Wait until we do *feel like* praying? It is easy to persuade ourselves that it is hypocrisy to pray when we do not feel like it; but we don't argue that way about other things in life. If you were in a room that had been tightly closed for some time you would, sooner or later, begin to feel very miserable—so miserable, perhaps, that you would not want to make the effort to open the windows, especially if they were difficult to open. But your weakness and listlessness would be proof that you were beginning to need fresh air very desperately—that you would soon be ill without it.

If the soul *perseveres* in a life of prayer, there will come a time when *these seasons of dryness will pass away and the soul will be led out*, as Daniel says, *"into a large place"* (margin, *"into a moist place."*) Let nothing discourage you. If the soil is dry, *keep cultivating* it. It is said that in a dry time the harrowing of the corn is equal to a shower of rain.

When we are listless about prayer *is the very time when we need most to pray!* The only way we can overcome listlessness in anything is to put more of ourselves, not less, into the task. To pray when you do not feel like praying *is not hypocrisy— it is faithfulness to the greatest duty of life. Just tell the Father* that you don't feel like it—ask Him to show you what is making you listless. *He will help you to overcome your moods,* and give you courage to persevere in spite of them.

"When you cannot pray as you would, pray as you can."

If I feel myself disinclined to pray, then is the time when I need to pray more than ever. Possibly when the soul leaps and exults in communion with God it might more safely refrain from prayer than at those seasons when it drags heavily in devotion.
                                                        —Charles H. Spurgeon.

November 21

"...In the selfsame day, as God had said unto him."
                                                        (Gen. 17:23.)

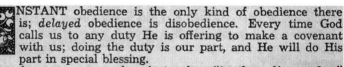

INSTANT obedience is the only kind of obedience there is; *delayed* obedience is disobedience. Every time God calls us to any duty He is offering to make a covenant with us; doing the duty is our part, and He will do His part in special blessing.

The only way we can obey is to obey *"in the selfsame day,"* as Abraham did. To be sure, we often postpone a duty and then later on do it as fully as we can. It is better to do this than not to do it at all. But it is then, at the best, only a crippled, disfigured, halfway sort of duty-doing; and *a postponed duty never can bring the full blessing that God intended, and that it would have brought if done at the earliest possible moment.*

It is a pity to rob ourselves, along with robbing God and others, by procrastination. *"In the selfsame day"* is the Genesis way of saying, "Do it now."
                                                        —Messages for the Morning Watch.

"Keep your obedience at the extreme verge of your illumination!"

November 22

"I am crucified with Christ: nevertheless I live; yet not I, but Christ liveth in me: and the life which I now live in the flesh I live by the faith of the Son of God, who loved me, and gave himself for me." (Gal. 2:20.)

CROWNED OR CRUCIFIED

I stood alone at the bar of God,
In the hush of the twilight dim,
And faced the question that pierced my heart:

What will you do with Him?
Crowned or crucified? Which shall it be?
No other choice was offered to me.

I looked on the face so marred with tears,
  That were shed in His agony,
The look in His kind eyes broke my heart—
  'Twas full of love for me,
"The crown or the cross," it seemed to say;
  "For or against Me—choose thou today."

He held out His loving hands to me,
  While He pleadingly said, "Obey;
Make Me thy choice, for I love thee so,"
  And I could not say Him nay.
Crowned, not crucified, thus it must be;
  No other way was open to me.

I knelt in tears at the feet of Christ,
  In the hush of the twilight dim,
And all that I was, or hoped, or sought,
  Surrendered unto Him.
Crowned, not crucified; my heart shall know
  No king, but Christ who loveth me so.
                                      —Selected.

There are some who would have Christ cheap. They would
have Him without His cross. But the price will not come down!
                              —Samuel Rutherford.

November 23

"...This one thing I do,..." (Phil. 3:13.)

THE rivers of life cannot often be both deep and wide.
Quantity and quality limit each other. Excellence demands concentration. Edison was a wizard at elec-
tricity but had no time for Greek and Hebrew roots.
When Victoria Booth Demarest began to preach and
could no longer concentrate laboriously upon the piano, she felt
the old technique slipping away. She sacrificed her music to her
preaching. "Art," writes Michael Angelo, "is a jealous mistress;
she demands the whole man." We prune vines and trees to produce better fruit; we sacrifice quantity for quality. Nowhere is
that truer than in Christian experience. The living water must
run in a narrow channel. For large and luscious fruits of the
Spirit the life must be pruned. "He *purgeth it, that it may bring
forth more fruit."* This one thing I do! We cannot have all of

Christ and all of the world. We cannot have all of Christ and some of the world. Choice Christians are not Christians plus *something* else! To scale the heights, we must lay aside every weight; we must possess "heavenly perspective," embrace *one* objective, do but *one* thing, have but *one passion!*

Said Count Zinzendorf, "I have but one passion; it is HE."

November 24

"And they came to the place which God had told him of;..." (Gen. 22:9.)

> *"Up, up the hill, to the whiter-than-snow shine,*
> *Help me to climb, and dwell in pardon's light.*
> *I must be pure as Thou, or ever less*
> *Than Thy design of me—therefore incline*
> *My heart to take men's wrongs as Thou tak'st*
> *mine."*

Have you come to the place God *told you of?* Have you gone through the sacrifice of death? Are you willing to make the moral decision that the thing die out in you which never was in Jesus?

Are you up to that whiter-than-snow shine, up to that place that is as strong and firm as the Throne of God? Do not say, "That pure, white, holy life is never for me!" Let God lift you; let Him take the shrouds away; let Him lift up—up to the hill— to *the whiter-than-snow shine.* And when you get to the top what do you find? A great, strong tableland, where your feet are on a rock, your steps enlarged under you, your goings established.

—*Oswald Chambers.*

Jesus offers you "life more abundantly." Grasp the offer! Quit the boggy and dark low ground, and let Him lead you up higher! —*Mountain Tops With Jesus*

Take the Supreme Climb!

> *"Jesus lead me up the mountain,*
> *Where the whitest robes are seen,*
> *Where the saints can see the fountain,*
> *Where the pure are keeping clean.*

> *"Higher up, where light increases,*
> *Rich above all earthly good,*
> *Where the life of sinning ceases,*
> *Where the Spirit comes in floods.*

"Lead me higher, nothing dreading,
  In the race to never stop;
In thy footsteps keep me treading,
  Give me grace to reach the top."

Courage, my soul, and let us journey on!

November 25

". . . To the uttermost . . ." (Heb. 7: 25.)

JOHN B. GOUGH, the world's greatest temperance lecturer, was given a text by his godly mother, which indeed became like a buried treasure, for it lay hidden within his heart for seven long years of dissipation. It was:

> *"He is able to save them to the uttermost*
> *that come unto God by Him."*

His sins rose mountain-high before him; they seemed indelible; the past could not be undone! But he met Jesus Christ and found that His blood availed for even him. "I have suffered," he cried, "and come out of the fire scorched and scathed with the marks upon my person and with the memory of it burnt right into my soul." He likened his life to a snowdrift that had been badly stained; no power on earth could restore its former whiteness and purity. "The scars remain! The scars remain!" he used to say with bitter self-reproaches.

Giant Yesterday pointed to the black, black past derisively, held it a threat over the poor penitent's bowed and contrite head, told in tones that sounded like thunder-claps that there was no escape.

> *"Wounds of the soul, though healed, will ache;*
>   *The reddening scars remain*
>   *And make confession.*
>   *Lost innocence returns no more,*
>   *We are not what we were*
>   *Before transgression!"*

Forty-four years have passed away since he had that grim struggle with sin. Gough is again in America, addressing a vast audience of young men in Philadelphia.

"Young men," he cries, perhaps with a bitter memory of those seven indelible years—"Young men, keep your record clean!" He pauses—a longer pause than usual, and the audience wonders. But he regains his voice.

"Young men," he repeats, more feebly this time, "keep your record clean!" Another pause—longer than the previous one. But again he finds the power of speech.

"Young men," he cries the third time, but in a thin, wavering voice, "Young men, keep your record clean!"

He falls heavily on the platform. Devout men carry him to his burial and make lamentation over him. His race is finished, his voyage completed, his battle won. The promise has been literally and triumphantly fulfilled. The grace that saved him has kept him *to the very last inch, of the very last yard, of the very last mile; to the very last minute, of the very last hour, of the very last day!* For "He is able to save them to the *uttermost* that come unto God by Him!"

—*Selected.*

November 26

"...Ye ought to be quiet,..." (Acts 19:36.)

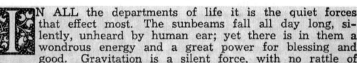 IN ALL the departments of life it is the quiet forces that effect most. The sunbeams fall all day long, silently, unheard by human ear; yet there is in them a wondrous energy and a great power for blessing and good. Gravitation is a silent force, with no rattle of machinery, no noise of engines, no clanking of chains, and yet it holds all the stars and worlds in their orbits and swings them through space with unvarying precision. The dew falls silently at night when men sleep, yet it touches every plant and leaf and flower with a new life and beauty. It is in the lightning, not in the thunderpeal, that the electric energy resides. Thus even in nature, strength lies in quietness, and the mightiest energies move noiselessly."   —*Dr. J. R. Miller.*

Nature's greatest miracles are wrought in silence. The wheels of the universe do not creak. Confusion and noise are man-made. In a jangling age such as this there must daily be found a place of solitude if we are to keep our sanity. The admonition of Christ, *"Enter into thy closet and shut thy door,"* was faithfully followed in His own life. If the quiet hour was such a necessity in Christ's life, how much more so in our own!

> *Lord, I have shut my door;*
> *Shut out life's busy cares and fretting noise,*
> *Here, in this silence, they intrude no more;*
> *Speak Thou, and heavenly joys*
> *Shall fill my heart with music sweet and calm,*
> *A holy Psalm.*

Yes, I have shut my door
On deathly passions, all its yearning love,
Its tender friendships, all the priceless store
Of human ties. Above
All these my heart aspires. O Heart Divine,
    Stoop Thou to mine.

Lord, I have shut my door!
Come Thou and visit me. I am alone!
Come as when doors were shut Thou cam'st of yore,
And visited Thine own!
My Lord, I kneel with reverent love and fear
    For Thou art here!
                                        —Selected.

The Master always kept a space of silence around His soul;
that inner serenity which is, perhaps, one of the most important
things a busy life can possess.

November 27

*From henceforth let no man trouble me: for I bear in my
body the marks of the Lord Jesus."* (Gal. 6:17.)

DURING the last century it was the custom at Scottish
universities that the recipient of an honorary degree was
fair sport for the students and must run the gauntlet of
their raucous remarks. The students sat in the balcony,
calling out what they pleased. "Is the candidate for honors
who is to become doctor of laws a miner?" No gift of the university could silence the greeting, "Hi, old miner!"

On one occasion David Livingstone was chosen to receive a
degree. Many wondered what the students would do. But as he
stood there, one arm hanging at his side, his shoulder torn by
a lion in the forest of Africa, his skin like leather, the students
arose of one accord and stood in absolute silence.

What nobler decoration of honor can any godly man seek
than his scars of service, his losses for the crown, his reproaches
for Christ's sake, his being worn out in his Master's service!

Of an old hero the minstrel sang—

"With his Yemen sword for aid;
    Ornament it carried none,
But the notches on the blade."

November 28

"And Terah took Abram his son...to go into the land of Canaan; and they came unto Haran, and dwelt there."
(Gen. 11:31.)

HARAN was reached.... There they halted, and there they stayed until Terah died.... Probably for as many as fifteen years Abraham's obedience stayed; and for that period there were no further commands, no additional promises, no hallowed communings between God and His child. It becomes us to be very careful as to whom we take with us on our pilgrimage. We may make a fair start from our Ur; but if we take Terah with us, we shall not go far. Take care, young pilgrim to Eternity, to whom you mate yourself in the marriage bond! Beware, man of business, lest you find your Terah in the man with whom you are entering into partnership! Let us all beware of that fatal spirit of compromise, which tempts us to tarry where loved ones bid us to stay. "Do not go to extremes," they cry; "we are willing to accompany you on your pilgrimage if you go only as far as Haran! Why think of going farther on a fool's errand—and whither you do not know?" Ah! this is hard to bear, harder far than outward opposition. Weakness and infirmity appeal to our feelings against our better judgment. The plains of Capua do for warriors what the arms of Rome failed to accomplish. And, tempted by the bewitching allurements which hold out to us their siren attractions, we imitate the sailors of Ulysses and vow we will go no farther in quest of our distant goal.   —F. B. Meyer.

"Be ye not unequally yoked together with unbelievers:..."
(2 Cor. 6: 14.)

November 29

"...Even as Christ forgave you, so also do ye." (Col. 3:13.)

HOW beautiful, and yet how rare, is forgiveness! Christ taught His disciples to forgive their enemies, and He is our great example. He said amid the agonies of the crucifixion, "Father, forgive them!"

A custom away out in the African bush which has no equivalent in this part of the world is *"Forgiveness Week."* Fixed in the dry season, when the weather itself is smiling, this is a week when every man and woman pledges himself or herself to forgive any neighbor any wrong, real or fancied, that may be a cause for misunderstanding, coldness, or quarrel between the parties.

A deaf mute, being asked, "What is forgiveness?" took a pencil and wrote, "It is the odor which a flower yields when trampled upon," and the Persian poet, Sadi, has given us these lines:

> "The sandal tree perfumes, when riven,
> The ax that laid it low;
> Let man, who hopes to be forgiven,
> Forgive and bless his foe."

November 30

"A little leaven leaveneth the whole lump." (Gal. 5:9.)

ONCE there was an abbot who desired the use of a piece of ground that lay conveniently near his own, but the owner refused to sell. After much persuasion he was content to lease it. The abbot covenanted only to farm it for one crop. Now his bargain sealed, he planted his field with acorns— a crop that lasted not one year, but three hundred!

So Satan seeks to get possession of our souls by asking us to permit some small sin to enter, some one wrong that seems of no great account. But when once he has entered and planted the seeds and beginnings of evil, he holds his ground, and sins and evils amazingly multiply.

The dangerous thing about a little sin is that it won't stay little.

> Each sin has its door of entrance.
> Keep—that—door—closed!
> Bolt it tight!
> Just outside, the wild beast crouches
> In the night.
> Pin the bolt with a prayer,
> God will fix it there.
> —Bees in Amber.

December 1

"So teach us to number our days, that we may apply our hearts unto wisdom." (Psalm 90:12.)

EARTH Rolls Onward into Day," and when the shadows fold me in again at the evening time, this day will have slipped away forever into the past. Each hour is given me to live but once. Minutes can trickle through my fingers carelessly, unused, and be lost. This day is entrusted to me but once. Shall I spend my portion of time carefully, or waste it, or lose it through careless fingers?

Frances Willard, when a student in Northwestern College for women, wrote in her journal: "Dr. Foster closed the Bible after his discourse at the university chapel yesterday, with these words: 'Brothers, with most men life is a failure.' The words impressed me deeply; there is sorrow in the thought; tears and agony are wrapped up in it. 'Oh, Thou who rulest above, help me that my life may be valuable—that some human being shall yet thank Thee that I have lived and toiled!'"

If I had a dozen lives to live I might afford to waste one of them, but I have only one life to invest or lose.

"Only one life, 'twill soon be past
Only what's done for Christ will last."

*Let us with faith consecrate ourselves as liv-
ing sacrifices,*
With vision to look beyond the stars,
*With love for his Kingdom to suffer with Him
on the Cross,*
With courage to reach the millions.
With hope we expect greater things for Christ,
*With joy we dare to attempt great things in
the uncharted voyage of God.*
—Newton H. Chiang.

December 2

"Give, and it shall be given unto you;...For with the same measure that ye mete withal it shall be measured to you again." (Luke 6:38.)

THE heathen have a fable of a selfish chief who dug a well and posted a law that none should drink of it but his own family. The well, however, failed to have any water. At length he appealed to the oracle, and the oracle told him that it would be dry until he shared it with the people. Even then he contrived to hold on to his selfishness, but in another form, by announcing that the people could have it all night, but he should have it all day. The following day the water failed to come until the sun went down, and then as the multitudes gathered around with their empty vessels, lo! the gurgling waters came bursting from the springs beneath and filled the well to the brim. They drank and filled their vessels and went away rejoicing. But when the morning came the waters disappeared again until the selfish monster learned the truth that we gain by giving and live by loving.

"Give, though thy gifts be small, still be a giver;
Out of the little founts proceeds the river;
Out of the river's gifts gulfs soon will be
Pouring their waters out, making a sea.
Out of the sea again Heaven draws its showers,
And to the fount imparts all its new powers.
Thus in the circle born, gifts roll around,
And in the blessings given, blessing is found."

December 3

"O the depth of the riches both of the wisdom and knowl-
edge of God! how unsearchable are his judgments, and his
ways past finding out!" (Rom. 11: 33.)

Dear Lord, as they who from the mountain crest
See in exultant sweep from east to west,
So would we turn from every lesser height
That with Thy vision we may see aright.
—A. W. C.

OH, FOR OPENED EYES!

TO TURNER, the artist, a lady remarked, "Mr. Turner, I cannot see in nature what you put into your pictures." "Don't you wish you could, madam?" was the artist's reply. And when the skeptic sneeringly says of one transported by the raptures of Christian faith and hope and love, "I can't see any joy in Christianity," the fitting reply is, "Don't you wish you could?" Love gives one eagle eyes to pierce heights and depths unscanned by those of sluggish heart; but those who love Him best are the very ones who cry, "The half was never told," of the unsearchable riches of Christ.

Our God is a God of tender, compassionate, unchangeable, and limitless love. And the God of limitless love is worthy of limitless trust.

"Could we with ink the ocean fill,
And were the skies of parchment made;
Were ev'ry stalk on earth a quill,
And ev'ry man a scribe by trade;
To write the love of God above
Would drain the ocean dry,
Nor could the scroll contain the whole
Though stretched from sky to sky."

The scarred hand, the thorn-pierced brow, the tear-marred face—these are the marks of love which passeth knowledge.

December 4

". . . Thy love to me was wonderful, . . ." (2 Samuel 1: 26.)

IS IT too much to hope that when we see our blessed Lord in the glory, when the trials and the toils and the sacrifices are all at an end—is it too much to desire that He should say something like this to us: *"Thy love to me was wonderful"?* I tell you it will make the toils of the road and all the renunciations and willing sacrifices of life seem as nothing to have some such words of commendation from the lips of our Saviour and to hear him say to the one who has sought to be faithful at all cost: "Well done! You were never popular on earth, and nobody knew much about you. The life you lived to My glory in the uninspiring sphere of duty seemed to be wasted and its sacrifice to be worthless by those who knew it; *but your love to Me was wonderful!* Men said you made mistakes and were narrow-minded and did not catch the spirit of the age. Men thought you were a fanatic and a fool and called you so. Men crucified you as they crucified Me, but *your love to Me was wonderful!"*

> *"Saviour, Thy dying love Thou gavest me,*
> *Nor should I aught withhold,*
>   *Dear Lord, from Thee:*
> *In love my soul would bow,*
> *My heart fulfill its vow,*
> *Some offering bring Thee now,*
>   *Something for Thee."*

I love Him because He first loved me!

———

December 5

"Thou hast made known to me the ways of life...."
                                            (Acts 2:28.)

I BELIEVE the Bible to be the inspired Word of God—inspired in a sense utterly different from that of any mere human book.

I believe Jesus Christ to be the Son of God, without human father, conceived by the Holy Spirit, born of the Virgin Mary. I believe that all men, without exception, are by nature sinners, alienated from God and thus utterly lost in sin. The Son of God Himself came down to earth, and by shedding His blood upon the Cross, paid the infinite penalty of the guilt of the whole world. I believe he who thus receives Jesus Christ as his Saviour is born again spiritually as definitely as in his first birth, and so born spiritually has new privileges, appetites, and affections, and is a completely changed being. I believe no man can save himself by good works, or what is commonly known as a "moral life." Such works, being but the necessary fruit and evidence of the faith within, come *after* salvation.

"Satan I believe to be the cause of man's fall and sin and rebellion against God as rightful Governor. Satan is the prince of all the kingdoms of this world, yet will in the end be cast into the pit and made harmless. Christ will come again in glory to earth to reign, even as He went away from earth, and I look for His return day by day. I believe the Bible to be God's Word, because as I use it as spiritual food I discover in my own life, as well as in the lives of those who likewise use it, a transformation, correcting evil tendencies, purifying affections, giving pure desires, and teaching that concerning the righteousness of God which those who do not so use it cannot know anything about. It is really food for the spirit as bread is for the body.

"Perhaps one of my strongest reasons for believing the Bible is that it reveals to me, as no other book in the world could do, that which appeals to me as a physician, a diagnosis of my spiritual condition. It shows me clearly what I am by nature—one lost in sin and alienated from the life that is in God. I find it a consistent and wonderful revelation of the character of God, a God far removed from any of the natural imaginings.

"It also reveals a tenderness and a nearness of God in Christ which satisfies the heart's longings and shows me that the infinite God, Creator of the world, took our very nature upon Him that He might in infinite love be one with His people to redeem them. I believe in it because it reveals a religion adapted to all classes and races, and it is intellectual suicide, knowing it, not to believe it."

—Dr. Howard A. Kelly.

December 6

"And they shall be mine, saith the Lord of hosts, in that day when I make up my jewels; . . ." (Mal. 3: 17.)

SOME scars are ornaments. I do not know a more splendid word in all the supremely splendid epistles of Paul than 'I bear about in my body the marks of the Lord Jesus.' 'Do you see this,' he said; 'I was stoned there'; and then he would pull up his sleeve and say, 'Do you see that? It is the mark of the scourge. If you could only see my back! I bear in my body the marks of the Lord Jesus.' He exhibited them as some men parade their degrees. His scars were his crown."

A youthful Mexican convert who had escaped the bondage of a false religion was listening to a missionary as she told of her visit to the Tower of London where the crown jewels are kept. She had seen the famous Kohinoor diamond which adorns the crown of the British King at his coronation. The crown is set with the most precious gems! They dazzle! They sparkle! They are priceless! Following this description, the process of polishing these gems was enlarged upon, and the words in Malachi 3 were quoted. Every word was being absorbed by this earnest, dark-eyed lad. At the close of the service he came to the missionary saying, "Pray for me that I may endure the polishing and be worthy of being even the smallest gem in my Saviour's crown. I do not want to wear a cheap crown." A few months later he suffered martyrdom.

Few have been the martyrs on whose heads crowns have alighted *while they were asleep.* Their preparatory school has ever been persecution, suffering, and the true, patient, yearlong fulfillment of duty.

> *"God has need of outstanding gems,*
> *There is work for all to do.*
> *God's vessels are chosen, but few become choice.*
> *I'd love to be choice. Would you?"*

December 7

"And the twelve gates were twelve pearls; every several gate was of one pearl: . . ." (Rev. 21: 21.)

"EVERY gate a pearl!" Every entrance into the heavenly life is through a pearl! What is a pearl? A wound is made in an oyster shell. A grain of sand, perhaps, is imbedded in the wound. Then all the resources of repair are rushed to the place where the breach was made. When the breach is closed, and the process of repair is completed, a pearl is found closing the wound. The break calls forth unsuspected resources of the shell, and a beauty appears that is not otherwise brought out. A pearl is a healed wound! No wound, no pearl.

Misfortune in our lives can be transformed into blessings, hurts changed into pearls of precious value. Look with Edison at his deafness, with Milton at his blindness, with Bunyan at his imprisonment, and see how these very misfortunes were converted into good fortunes. Even a grievous handicap may become a lifesaving power. Do you remember the story of Nydia, the blind flower girl in *The Last Days of Pompeii"?* Nydia had not become bitter about her blindness; nor had she sulked and sat at home. She had gone about the business of living and had earned a living as best she could. Then came the awful day of the eruption of Vesuvius, with the doomed city as dark as midnight beneath a thick pall of smoke and falling ashes. The terror-stricken inhabitants rushed blindly to and fro, and lost themselves in the awful blackness. But Nydia did not get lost; because of her cross of blindness she had learned to find her way by touch and hearing, and now she could go straight to rescue the life of the one she loved best. "Every gate a pearl!" Every misfortune, every failure, every loss, may be so transformed. God has the power to transform all "misfortunes" into godsends. So Jesus transformed the Cross from a criminal's badge of shame into the sign of the love of God. Often it takes a wound to transform a denying Peter into a fearless rock of a man. "No wound, no pearl!"—out of life's buffetings may come our richest rewards.

—*Selected.*

December 8

"...Freely ye have received, freely give." (Matt. 10:8.)

"Take heed therefore . . . for whosoever hath, to him shall be given; and whosoever hath not, from him shall be taken even that which he seemeth to have." (Luke 8:18.)

AS WE give our time, our substance, our very lives for others, so shall we be blessed. To receive and take and hold, without an outflowing, is to be as dead and dismal as the Dead Sea. Though watered by the dew of Hermon and the rain of Lebanon, the Dead Sea to this day is so bitter and vile that not a single living thing can be found in it. How loud is its message to us! The Dead Sea has no outlet. The waters of the many rivers would soon purify the Dead Sea did it but have an outlet to the ocean. But all the fresh and sparkling water flowing into it cannot heal its death and vileness while it does not pass on the blessing which comes into its basin.

—*L. S.*

"Hearken then thou deep,
thou Dead Sea,
I have now thy secret
learned!
Why in thee the dew of
Hermon
Is to gall and wormwood
turned."

In an old churchyard you may read this epitaph and epigram:
"What I gave, that I have;
What I kept, that I lost."

God might have used His sunset gold so sparingly;
He might have put but one wee star in all the sky—
He might have doled His blossoms out quite grudgingly;
But since He gave so lavishly, why should not I?
                                        —A. C. H.

December 9

"Therefore are they before the throne of God, and serve him day and night in his temple: and he that sitteth on the throne shall dwell among them." (Rev. 7:15.)

JOHN and Betty Stam, Moody Bible Institute graduates, were martyred in China on December 8, 1934. On December 6, John Stam wrote, "My wife, baby, and myself are today in the hands of communists. All our possessions and stores they have taken, but we praise God for peace in our hearts and a meal tonight. God grant you wisdom in what you do and us fortitude, courage, and peace of heart. He is able, and a wonderful Friend at such a time." And in closing, he said, "The Lord bless and guide you, and as for us, may God be glorified, whether by life or death."

"A martyr is not a martyr because he dies;
he dies because he is a martyr."

"For me is ordained the red robe of martyrdom," said Savonarola.

"A martyr's crown is worth its cost;
To reign with Christ will all repay;
No tongue can tell, no heart conceive
The joys of that celestial day."

O ye martyrs, be not impatient; there is another company of martyrs coming on; wait for them!
                                        —A. J. Gordon.

December 10

"Ponder the path of thy feet, and let all thy ways be established." (Prov. 4: 26.)

THINK a Christian can go anywhere," said a young woman who was defending her continued attendance at some very doubtful place of amusement.

"Certainly she can," rejoined her friend, "but I am reminded of a little incident that happened last summer when I went with a party of friends to explore a coal mine. One of the young women dressed in a dainty white gown. When her

friends remonstrated with her, she appealed to the old miner who
was to act as guide of the party.

"Can't I wear a white dress down into the mine?" she asked
petulantly.

"Yes'm," returned the old man. "There's nothin' to keep you
from wearin' a white frock down there, but there'll be consider-
able to keep you from wearin' one back."

There is nothing to prevent the Christian from wearing his white
garments when he seeks fellowship of that which is unclean, but
there is a good deal to prevent his wearing white garments
afterward.

"Beware of going to places where Christ is not allowed! Do
you not think it argues very badly for Christianity when a believer fancies it needful to go down to the world's level to get
an hour or two of enjoyment? Rather, let worldlings see that our
joy in Christ is so much superior to what they have that we are
spoiled for anything besides."

—Franklin Ferguson.

Am I not enough, Mine own? Enough,
Mine own, for thee?
Hath the world its palace towers,
Garden glades of magic flowers,
Where thou wouldst be?
Fair things and false are there,
False things but fair,
All things thou find'st at last
Only in Me.
Am I not enough, Mine own? I, forever
And alone? I, needing thee?

—Suso.

December 11

*"Let nothing be done through strife or vainglory; but in
lowliness of mind let each esteem other better than themselves."* (Phil. 2: 3.)

THE day was cold and bleak. Washington, starting out
from his headquarters, drew on his greatcoat, turned up
the collar, and pulled his hat down to shield his face
from the biting wind. As he walked down the road to
where the soldiers were fortifying a camp, no one would
have known that the tall, muffled figure was the commander in
chief of the army.

As he came near the camp he stopped to watch a small company
of soldiers who, under command of a corporal, were building a
breastwork of logs. The men were tugging at a heavy log;

the corporal, important and superior, stood at one side giving orders.

"Up with it!" he cried. "Now altogether! Push! Up with it, I say! Now!" The men gathered new strength. A great push all together, and the log was nearly in its place, but it was too heavy, and just before it reached the top of the pile it slipped and fell back. The corporal shouted again. "Up with it, now! What ails you? Up with it, I say!"

The men tugged and strained again; the log nearly reached the top, slipped, and once more rolled back.

"Heave hard!" cried the corporal. "One, two, three! Now all together! Push!"

Another struggle, and then, just as the log was about to roll back for the third time, Washington ran forward, pushed with all his great strength, and the log rolled into place on top of the breastwork. The men, panting and perspiring, sought eagerly to thank him, but he turned toward the corporal.

"Why don't you help your men with this heavy lifting when they need another hand?" he asked.

"Why don't I?" asked the man. "Don't you see I am a corporal?"

"Indeed!" replied Washington, throwing open his greatcoat and showing his uniform. "I am only the commander in chief. Next time you have a log too heavy for your men to lift, send for me!"

December 12

"...What things soever ye desire, when ye pray, believe that ye receive them, and ye shall have them." (Mark 11: 24.)

WHEN my little son was about ten years of age, his grandmother promised him a stamp album for Christmas. Christmas came, but no stamp album and no word from grandmother. The matter, however, was not mentioned; but when his playmates came to see his Christmas presents, I was astonished, after he had named over this and that as gifts received, to hear him add,

"And a stamp album from grandmother."

I had heard it several times, when I called him to me, and said, "But, Georgie, you did not get an album from your grandmother. Why do you say so?"

There was a wondering look on his face, as if he thought it strange that I should ask such a question, and he replied, "Well, Mamma, grandma *said*, so it is the same as." I could not say a word to check his faith.

A month went by, and nothing was heard from the album. Finally, one day, really wondering in my heart why the album had not been sent, I said, to test his faith:

"Well, Georgie, I think grandma has forgotten her promise."

"Oh, no, Mamma," he quickly and firmly said, "she hasn't."

I watched the dear, trusting face, which, for a while, looked very sober, as if debating the possibilities I had suggested. Finally a bright light passed over it, and he said,

"Mamma, do you think it would do any good if I should write to her *thanking* her for the album?"

"I do not know," I said, "but you might try it."

A rich spiritual truth began to dawn upon me. In a few minutes a letter was prepared and committed to the mail, and he went off whistling his confidence in his grandma. In just a short time a letter came, saying:

"My dear Georgie: I have not forgotten my promise to you, of an album. I tried to get such a book as you desired, but could not get the kind you wanted; so I sent on to New York. It did not get here till after Christmas, and it was still not right, so I sent for another, and as it has not come as yet, I send you three dollars to get one in Chicago. Your loving grandma."

As he read the letter his face was the face of a victor. "Now, Mamma, didn't I tell you?" came from the depths of a heart that never doubted; that *"against hope, believed in hope"* that the stamp album would come. While he was trusting, grandma was working, and in due season faith became sight.

It is so human to want sight when we step out on the promises of God, but our Saviour said to Thomas, and to the long roll of doubters who have ever since followed him: *"Blessed are they who have not seen, and yet have believed."—Mrs. Rounds.*

December 13

"Take us the foxes, the little foxes, that spoil the vines: for our vines have tender grapes." (Song of Sol. 2:15.)

ASK then the question, "What has driven Christ from me?" He hides his face behind the wall of thy sins. That wall may be built up of little pebbles, as well as of large stones. If thou would'st live with Christ, walk with Christ, see Christ, and have fellowship with Christ, take heed of the little foxes that spoil the vines, "for our vines have tender grapes." The Lord invites you to go with Him and take them. He will surely, like Samson, take the foxes at once and easily. Go with Him and He will *keep* you.

FOXES AND FAULTS

If I had a grapevine tender and green
Growing taller and taller each day,
And a little fox tried to spoil that vine,
I'd drive that fox away.

If I had a life all clean and pure,
   Growing sweeter and sweeter each day,
And a little fault tried to spoil that life,
   I'd drive that fault away.
                  —Florence Harrell.

December 14

"And so, after he had patiently endured, he obtained the promise." (Heb. 6:15.)

GOD'S Word is as full of promises as the heavens are full of stars. All of them are payable upon demand according to the conditions named. They are made freely, and they are paid fully. Spurgeon calls a book of God's promises "The Check Book of the Bank of Faith." We do not have check books for an ornament or for meditation, but for use. A promise of God is given to be presented and paid in full. The believer's capital for the King's business is all lodged in the Lord's treasury, and the only way to secure it for use is to make daily drafts upon the unfailing supply. God writes no names upon His promises, only conditions upon which they will be honored. Put your name in, fulfill the condition, and draw upon God for all that He promises!

Some promises are payable upon demand. Others are dated farther on. But a long-time promise of God is as sure of payment as one payable on demand. Be sure of the time limitation of God's promises, and if delayed, look at your dates.
               —A Daily Thought for a Daily Endeavor.

"The possibilities of prayer are bounded by the promises of God."
                        —Bounds.

I will not therefore minimize my prayer,
But make it large as are the promises.
Since God is willing thus to bless,
No less an answer would I share.
Alas, for my small faith,
Compared with what He saith.

Therefore, henceforth, shall prayer be heard
From me according to God's word.
I will request, as long as I shall live,
All God has shown His willingness to give.
As are the love and power His truth declares,
So shall faith make the measure of my prayers.
                 —Wm. Olney.

December 15

"...He will beautify the meek with salvation."
(Psalm 149: 4.)

THE SOURCE OF ITS BEAUTY

ONCE there was a brier growing in a ditch, and there came along a gardener with his spade. As he dug around it and lifted it out, the brier said to itself, 'What is he doing that for? Doesn't he know that I am a worthless brier?' But the gardener took it into the garden and planted it amid his flowers, while the brier said, 'What a mistake he has made, planting a brier like myself among such rose trees as these!' But the gardener came once more with his keen-edged knife, made a slit in the brier and *budded* it with a rose, and by and by, when summer came, lovely roses were blooming on that old brier! Then the gardener said, 'Your beauty is not due to that which came out, but to that which I put into you.' That is just what Christ is doing all the time with our human lives."

> *"Let the beauty of Jesus be seen in me,*
> *All His wondrous compassion and purity;*
> *O Thou Spirit Divine, all my nature refine*
> *Till the beauty of Jesus be seen in me."*

December 16

"...The Father hath not left me alone; for I do always those things that please him." (John 8:29.)

IT IS human to stand with the crowd; it is divine to stand alone. It is manlike to follow the people, to drift with the tide; it is Godlike to follow a principle, to stem the tide.

It is natural to compromise conscience and follow the social and religious fashion for the sake of gain or pleasure; it is against nature to sacrifice both on the altar of His will.

"No man stood with me, but all men forsook me," wrote the battle-scarred apostle in describing his first appearance before Nero to answer with his life for believing and teaching contrary to the Roman world.

Truth has been out of fashion since man changed his robe of fadeless light for a garment of fading leaves.

Noah built and voyaged alone. His neighbors laughed at his strangeness and perished in style.

Abraham wandered and worshiped alone. Sodomites smiled at the simple shepherd, followed the fashion and fed the flames.

Daniel watched and prayed alone. Elijah sacrificed and witnessed alone. Jeremiah prophesied and wept alone. JESUS loved and died ALONE.

I'M NOT ALONE

I'm not alone, though others go
  A different way from what I choose;
I'm not alone, though I say "No!"
  I know that I will never lose.
I'm not alone, though others tease
  And urge that I should go their way;
I'm not alone, though I displease
  My friends by what I'll never say.
I'm not alone, for I now choose—
  Though other folk may call me odd,
Though now it seems that I might lose—
  To go the way that Jesus trod.
                    —L. E. Dunkin.

December 17

"And he led them forth by the right way . . ." (Psalm 107: 7.)

ONCE, in going down an Alpine path, the travelers found their way wholly closed. The little path by the mountain torrent suddenly ended in a vast ice cliff under which the torrent plunged and disappeared. What were they to do? Suddenly the guide leaped into the stream and bade his companions follow. For a moment there was darkness and fear, then they were carried under the ice mountain and a moment later flung on the banks of green in the valley of Chamouni.

"O Lord, Thou art the Pathfinder. Glorious outlines of some great plan of Thine pass, into which we may fit if we will.

What room is there for troubled fear?
  I know my Lord, and He is near;
And He will light my candle, so
  That I may see the way I go.

There need be no bewilderment
  To one who goes where he is sent;
The trackless plain, by night and day
  Is set with signs lest he should stray.

My path may cross a waste of sea,
  But that need never frighten me—
Or rivers full to very brim,
  But they are open ways to Him.

My path may lead through wood at night,
 Where neither moon nor any light
Of guiding star or beacon shines;
 He will not let me miss my signs.

Lord, grant to me a quiet mind,
 That, trusting Thee—for Thou art kind—
I may go on without a fear,
 For Thou, my Lord, art always near.
                              —Author unknown.

December 18

"For it is God which worketh in you both to will and to do
of his good pleasure." (Phil. 2:13.)

IF WE would have Christ dwell in our hearts there must
be something more than a guest room set aside for Him.
He desires to dwell with us, to abide in us. The transient guest is hedged about by certain limitations. But
there can be no secrets from one who has a permanent
home with us. This is so with Christ in the heart. From attic to
basement in the whole house of life there must be no room that
is closed to Him. There may be rooms of the soul we would not
throw open to the world, but if the Lord is to abide with us, the
key even to these must be placed in His hands. Only so can we
know the joy and peace and strength of His abiding presence in
the heart.   —Christian Observer.

AN EXCHANGE OF WILLS

I want my heart so cleared of self
That my dear Lord can come
And set up His own furnishings,
And make my heart—His home.

And since I know what this requires,
Each morning while it's still,
I slip into that secret room,
And leave with Him—My WILL,

He always takes it graciously,
Presenting me with His;
I'm ready then to meet the day —
And any task there is.

And this is how my Lord controls
My interest, my ills,
Because we meet at break of day,
For an EXCHANGE OF WILLS.
                              —Anna Jane Granniss.

December 19

"...Go ye into all the world, and preach the gospel to every creature." (Mark 16:15.)

> *O Zion, haste, thy mission high fulfilling,*
> *To tell to all the world that God is Light;*
> *That He who made all nations is not willing*
> *One soul should perish, lost in shades of night.*
>
> *Behold how many thousands still are lying,*
> *Bound in the darksome prison-house of sin,*
> *With none to tell them of the Saviour's dying,*
> *Or of the life He died for them to win.*
>
> *'Tis thine to save from peril of perdition*
> *The souls for whom the Lord His life laid down;*
> *Beware, lest, slothful to fulfill thy mission,*
> *Thou lose one jewel that should deck His crown.*
>
> *Proclaim to ev'ry people, tongue and nation*
> *That God, in whom they live and move, is love:*
> *Tell how He stoop'd to save His lost creation,*
> *And died on earth that man might live above.*
>
> *Give of thy sons to bear the message glorious;*
> *Give of thy wealth to speed them on their way;*
> *Pour out thy soul for them in prayer victorious;*
> *And all thou spendest Jesus will repay.*
> —*Hymnal.*

The whole wide world with its restless millions waits for the "beautiful feet" of triumphant mountaineers. (Isa. 52: 7.)

December 20

"...I will uphold thee with the right hand of my righteousness." (Isaiah 41:10.)

"Then shalt thou walk in thy way safely, and thy foot shall not stumble." (Prov. 3:23.)

FEAR of falling is wholesome. To be venturesome is no sign of wisdom. Times come to us when we feel we must go down unless we have very special support. God's right hand is a grand thing to lean upon. It is not only His hand but His right hand; His power united with skill, His power where it is most dexterous! Fearful is our danger, but joyful is our security. The youth whom God upholds, devils cannot throw down. He will hold me fast! Our worst peril is in our own carelessness, but against this the Lord Jesus has put us on our guard, saying, "Watch and pray."

Oh, for grace to walk this day without a single stumble! It is not enough that we do not actually fall; our cry should be that we may not make the smallest slip with our feet, but may at the last adore Him "who is able to keep us from stumbling."
—C. H. Spurgeon.

Some stumble because they do not see the stone in the way.

The Lord will give us *sure-footedness*. The hinds leap over rock and crag, never missing their foothold. Our Lord will give us grace to follow the most difficult paths of duty without a stumble. He can fit our feet for the crags, so that we shall be at home where apart from God we should perish.

Oh, what feet are the feet of faith, by which, following the "Hind of the Morning" we shall ascend into the hill of the Lord!

> *He holdeth the waters in the hollow*
> *Of His hand,*
> *This mighty restless seething sea*
> *In His hand.*
> *Oh, hand so sure, so safe, so strong*
> *That it can hold the sea,*
> *Mid the storm-tossed waves of the sea*
> *of life*
> *It can, it will, hold me.*
> —M. Slattery.

December 21

"O satisfy us early with thy mercy; that we may rejoice and be glad all our days." (Psalm 90:14.)

YOUR AFTERSELF

YOUR first duty in life is toward your afterself. So live that the man you ought to be may, in his time, be possible, be actual. Far away in the years he is awaiting his turn. His body, his brain, his soul, are in your boyish hands. He cannot help himself. What will you leave for him? Will it be a brain unspoiled by lust or dissipation, a mind trained to think and act, a nervous system true as a dial in its response to the truth about you? Will you, boy, let him come as a man among men in his time? Or will you throw away his inheritance before he has had the chance to touch it? Will you turn over to him a brain distorted, a mind diseased, a will untrained to action, a spinal cord grown through and through with

"devil-grass, with "wild oats"? Will you let him come and take
your place, gaining through your experience, happy in your
friendships, hallowed through your joys, building on them his
own? Or will you fling it all away, decreeing, wantonlike, that
the man you might have been shall never be? This is your problem in life—the problem which is vastly more to you than any or
all others! How will you meet it, as a man or as a fool? It comes
before you today and every day, and the hour of your choice is
the crisis of your destiny!   —*David Starr Jordan.*

Our mark is always our magnet.

———

December 22

"... Pray for them which despitefully use you ..."
(Matt. 5:44.)

IT IS so easy to become jealous, to believe false rumors,
to form unfair opinions, and to say harsh things about
our neighbors and associates. People are all so prone to
answer such attacks in a like manner.

On one occasion Bishop Francis Asbury received an
abusive anonymous letter. In his journal he wrote as follows:
"I came from my knees to receive the letter, and having read it,
I returned whence I came."

How can I live this day so that people will say as they said in
the early period of the church, "Behold, how the Christians love
one another!"

IF I WERE YOU

It is easy to say the quick, sharp word
   That will hurt him through and through—
The friend you have always held so dear—
   But I wouldn't, if I were you.

It is easy to spread an idle tale
   That perhaps may not be true,
And give it wings like the thistledown,
   But I wouldn't, if I were you.

To words once spoken, if harsh, unkind,
   You must ever bid adieu,
And though you may speak them if you will,
   Yet I wouldn't, if I were you.
—Florence Jones Hadley.

"Drop the subject when you cannot agree; there is no need to
be bitter because you know you are right."

Leave it all quietly with Him!

December 23

"...*We have seen his star in the east, and are come to worship him.*" (Matt. 2:2.)

STAR TRAILS

"Star of wonder, star of night,
Star with royal beauty bright,
Westward leading, still proceeding,
Guide us to Thy perfect light."

 DID you ever hear the story of the boy who was left by his father on the sailing vessel to handle the rudder while his father went below? He said to the boy: "Now, my boy, keep your eye on the North Star right there and all will be right." The boy answered: "Yes, Sir, I will." After a while the boy called down the hatchway, "Father, come up, I have passed the star."

The world is full of folk who run past the star, but you cannot run away from the stars that are there to guide you and not run on the rocks. If you do not mind the rudder you will have to mind the rocks.

Map your course by heavenly lights!

"When crossing Niagara on a tight rope, Blondin always had a star fixed in the opposite direction and kept his eye on the star."

"When the wanderer has lost his path in the storm of dust there is nothing to do but wait till the stars come out."

December 24

"... *Let us now go even unto Bethlehem, and see* . . ."
(Luke 2:15.)

THEY came that night to Bethlehem, the simple and the wise. The shepherd and the scholar saw the glory in the skies—and sought the holy manger bed, that place of mystery—where God Himself had broken in upon humanity.

The greatest men who walk the earth can offer us today—no diviner revelation. This then is the Way. . . . Though to knowledge high and vast the human mind may soar, every man must come at last unto the stable door.

—*Patience Strong.*

"They all were looking for a King,
To slay their foes and lift them high:
Thou cam'st, a little baby thing
That made a woman cry."

IF HE HAD NOT COME

There would have been no Christmas Day, there would have been no revelation of God in understandable human hearts, there would have been no living faith to encourage us each new day, there would have been no everlasting doctrine of Peace-on-earth, Good will to men!

"*O come all ye faithful, joyful and triumphant,*
O come ye, O come ye to Bethlehem;
Come and behold Him, born the King of angels.
O come, let us adore Him, Christ, the Lord!

Sing, choirs of angels, sing in exultation,
O sing, all ye bright hosts of heav'n above;
Glory to God, all glory in the highest
O come, let us adore Him, Christ the Lord!

Yea, Lord, we greet Thee, born this happy morning,
Jesus, to Thee be all glory giv'n; Word of the Father,
Now in flesh appearing
O come, let us adore Him, Christ, the Lord!

"O night divine, the night when Christ was born!"

December 25

"*...Unto us ...*" (Isa. 9: 6.)

THE wonder of Christmas is its *simplicity*. There is Mary, the mother, and there is Joseph to whom she was betrothed. Plain and simple folk, these, even as you and I. There are the Shepherds—the first Christmas congregation. Humble folk, these, folk who lived close to the things God made—the earth, the carpet for their feet; the sun and stars, their covering.

Yes, and the Child, too. Nothing here of the pomp and circumstance of life, only the simplicity of the divine. It is this simplicity which makes Christmas wonderful. Here may we all come, suppliant—not to a throne of human exaltation, but to a throne of divine simplicity.

Here may we worship, recognizing in the simplicity of the Child the meaning of God's redeeming love. Here may we bring our joys and our sorrows; our joys will be hallowed, our sorrows will be lightened. Here may we receive strength for the days to come, light for the time that shall be. And the Light that shines from the humble manger is strong enough to reach to the end of our days.

Here, then, we come—the young, the old; the rich, the poor;

the mighty, the servant—worshipping in the beauty of divine
simplicity, marvelling at its simple love. *This is the wonder of
Christmas!*

> *"Unto you is born this day a Saviour"*
> *Which is Jesus Christ the wondrous Lord;*
> *Not a "teacher," not a "good example,"*
> *But the Son of God, the Living Word.*

> *No "philosopher," his fancies weaving,*
> *Warp of dreams and woof of visions vast,*
> *Not a "prophet," peering down the future,*
> *Not a "scholar," delving in the past.*

> *"Unto you is born this day a Saviour";*
> *Shine, O star! and shout, O angel voice!*
> *Unto you this precious gift is given;*
> *Sing, O earth! and all ye Heavens, rejoice!*

> *Long the world has waited such a Saviour,*
> *Sunk in sin and torn by fear and doubt;*
> *Long in darkness groped for truth and wisdom;*
> *Glory, glory, now the light shines out!*

> *"Unto you is born this day a Saviour,"*
> *Earth's one hope, the Life, the Truth, the Way,*
> *Mighty God and glorious Redeemer,*
> *Jesus Christ the Lord is born today.*
>   —*Annie Johnson Flint.*

December 26

*"Thou shalt guide me with thy counsel, and afterward re-
ceive me to glory."* (Psalm 73:24.)

WONDERFUL COUNSELLOR

ONE of the offices which our Lord Jesus sustains is
"Counsellor" (Isaiah 9:6).
    Now there are numberless things before us contin-
ually in our earthly pilgrimage regarding which we
need counsel, we need advice; and then under these
circumstances we should go to our Lord Jesus Christ and say to
Him: "My Lord, I am ignorant; now what am I to do? Thou art
my Counsellor, now show me clearly and distinctly how to act
under these circumstances." And what will be the result? We
shall be taught!
You need never take a step in the dark. If you do, you are

sure to make a mistake. Wait! Wait till you have light. Remind
the Lord Jesus that as He is Counsellor to the Church of God,
He will be, in your particular case, Counsellor and Guide, and
will direct you, and if you patiently wait, believingly, expectantly,
you will find that the waiting is not in vain, and that the Lord
will prove Himself a Counsellor both wise and good.

—*George Mueller, of Bristol.*

December 27

"...*God also hath highly exalted him, and given him a
name which is above every name.*" (Phil. 2:9.)

HEAVEN'S GREATEST GIFT

 OD [the greatest lover] so loved [the greatest degree]
the world [the greatest number] that he gave [the greatest act] his only begotten Son [the greatest gift] that whosoever [the greatest invitation] believeth [the greatest
simplicity] in him [the greatest person] should not perish
[the greatest deliverance], but [the greatest difference] have [the
greatest certainty] everlasting life [the greatest possession]."

(John 3:16.)

Christ never looks greater than when you put some great man
by His side.

"I paint," cried Raphael.
"I build," was the boast of Michael Angelo.
"I rule," cried Caesar.
"I sing," cried Homer.
"I conquer," cried Alexander.
"I *seek and save*," cried Jesus Christ.

This is the glory of the Master of His Gospel!

"O come, let us adore Him,
Christ the Lord."

An African in a jungle village was one of a crowd listening
to a missionary tell of Jesus Christ, His matchless personality
and sacrificial life of service. The African could not contain his
joy. Breaking in on the missionary's message, he cried: "I always
knew there ought to be a God like that, but never before did I
know His name!"

"*His name shall endure for ever: ...*" (Psalm 72:17.)

MIRACLE

I heard the bells of Bethlehem ring out this Christmas Day!
Men scoff at miracles. "They cannot be," they say;
"Christ was not born of Mary: there could be no virgin birth.
'Tis but a lovely legend of the Godhead come to earth."

*And yet, I heard the bells of Bethlehem ring out this Christmas
          Day,
And the clangor of their ringing was ten thousand miles away!*
                                        —Alice Gay Judd.

December 28

"... Whose names were not written in the book of life ..."
                                        (Rev. 17:8.)

YOUNG man, a high-school graduate, having arrived
at the college where he intended to finish his education,
was greeted by the president, a godly old man and a
great friend of the boy's father. Having an interest in
him, he said to the boy: "Well, my boy, after you have
finished your college course here—what then?"

"Oh, I may be elected to the Senate."

"Fine ambition. What then?"

"I suppose that I will get old and retire to a well-earned rest."

"Yes — and what then?"

Very quietly and subdued the boy replied: "Some day I shall
die."

"Yes," said the old man seriously, "and after death, what?"

But there was no answer.

> *"When the choir has sung its last
>   anthem,
> And the preacher has made his
>   last prayer;
> When the people have heard their
>   last sermon
> And the sound has died out on
>   the air;
> When the Bible lies closed on the
>   altar
> And the pews are all empty of
>   men
> And each one stands facing his
>   record—*
> *And the great Book is opened—
>   WHAT THEN?"*

When the great angel announces that time shall be no more—
What Then?

> *"TOMORROW'S sun may never rise
> To shed its beams upon the way;
> This is the TIME, O then be wise,
> Thou wouldst be saved, why not
>   TODAY?"*

"Now is the accepted time, now is the day of salvation."

December 29

"The place whereon thou standest is holy ground."
(Exodus 3: 5.)

IN Nottingham, England, there is a little chapel, on the wall of which is a bronze tablet that marks the spot where William Booth, the leader and founder of the Salvation Army, is said to have received the vision, and been *swept* with the passion that sent him as God's restless missionary to the very ends of the earth. It is said that one day a humble African wandered into the little chapel. He seemed to be searching for something, and at length he came to this tablet, and there he stood transfixed. And then, looking around him again, he discerned the janitor, and said to him, "Is this the spot where William Booth knelt and prayed?" The janitor said, "This is it!" Then said the humble African, "Can a man be permitted to kneel down here?" The janitor said, "You can. It is a place for prayer." And the old African, falling upon his knees, with uplifted arms and streaming face, said, "Lord God, do it again! Do it again!"

A vision of the Risen Christ and His plan for your life and for the world and your obedience to it is the most significant thing that can come into your life! Will you not reverently kneel in the presence of Him, who only has the right to reign, and say, "Lord Jesus, do it again! by putting Thy redeeming passion upon *me*"?

It is at the Trysting-Place of the Cross that we shall see the vision, receive our orders, and in the power of the Holy Spirit be enabled to respond, "Lord, here am I; send me!" (Isa. 6: 8.)

You may belong to the generation of great souls in your day.

December 30

". . . But this one thing I do, forgetting those things which are behind, and reaching forth unto those things which are before, I press toward the mark for the prize of the high calling of God in Christ Jesus." (Phil. 3: 13, 14.)

WHILE we were students in the seminary several of us camped in the Catskill mountains. One day we selected a certain mountain that we were going to climb. After we had started, we looked up and thought we saw the top, and we climbed for it. When we finally reached that point we found that we had not yet reached its summit. Again we started to climb to what looked to be the top, and when we reached that point

we found to our surprise that there was still a higher peak. So it is
with our life of faith. We go from "strength to strength," "abound
more and more," and go from "glory to glory."

ON THE SUMMIT

The path was steep and snowy—the way was hard and cold,
The wind rushed fiercely at us like a wolf upon the fold;
And we bit our lips and struggled in the terror of the blast,
And we blessed our staffs and wondered if the storm would
                soon be past.
Sometimes our feet slipped backward on the crusty ice and
                snow,
Sometimes we stumbled, helpless, for the way was hard to go;
Sometimes we fell, and falling, we were sorry we had tried
To reach the mountain's summit, and the hope within us died.

The path was steep and snowy—the way was hard and cold,
But we struggled ever forward, half afraid—no longer bold;
And with dogged perseverance, we pushed up the hidden trail,
And we seemed but children playing with the elements—
                too frail
To live long in the displeasure of the wind and hail and sleet,
And the snowy down-like blanket seemed a mammoth winding
                sheet—
And we almost started homeward with a weary broken sigh,
But we flinched and struggled forward 'neath the scorn that
                cleft the sky.

The path was steep and snowy—the way was hard and cold,
But at last we reached the summit, and it glittered with the
                gold
Of the sun that had been shining, with a perfect, glowing
                light
From behind the heavy storm clouds that had turned the day
                to night.
And standing on the summit, we looked down and tried to pray,
For we wished to thank the Father who had kept us on our way;
For the snow and sleet and windstorm were but trifles in the
                past,
And they made the sunshine brighter when we reached the
                top at last.
                                —Margaret E. Sangster, Jr.

A bracing exploration and a magnificent discovery!

December 31

"So will not we go back from thee: . . ." (Psalm 80: 18.)

Oh, there are heavenly heights to reach
In many a fearful place,
While the poor, timid heir of God
Lies blindly on his face;
Lies languishing for light Divine
That he shall never see
'Til he goes forward at Thy sign,
And trusts himself to Thee.
—Rev. C. A. Fox.

When Mallory and Irvine were last seen on Mt. Everest—the highest peak in the world—they were "going strong for the top." Bitter cold, raging winds, blinding blizzards, engulfing avalanches of snow and rock—all these dangers stood between these brave climbers and the top of that towering mountain. Nothing could turn them back!

What a great way to close the old year, and crossing the threshold into the new to say with these heroic climbers, "We will not go back from Thee!"

Let us fare forth bravely, our feet on solid ground, our eyes to the stars, for we walk with Him whose promise is: "Lo, I am with you alway, even unto the end of the age."

Press on! Surmount the rocky steeps,
Climb boldly o'er the torrent's arch;
He fails alone who feebly creeps,
He wins who dares the hero's march.
Be thou a hero! Let thy might
Tramp on eternal snows its way
And through the ebon walls of night
Hew down a passage unto day.
—Park Benjamin.

This generation will complete the task of world-evangelization by the youth who were last seen "heading toward the summit."

Now must I hence!
Through the thick night I hear
the trumpet blow.
—Tennyson.

Onward and Upward!

Every Reader of "Mountain Trailways for Youth"
Should Also Have

"STREAMS IN THE DESERT"
A Book of Daily Devotional Reading in Nine Languages

Why "Streams in the Desert" Was Written

By Mrs. Charles E. Cowman

Letters pour into our missionary office from the four corners of the world asking for copies of "Streams in the Desert." We have come in touch with thousands of dear fellow Christians, weighted with burdens too heavy to bear, to whom the daily devotional readings have brought comfort and cheer. Many of the letters contain such sentences as, "What led you to compile 'Streams'?" "Where did you find the helpful messages?" "Were you ever a great sufferer or a shut-in?" May I take this opportunity to reply to these personal questions?

My beloved companion, the founder of the Oriental Missionary Society, and I, had the unspeakable privilege of spending a number of years in the Orient as missionaries of the Cross. It was a delightful service; but where is the missionary, possessed with a passionate passion for souls, who is able to take life easy? Twenty years of Bible Training Institute work in Japan and Korea, then five years with one hundred workers in the villages of Japan, placing the Word of God into the 10,300,000 homes of the Mikado's Empire, seeing hundreds inquiring their way to Zion—what blessed days! In the midst of these wonderful times came the angel of pain, dressed in her somber robes. We were afar in the mountain fastnesses of Japan, engaged in evangelistic work, when one evening, like a bolt out of the blue, came the stroke that completely changed everything in our lives. A doctor was summoned hastily, and after a hurried examination he said to me, "Your husband's work is finished. Take him to the homeland immediately, if you would not bury him in heathen soil." *"Worn out"* was the term that the physician used. His only human hope was across the deep blue in the homeland. We boarded a steamer that lay at anchor, and put out to sea. What lay ahead of us? We could only trust and wait.

Several times during the twenty years of missionary service, the climate of sunny Southern California had restored the tired nerves and renewed his strength. Would it not do so again? He never ceased to pray and believe that it might, but his closest friends knew

309

that his missionary career was ended. Activity is not the only kind of service that fulfills God's will. "They also serve who only stand and wait," wrote blind Milton. Not always, however, do we accept the Master's guidance with submission and joy, when He calls away from the white fields to the lonely desert. What a change for this keen, active man! From the din of the battle to the seclusion of the sick chamber. From the glow and glory of the work he loved so dearly, to the utter abandonment of it all. Would his faith fail now, at this crucial point? Would he still trust on through God's silences? Ah, a triumphant faith was needed just here. God gave it, and he found that it was possible to praise God in the darkest hour that ever swept a human life. If God was to give him songs in the night, He must first make it night. The refining fires never raged beyond His control. The billows, which, in their approach, threatened to submerge him as they came on, lifted him up to the heaven he was bound for. All the waves were crested with God's benediction. God answered his prayer in His own way, permitting him to be shut in with Himself that he might find the treasures of darkness, delivering him with such a mighty hand that he was glad that the tempest arose, for the furious winds and tumbling seas revealed to him "*what manner of man is this.*"

If the great adversary sought by that stroke to mar or bruise a chosen instrument, he was certainly disappointed; and if he thought, by making the Lord's servant often go heavily, to arrest the work, he was foiled. Charles Cowman stood still beneath the shadow of the Cross.

It was my privilege to be by his side through the six long, pain-filled years. Often Satan came, tempting us to faint under the pressure, but each time when the testings reached their utmost limit, God would illumine some old and familiar text, or a helpful book or tract would providentially fall into our hands which contained just the message needed at that moment.

On day, while walking along the seashore, wondering almost if "*God had forgotten to be gracious,*" we noticed a leaflet lying at our feet. We eagerly picked it up and found the exquisite poem, "God smiles on His child in the eye of the storm." We caught anew a glimpse of His loving face. His choicest cordials were kept for our deepest faintings, and we were held in His strong, loving arms throughout those years, till we learned to love our desert, with its refreshing streams, because of His wonderful presence with us.

"*The way was long, and the shadows spread, far as the eye could see.*

I stretched my hands to a human Christ, who walked through the night with me,

Out of the darkness we came at last, our feet on the dawn-warm sod,

And I knew by the light in His wondrous eye, that I walked with the Son of God."

310

"God does not comfort us to make us comfortable, but to make us comforters," wrote Dr. Jowett. One day, when lonely and bereft, a sweet Voice whispered to me, "Pass on to other troubled hearts some of the messages that were helpful to you throughout the years of testing." So a book was compiled, and the first edition of "Streams in the Desert" was sent on its errand of love. There came a call for a second edition and letters were received, not only from America and England, but from Japan, Korea, China, India, Africa, The Congo, Egypt, Australia, Alaska, Siam, and from the islands of the sea, from other missionaries and Christian workers, asking for copies of the book. Another edition was published, but soon exhausted; then followed the fourth, fifth, sixth and seventh. The eighth edition was entirely exhausted within three months, and the ninth edition, five times the number of the eighth, was likewise soon sent out. The twenty-eighth edition is now off the press. My desk is piled up with letters, many of them from leading ministers and workers of the world, telling of the blessing that has come to them through reading "Streams in the Desert." I have learned this little secret—to

> *"Measure thy life by loss and not gain;*
> *Not by the wine drunk, but the wine poured forth;*
> *For love's strength standeth in love's sacrifice,*
> *And he who suffers most has most to give."*

"*Streams in the Desert*" can be obtained from THE ORIENTAL MISSIONARY SOCIETY. American Headquarters, 900 North Hobart Blvd., Los Angeles 27, California.

Price, $2.00

The profits from the sale of all of Mrs. Cowman's books are used in world-wide missionary work.

INDEX

27. "For Their Sakes I Sanctify Myself."
28. "Life Victorious!"
29. "Beethoven and an Old Harpsichord."
30. "We Must Empty by Filling."
31. "Your Opportunity the Greatest."

SEPTEMBER

1. "Dr. Bushnell Finds God."
2. "If Radio's Slim Fingers, etc."
3. "Daniel Purposed in His Heart."
4. "I Simply Take Him at His Word."
5. "The Lord's Song in a Strange Land."
6. "Hasty Praying."
7. "A Brazilian Girl's Consecration."
8. "The Cowboy's Prayer."
9. "All the Promises of God Are Yea."
10. "Believing God."
11. "Give Attendance to Reading."
12. "Temptation in Fine, Gay Colors."
13. "Indian Lay Down Blanket."
14. "Recognize God's Right."
15. "The Morning Hour with God."
16. "He Will Keep the Feet."
17. "Your Goal Was Not Some Island."
18. "Our Life Is but a Little Holding."
19. "The Cross the Crowning Service."
20. "Once in an Eastern Palace."
21. "Trifling With the Serpent."
22. "Garibaldi's Challenge."
23. "He Found His Place in God's Plan."
24. "The Sun-Bird and God's Care."
25. "The Rich Young Ruler."
26. "God Spoke."
27. "The Yellow Rosebush."
28. "I Have Prayed That Your Faith."
29. "Let Us Go Into the House."
30. "The Wings of the Morning."

OCTOBER

1. "Living a Great Life."
2. "Young African Convert."
3. "I See My Way as Birds."
4. "Sin as a Caterpillar and a Butterfly."
5. "You Can Conquer Temptation!"
6. "The Need of God-Consciousness."
7. "Buying Up Your Opportunity."
8. "His Lamps Are We."
9. "What Think Ye of Christ?"
10. "The Value of a Single Soul!"
11. "The Spider and the Doorbell."
12. "One of God's Farmers."
13. "God Can Make a Stepping-Stone."
14. "Never Defend Yourself."
15. "He Was Tired of the Rope."
16. "Every Youth Has a Quest to Make."
17. "Watch the Morning Watch."
18. "Make Me a Captive, Lord!"
19. "A Lady's Rank Is Not Dependent."
20. "Walking in the Spirit."
21. "Mind the Light!"
22. "The Language Jesus Spoke."
23. "To Know All Is to Forgive All."
24. "Livingstone, on Sacrifice."
25. "I'm Yielded, Lord."
26. "Guard Your Discernment."
27. "As John Upon the Dear Lord's Breast."
28. "Life Is All a Pilgrim's."
29. "The Boy Who Made a Bridge."

30. "Antonio Stradivari and His Violin."
31. "Love Through Me, Love of God."

NOVEMBER

1. "Alone With Thee—The Peep O' Day."
2. "Faithful in a Very Little."
3. "We Mean a Lot to Someone."
4. "A Strange Bonfire."
5. "Weaving—White and Black."
6. "Open the Door!"
7. "Have You an Ancient Wound?"
8. "Hast Thou Heard Him, Seen Him?"
9. "Emancipation Day for the Slaves."
10. "Where Are You, God?"
11. "With God NOTHING Shall Be Impossible."
12. "In the Secret of His Presence."
13. "Jesus, Saviour, Pilot Me!"
14. "Mine Were the Streets of Nazareth."
15. "Be What Yo' Am!"
16. "God Delivered a Young Christian."
17. "March We Forth."
18. "Is Not This the Carpenter?"
19. "I Refuse to Criticize, Find Fault!"
20. "Instant Obedience."
21. "Men Ought Always to Pray."
22. "Crowned or Crucified."
23. "This One Thing I Do!"
24. "Jesus, Lead Me Up the Mountain!"
25. "The World's Greatest."
26. "Lord, I have Shut My Door!"
27. "David Livingstone Receives a Degree."
28. "Be Not Unequally Yoked Together."
29. "Forgiveness Week in Africa."
30. "One Acorn and Many Oaks."

DECEMBER

1. "Only One Life—'Twill Soon Be Past."
2. "Give, Though Thy Gifts Be Small!"
3. "Could We With Ink the Ocean Fill!"
4. "Thy Love to Me Was Wonderful."
5. "Testimony of Dr. Howard A. Kelly."
6. "They Shall Be My Jewels!"
7. "Every Gate a Pearl!"
8. "He Might Have Doled His Blossoms."
9. "Martyrdom of John and Betty Stam."
10. "Wearing a White Frock in a Mine."
11. "Washington Assisting His Soldier."
12. "The Stamp Album and the Promise."
13. "Foxes and Faults."
14. "God's Word—Full of Promises."
15. "The Source of Its Beauty."
16. "It Is Human."
17. "What Room Is There?"
18. "An Exchange of Wills."
19. "O Zion, Haste!"
20. "The Fear of Falling Is Wholesome."
21. "Your Afterself."
22. "It Is Easy to Say."
23. "Star of Wonder, Star of Night."
24. "Let Us Now Go Even to Bethlehem."
25. "Unto You Is Born This Day."
26. "Wonderful, Counsellor!"
27. "I Heard the Bells of Bethlehem."
28. "What Then? What Then?"
29. "He Might Have Reared a Palace."
30. "On the Summit."
31. "Press On!"

314

CPSIA information can be obtained
at www.ICGtesting.com
Printed in the USA
LVHW081637130522
718730LV00026B/255

9 781014 751041